AutoBioPhilosophy

An intimate story of what it means to be human

ROBERT ROWLAND SMITH

Robert Rowland Smith

4th ESTATE • *London*

4th Estate
An imprint of HarperCollins*Publishers*
1 London Bridge Street
London SE1 9GF
www.4thEstate.co.uk

First published in Great Britain by 4th Estate in 2018

1 3 5 7 9 8 6 4 2

A catalogue record for this book is available from the British Library

ISBN 978-0-00-821846-1

Printed and bound by CPI Group (UK) Ltd, Croydon, CR0 4YY

MIX
Paper from
responsible sources
FSC™ C007454

This book is produced from independently certified
FSC paper to ensure responsible forest management

Find out more about HarperCollins and the environment at
www.harpercollins.co.uk/green

Contents

Foreword

Foreword

When such a spacious mirror's set before him
He needs must see himself.

William Shakespeare

What is it to be human? That is the question. This book offers nine answers, each mapping on to one of the nine chapters. Being human means:

1. Dealing with our fate
2. Standing in the flow of time
3. Needing a purpose
4. Living amongst others
5. Making mistakes
6. Belonging to groups
7. Facing mortality
8. Not knowing it all
9. Looking for love

Needless to say, there are far more potential answers than those on the above list. The nine offered here correspond broadly to the nine phases of my own life, from my origins to the present day. For I have used my own experience as the source material for answering the question of what it is to be human. To arrive at the general, I go via the specific.

What results is an autobiographical narrative that serves up philosophical insights along the way. But I should stress that the narrative has many gaps. It is not supposed to be a complete life story. My criterion for selecting content was how fertile it appeared to be from a philosophic point of view. If people or periods are represented unevenly, that is why. For example, because of circumstances unique to him, my father Colin plays a more leading role in the text than does my mother. In real life, she is no less important. This book is dedicated to them both.

Author's Note

In the vast majority of cases, I have changed people's names for the sake of anonymity. When talking about individuals, disguised or otherwise, I have been as even-handed as I can be. I recognise that judgements are hard to keep out of one's descriptions of other people, but the agenda here is philosophical rather than personal. Besides, it is the flaws in my own character that will be the most conspicuous by far.

The specific weight of the soul is equal to the weight of what has been dared.

Bert Hellinger

1

Blood and Water

My formula for greatness in a human being is 'amor fati': that one wants nothing to be different, not forward, not backward, not in all eternity. Not merely bear what is necessary, still less conceal it . . . but love it.

Friedrich Nietzsche

At the brow of a hill in Norwood, south London, stands an imposing red-brick building. It is called The British Home and Hospital for Incurables. The word 'incurable' sounds strikingly Victorian, and indeed it was during Victoria's reign, in 1894, that the building was officially opened. Just as striking is the word's directness. *Incurable.* The people who come here aren't going to get better, it says. We might mock the Victorians for their stiff upper lips and prudery, but in their choice of this word, they showed a frankness that we would balk at today.

Among the seventy-odd residents of this Victorian terminus is my father, Colin Rowland Smith. His particular incurability is multiple sclerosis. It is his story that will provide the framework for this first chapter.

The reasons for choosing my father are threefold. First, he

1

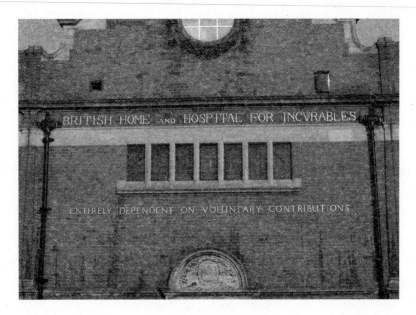

represents the origin, along with my mother, of my own life. He is therefore the starting point of my story, which unfolds in the chapters ahead.

The second reason is that, by bringing a real person into the picture, we can gain some initial purchase on what a human being might actually be. For a human being is always a particular human being, not some vague notion of a human being. I often think of an article by the British novelist Zadie Smith, reflecting on the process of writing. She talks about how you always start out with the ambition of penning the perfect book. From the moment you write the first word, however, it becomes *this* book and no other.

Behind the idea lies, I suppose, a simple logic. That first word limits the range of options for the second word, the second for the third, and so on, until you have a paragraph which determines the next paragraph which determines the next, until you have a chapter. Then each chapter conditions the chapter after it, until the whole thing is done. A book has to follow an internal sequence to reveal its own identity. By definition, this identity will differ from the identity of other books, and so become unique.

As the book, so the human being. None of us has an ideal, perfect or general self. We have the self that we have, with its irreducible specificity, its one-of-a-kind combination of history, biology and character. What's more, our choices narrow as we grow older, making us even less likely to deviate from who we are. The golden thread that leads from the beginning to the end of our lives only becomes finer along the way. So that is why in this chapter I'm looking at a human being in all his book-like individuality.

The third and most important reason for choosing my father is that his story gives us a first answer to the question that will serve as a prompt to all the chapters ahead. The question is: 'What does it mean to be a human being?' Each chapter will offer a different response. In the case of my father, that response goes something like this: 'Being human means dealing with our fate.'

My father's fate was a heavy one. It wasn't just the MS with which he had to contend. Yet how he contended is what matters. It matters for us all. Whether our fate is lucky or unlucky, we are dealt a hand. We might be born into poverty or affluence, good or bad health, peace or war – but the playing of that hand is up to us. And so it is that tension between being determined by our circumstances and determining ourselves which is an essential part of being human.

Mutiny in the body

The 'sclerosis' in multiple sclerosis or MS refers to lesions resulting from damage done to the sheaths encasing the nerve cells in the brain and spinal cord. This damage affects physical coordination, speech, ability to concentrate, memory and more. Maybe all diseases are strange, travelling as covertly as spies and silently infiltrating our systems. What makes MS especially mysterious is that it seems to result from a mutiny in the autoimmune system. Rather than do its job of protecting the body, the autoimmune system revolts and attacks. But not only that:

- women get it more than men;
- you're more susceptible to it the further your origins lie from the Equator;
- there is no available cure; and
- its causes are unknown.

Unknown but not unguessed at. The medical literature points to both genetic and environmental factors, though the evidence for either remains inconclusive. It is not a lifestyle disease. Nor is it considered heritable, even though there's some debate about your increased likelihood of getting it if you're related to a sufferer. As Colin's son, I am acutely aware of this possibility, though I've never shown any symptoms and have reached an age at which they're less likely to appear. That does, however, raise the question of just how closely related he and I are.

Institutionalised

Colin's parents, Rowland and Beatrice, divorced early in his life. At the tender age of eight, Colin, an only child, was packed off to an English boarding school in leafy Sussex, called Hurstpierpoint College. This was in 1945, just as the war was ending. I picture the school as a rural haven from the disarray in cities to the north. It was set, as if to a metronome, to the consoling tempo of public-school life – cricket matches, prayers, tea, weekly baths. But rationing was still in force, those baths were cold, and the school will have had its share of bullies. Female presence was limited, and academic study came a long way ahead of emotional development.

Beatrice, his mother, went to live a hundred and fifty miles away in Birmingham. Rowland took a new wife and had four more children. To begin with, they set up in Hove, adjoining Brighton, and a mere ten miles from Hurstpierpoint. Later, they moved to handsome surroundings in Bungay, Suffolk, which was scarcely any nearer than Birmingham, and required of my grandfather a lengthy commute into Liverpool Street station.

Hurstpierpoint College

So, from the age of eight to eighteen, the Neo-Gothic flint castle of Hurstpierpoint College would have been my father's entire world, a colony unto itself. Apart from school holidays, that is. These he spent with his mother in Birmingham. There, as a fifteen-year-old, Colin met his wife-to-be, Patricia. A year younger than Colin, Patricia had already left school, and was doing a clerical job in the Midland Bank not far from the Bull Ring. As a girl in the 1940s and 50s, her education wasn't deemed important, though that didn't suppress her aspirations to improve her working-class lot. She dreamed about one day having a son and sending him to Dulwich College, the famous public school of which she had once heard as in a legend. With his Queen's English, shiny bicycle and public-school credentials of his own, Colin appeared in Patricia's life like the key to a door. For his part, he found a first meaningful female connection. The relationship flourished.

Trouble in paradise

Thanks to the class divide, however, neither family approved. By the time the couple reached their late teens, and Colin too had left school, Rowland, his father, was ready to take action.⬇ With a view to splitting them up, he packed Colin off again, only this time much farther afield. Colin was dispatched to an outpost of the family food business in Canada.

The plan backfired. From his exile Colin wrote to Patricia, imploring her to join him. He enclosed a ticket for the Atlantic sea crossing. The letter landed on the doormat of a terraced house in Bell Hill, Northfield, one of Birmingham's less well-to-do districts. Patricia opened it, made up her mind and set sail. Some months later, at a United Reformed church in Hamilton, Ontario, in a ceremony attended by no more than a handful of well-wishers, they married.

⬆ In the family, the name Rowland is sometimes used as a first name, sometimes as a middle name, and sometimes as part of a surname, with or without a hyphen. Some of the females have it too, as part of the surname. In my case, Rowland is my middle name, and Smith is my surname, meaning that to family and friends, I'm plain Robert Smith. However, I use all three names for my public profile.

Colin and Patricia might have settled in Canada for life, but a combination of factors drew them back to England. Here my mother was grudgingly accepted and subsequently patronised by her in-laws. The newlyweds set up home in south Croydon, then a still desirable suburb of London. Colin began commuting to the family business' head office on Tooley Street, opposite London Bridge station. Patricia gave birth to three children, two girls and one boy. She sent me to Dulwich College.

My two sisters were privately educated also. The combined fees can't have been cheap, but the business was doing well and paying Colin a tidy salary. In 1970 the family moved to a much-extended house with a large garden on a private road further into the suburbs. I had a pine tree outside my bedroom window. Colin bought himself Jaguars, Daimler Double Sixes and BMW 7 Series. For Patricia there was a gold Ford Escort, then a cherry red Opel Manta. The pinnacle was a white two-seater Triumph Spitfire with detachable roof. I would beg her to collect me from school in it. My parents shopped for clothes on Bond Street. One year we went on holiday to Chewton Glen in the New Forest, then the UK's fanciest hotel.

Yet by the end of that decade a serpent had slithered in. The economy was tanking. The family business was running out of the steam that had powered it since its heyday in the late 1960s. A major factor had been the death of 'Uncle Bob'. He had been the company's driving force. Robert Rowland Smith – after whom I was named – was my grandfather Rowland's brother, and my father's uncle. Tall, talented and magnetic, Uncle Bob was a legend. With no children of his own, he invested his energies not only in the firm but also in his extended family. So whilst he was happy to splurge on himself – a mansion in St John's Wood, a Rolls Royce – it was he who had bought Colin and Patricia that first house in south Croydon. What with his passing and the weather in the market turning squally, the business began to founder.

From Colin's perspective, the squeeze on company revenues wasn't the only challenge. Without Uncle Bob's mediating influence, Colin found himself working directly to a father whose *modus operandi* with his son was criticism. 'Useless' was his put-down of choice. Colin was conscious that his father had gone on to have a second family. The youngest of four among that second batch of children was another son, also named Rowland. This new Rowland was about fifteen years my father's junior and an incipient rival. My father was jealous not just in the way that any brother might be jealous of a half-brother, but also because Rowland – known as Rowley – was taking his own first steps in the family business.

The axe falls

There was a third man for Colin to worry about. This was David Cooke. As is obvious from his surname, Mr Cooke wasn't part of the family. He was an outsider. Like the owners of many family businesses, I suppose, the proprietors of Rowland Smith & Son Ltd. were aware that family ties could be a liability as well as an asset. They saw the value in an external perspective. Besides, David Cooke came with a reputation as a marketing genius. Before long, Colin perceived his father to be favouring the interloper over him, just as he had suspected his father of transferring his favour to young Rowley. Colin might have been made a director of the company, but psychologically he found himself twice displaced.

Meanwhile, in his thirties, Colin had been diagnosed with MS. He would complain of pins and needles, and of a recurrent ache down the left side of his body, starting in his shoulder. He acquired a slight limp. Mercifully, the disease stabilised at a low level, barely impinging on his capacity to function. Until, that is, the storm clouds that had been gathering over the business finally broke. The money began running out and desperate measures had to be taken. As the big boss, my grandfather decided on cuts. Having tallied up the golden salaries paid to the directors, particularly to my father and David Cooke, he chose to delete one. He sacked his son.

That was in 1979, when Colin was forty-three. He made some half-hearted efforts to set up a marketing enterprise. But, having been given a house and a job and a salary just by virtue of belonging to the Rowland Smith clan, he couldn't muster the initiative to make anything happen. Perhaps he had also internalised his father's verdict on his uselessness. He never properly worked again. He sold the big house and gave himself up to his disease.

His eyes were one of the first things to go. He developed a squint and had to wear an eye patch. He had trouble forming sentences. One day he lost control of the accelerator pedal on the Citroën to which he had downgraded. He rammed the vehicle in front, causing a minor accident. With great reluctance, he agreed not to drive again. The limp that had been with him since his thirties became unignorable. The staircase at home had become an abyss into which he risked tumbling from the top. Before long, the walking stick was traded for a wheelchair. Colin would trundle this contraption around the downstairs of the gingerbread cottage he now lived in with Patricia, smashing against the door jambs until they were splintery and raw. By the late 1990s he would fall down regularly getting in and out of it, and my small-framed mother was losing the strength to haul him up again. It was then that she approached the British Home and Hospital for Incurables.

Man's character is his fate

Colin's story shows just how singular was his fate. In its details it belongs to nobody else. That is what makes him different – different even from me, his son. The truth is that, having witnessed the onset of his MS, which terrifies me, I'm glad of it. For all the compassion I feel towards him, that his fate differs from mine is something for which I can only be thankful.

Maybe it would be nobler if I felt the urge to take on his disease in order to spare him. That would be a grand filial sacrifice. It is what sacrifice is, at heart – the loving instinct to take over somebody else's fate, to bear their cross. But that is a fantasy, and in any case doing so is impossible. We can never really stand in for anybody else. Even in the extreme case of offering up our own life to save another's, it is still our own death that we will die, not theirs. We can't actually spare them, we can merely buy them some time. What's more, sacrifice seems to flow more appropriately in the other direction. If anything, parents sacrifice themselves for their children, not the other way round, at least in the West. They cede to the flow of time, giving priority to newer life over older. Incurable is incurable, as the Victorians said.

Wrapped up inside fate is another element that makes family members other to us. It was identified by the Greek philosopher Heraclitus. In a precious fragment of text from the ancient world, Heraclitus is quoted as saying that 'man's character is his fate'. Who we are, as much as the action of any external influence, determines what will happen to us. To change our fate, therefore, requires changing who we are. But changing who we are is never easy. The drive to carry on being ourselves counts among the most powerful forces in the universe, rivalling gravity. After all, our character is what stops us from becoming other people. As if it were a repelling magnet, our character keeps others at arm's length, insisting on its own space.

I saw first hand just how much my father's character shaped his fate. Despite his education, his money, his family, and his luck in being given both a job and a house, he experienced life as a series of calamities. The slightest thing would vex him. If the traffic was bad, if he couldn't open a jar, if a utility bill arrived in the post, if the sink got blocked, if the lawnmower ran out of petrol, if the television picture went fuzzy – in all cases, an almost existential despair would wash over him. It was as if every red light on the road was a monstrous unfairness trained deliberately on him. In little things he saw large tragedies. Fate had seen that Colin's character was tragic, and decided to follow suit.

What overwhelmed him, I believe, was the sense of confronting his own resourcelessness. It wasn't just that he had been given a lot, but that both boarding school and the family business were institutions that ran life for him. True, he had shown initiative in bringing Patricia to Canada. But she was expected to be a stereotypical 1950s wife, managing his domestic infrastructure. In other words, he'd had precious few opportunities to develop agency of his own. So whenever something less than advantageous occurred, he looked into his cupboard of personal supplies for dealing with it, and saw that it was empty.

In such tiny moments, Colin exhibited a brief but bottomless despair. He would let out what the English Gothic writer Thomas de Quincey called a 'suspiria de profundis', a sigh from the depths. I remember this sigh filling the house like the exhalation of a wounded animal. So when something truly terrible finally did happen – his own father ousting him from what was purportedly a family business – one can only imagine the hollowness into which he stared. If it was hard enough for Colin to roll with the mishaps of everyday existence, how frightening it would have been to behold this once-in-a-lifetime tsunami.

In the jargon, Colin lacked the necessary 'coping mechanisms'. The want of resilience that he had shown in allowing minor inconveniences to flummox him became, when he was fired, his condition of being. Cruelly, it also provided the ideal environment for the MS to thrust upwards from beneath the ground, where it was only half buried, into the light. For whatever else multiple sclerosis might be, it is a disease that deprives its victims of the ability to cope. To someone whose coping mechanisms are already feeble, an incurable disease such as MS, mixed with unemployment, produces a fatal concoction. Paralysis was the result.

Other people might have responded differently. Stories abound of those who conquer or at least subdue their MS through a combination of attitude, diet and exercise. But my father responded in the way that only he could. He met the emptiness that faced him with an emptiness of his own. That was his character, and it became his fate.

Our parents are foreigners in time

Both character and fate set Colin apart. They even set him apart from me, his biological offspring. The straight genetic pipe from him to me contained leaks, so not everything got transmitted. Besides, there was another pipe coming in from the maternal side, although with leaks of its own, to be sure. It is by these twin leaky conduits that we're connected to our biological inheritance.

What that means in terms of our parents is that we're both the same and different. Such is the mystery of generation. When the human organism divides, it issues a copy of itself that's not quite perfect. The uncanny thing is to look into the face of anyone we know and see three people. Both parents flutter in the movements of that face, along with the unique combination of them that produces the third person, the person whom we erroneously think of as a discrete self.

That leakiness is not just biological. It also applies to what gets transmitted by way of narrative about our parents' lives. We hear a few details and they take on a magical quality, like photographs found in an attic. But so much of their lives leaks away, and we have to rely on their memories, which are leaky themselves. These memories can feel strange because they are both near and far. They are highly intimate and yet unavailable. They have a warm otherness to them, like a soil.

That soil is where we come to be planted. It is because they concern our own origin that our parents' stories, about their lives before us, take on the quality of fable. Origins are always mysterious. We hear this mystery in Colin's narrative. We get a picture of the 1950s, for example. It contains a post-war mixture of bereavement and hope; the recognition of a modernity finally burying the Victorian past; and a sense that the triple-towered edifice of class, gender and religion is cracking. But that is a historical view. Through it, the 1950s seem to be part of an objective account that people can write books or make documentaries about. This account is available to anyone who's interested. The other is the view of a child – me – learning about the time in which my parents lived, before the child was born. This view is far more private, and the time period it gazes at has a different feel. Different and more enigmatic.

The stories about our parents aren't quite history, therefore, even where there is plenty of historical data, because they produce in us a state of wonder. This wonder makes those parents all the stranger to us. Indeed, as much as those stories draw us in to the lives of father and mother, we can't help feeling a trace of repugnance. For all our natural, biological proximity to them, they are foreigners in time. Children come after their parents, by necessity, and we all live in a flow of time that none of us can interrupt. Time is like a motor beneath an hermetically sealed bonnet, always running.

So if our parents are strangely 'other' to us, their children – if their fate separates them from us, their closest kin – it's not just because the stories are exclusively theirs. It is also because those stories hail from a time that is not ours. Our parents are not of our generation, and so a quantum of alienation runs beneath every experience that we have of them. Even these twin origins of our becoming, our parents, remain other to us. In this respect, they are no more special than every other person on the earth – even the remotest, the never thought-of, those who come and go without us even having been aware of their existence.

Perhaps this semi-disconnect from the past of our parents is why our own lives can at times feel so random. In Existentialist philosophy, which examines the big questions of life and death, insisting on the arbitrariness of our birth is a commonplace. Martin Heidegger, for example, writing in the hush of the Black Forest in the 1920s, talks about how we are 'thrown' into the world. It is as if we were literally cast into a pine forest, fenced in by the tall, dark shapes of the trees and the silhouettes of strangers threading between them. There's nothing apparently necessary about how we got there. Whenever we get an intimation that, thanks to the separating effects of time and fate, some distancing even from our own parents is inevitable, it's little surprise that this sense of randomness can seize us so strongly.

Performance versus belonging

Colin himself would hardly have been unaware of all the factors that created distance between him and the members of his family.

First, there was the divorce of his parents. Though divorce wasn't unheard of at the time, it was scarcely the norm. Another half-century would have to pass before its stigma faded.

Second, there was being sent to boarding school. Again, this wasn't uncommon. It was even considered a reputable form of education for a boy – 'character-building' was the term used to endorse and/or excuse it. Wartime had in any case necessitated all sorts of makeshift arrangements for children, who were often dispatched to live with distant relatives or friends. Colin himself had been evacuated to sleepy Gloucestershire during the war proper. But emotionally, boarding school was a wrench. Just as other families whose fathers had come back from the war were reuniting, he, an only child, was torn away from parents who had torn away from each other.

Third, there was Rowland generating a second family to which Colin both did and didn't belong. Or rather, he continued to belong to his father as a son – that was his right – but belonging to the second family as a whole was something that would have to be done by invitation, as it was never quite a right in the same way.

Finally, there was the family business, where Colin's experience of separation would have been the most complex. The very phrase 'family business' holds a tension, even a contradiction. A family has no purpose beyond the affirmation of blood ties and the circulation of love. It can simply be and nobody has to justify its existence. Most importantly, everybody in a family has a right to belong. The sole entry requirement is being of the same blood. With a business, it's different. There is a test involved in joining a business: belonging is never automatic. As a commercial enterprise, the right to belong to it must be earned by supporting that commercial aim.

So when you merge 'family' and 'business' into the entity

known as a 'family business', a circle has to be squared. Do you have a right to belong to the family business just because you're a part of the family? Or do you have to prove yourself first, as anyone joining a conventional business would have to do?

Colin was tipped straight into the mesh of that ambiguity. He had been brought into the business as a young man by virtue of belonging to the family, even though his 'belonging' had already been rattled after his father remarried. But that was when the economic weather was still fair. When it turned foul, Colin was judged on his merits and found wanting. Now his card was set next to that of the non-family member, David Cooke, and his scores looked poor. No longer was being part of the family enough; performance was the new measure, and Colin's fell below par. When the chips were down, water was thicker than blood.

Put another way, businesses have an easier time excluding people than families do. It doesn't test their conscience in the same way. Unlike the right to belong to a family, which is granted once and for ever through the definitive act of birth, in a business you have to keep demonstrating how valuable you are. It never lets up. Belonging is secured by the collateral of performance; and explicitly or implicitly, performance is continuously monitored. Take the performance away, and the belonging falls apart too.

Of course, there are those individuals in certain businesses who become so much part of the furniture that, long after they have ceased to hold their own commercially, they're kept on like pets. But that is an indulgence. The only legitimate exception to the rule of belonging-conditional-upon-performance would be if the business were one that you founded. As the originating spirit, you are central. And you will be largely exempt from the scrutiny applied to the performance of those who come after. You created the enterprise, which makes you its 'father' or 'mother' in a more than metaphorical way. You gave it life. Where there had been nothing, you made something.

As acts of creation, these inaugurating gestures of the founding father share a life instinct with the making of a family. Which is why, in those rare cases when a company does turn on its founder and relieve him of his duties, everybody feels its moral portent. There is an unspoken question as to how natural it can be, like watching an eclipse. Nobody is totally sure that it's a legitimate move, even if the business reasons for the removal are sound. Taking such a dramatic step leaves a mark on the conscience of those who unseated the founder, as if they had committed parricide. (In the later chapter about organisations called 'Office Politics', I will say more about this uncanny power of the founder.)

No wonder the concept of a family business holds so much tension. Most of the time that tension remains obligingly latent, but when, as in the case of Rowland Smith & Son Ltd., market forces enjoin on the company the taking of drastic action, it appears like an unspeakable black animal on stage. It has to be addressed. Do you get rid of Colin or David? Between family and business, which comes first?

We know which way my grandfather, Rowland, called it. He chose in that moment to see my father less as his son than as an employee to be judged on a level playing field with his rival. No more was Colin an alternative but sympathetic expression of the same genetic wave, a variant of Rowland's own subjectivity. Rather, Colin had become an objective human asset to be evaluated against other human assets. To say that Rowland 'disowned' Colin would be a clear distortion, despite the feelings of abandonment that Colin must have suffered. Nevertheless, Rowland shook the family tree with sufficient vigour to make Colin fear that, like a rotten fruit, he would fall.

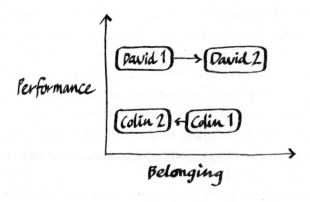

The diagram above describes the situation in graphic form. 'Colin 1' and 'David 1' refer to the starting positions, the point at which David was brought into the business. 'Colin 2' and 'David 2' refer to the later point at which Rowland, my grandfather, chose between them. This choice was made against two criteria: performance and belonging. In position one, David's performance was seen as strong, but as someone with the surname Cooke rather than Smith, his belonging could only be weak. In contrast, what was perceived as weak about Colin was his performance.

The fundamental problem was that even at the start Colin's belonging was less secure than it could have been. We know that Rowland's 'ownership' of his son had always been circumscribed. He was barely involved in Colin's childhood, and not for purely psychological reasons. For six of the eight years before Colin was sent to boarding school, 1939–1945, Rowland was at war, stationed in India and Burma. Not long after his return, he divorced, remarried and began his new family. In other words, Colin's belonging never was assured. It wasn't as if he had a full tank that got emptied: the tank peaked at around 70 per cent. Colin's aggregate score, even in position one, fell short.

What's most striking, however, is that despite his different blood, David actually increases his level of belonging. This is, first,

18

because he replaces Colin: doing so makes David a stand-in son, a family member. The second reason is that David doesn't carry the same baggage as Colin did from Rowland's previous marriage. That makes David a less problematic proposition when it comes to slotting him in. These two reasons facilitated the miracle that Rowland performed of turning water into blood.

That miracle doesn't have to happen under such special circumstances. There is a perfectly ordinary example of it. In the early 1930s, Rowland and Beatrice are a couple, and Colin is not even a glimmer in the eye. In order to marry, they must by law come from separate families. Marriage represents what anthropologists call 'exogamy'. Exogamy means that matrimony occurs with a spouse chosen from outside the family. Nothing unusual about that. And yet on the day of the wedding, husband and wife *become* each other's family. When Rowland and Beatrice tie the knot, they transmogrify into each other's next of kin. That happens despite *and* because of the absence of blood ties. It is an act of social alchemy. In marriage, water not only becomes blood: it can become blood *only if* it is water. To extend the metaphor, one could say that Colin's issue was that his blood and water were mixed. The result was a dilute mid-liquid that embarrassed all concerned.

The irony is that Rowland's own belonging might have been the tiniest bit in doubt too. I say this because stories about my grandfather suggest he was never quite the man that legendary Uncle Bob – Robert, his brother – had been. Bob always seemed the more able. There is a suspicion, then, of what Freud called 'projection'. This is the idea that we transfer onto other people those aspects of ourselves we find least congenial, thereby restoring a sense of our own flawlessness. In couples psychotherapy, for example, a wife might say of her husband, 'I don't trust him.' But unconsciously what she is indicating is, 'I am not to be trusted.'

So if, as second fiddle to Robert, Rowland felt inadequate, it's possible that he saw in the pairing of David and Colin an echo, psychologically speaking, of his own situation. Thus David was the superior and Colin the inferior partner. Expelling Colin represented the purging of an inferiority that was Rowland's own.

If that hypothesis is credible, then berating my father for his 'uselessness' was for Rowland an unconscious way of railing at a deficiency of his own, relative to his brother. It was a personal deficiency that he dealt with by contaminating his son with it. He then cited his son's deficiency as a justification for banishing that son like a leper. Unluckily, however, you do not get rid of a disease by passing it on to someone else. It sticks. In any case, Colin had already been invaded by a disease of his own that would derange him more completely.

The madness of decision

On the other hand, we could say that Rowland took the tough decision. From this perspective, he was acting like a true leader. After all, when decisions require little discretion, we are not really deciding at all. We are pushing at an open door. Say I'm checking into the Grand Hotel in Brighton and am offered a choice between two rooms at the same tariff. One is at the front with a sea view; the other is at the back, overlooking the car park. It is obvious which one I should take.

But when I quiz the receptionist further, I discover that the sea-view room is poky. Between it and the sea runs a noisy road. The back room, by contrast, is spacious and quiet. Now I have a genuine dilemma, which calls for a true decision. Choosing between family and business is a genuine dilemma too, because the arguments on both sides can never be exhausted. The decision can always be deferred. What's more, families and businesses are not two hotel rooms but apples and oranges. We are not comparing like with like, so how on earth are we to weigh them up?

So tricky are such genuine dilemmas that reason can take us only so far towards resolving them. That is why the Algerian-French philosopher Jacques Derrida, for example, writes about the 'madness of decision'.⬇ Whatever the logical steps involved in the run-up to it, the decision itself marks a leap into the dark. That leap is the point at which reason can no longer help, because now it's a matter of acting. You close your eyes and jump.

That's what Rowland did. He acted with the unavoidable madness of all action. By not ducking the decision, he was, for good or for ill, accepting accountability. Was this something that he had learned in wartime? He had won an OBE for his actions. If Colin was the poorer performer, keeping him on might have put the business at risk. That would have impacted everyone. We can choose to see Rowland's decision not as the cold-hearted rejection of his firstborn, but as a judicious move for the greater good. After all, the gravity of the decision can't not have affected him.

The contribution sextant

An organisation perishes if it doesn't work, so ultimately it has to put its own prosperity above the individuals in it. There is no autonomic system operating in a business such as there is in a human body. A business has no respiratory function that carries on regardless of the will of its owner. It must remember to breathe.

This need on the part of a business to keep its purpose at the front of its mind has an impact on the relationships among

---

⬆ Derrida's reference, in his book *The Gift of Death*, is to Abraham and Isaac – the original case of a father sacrificing his son. I shall say more about Derrida in Chapter 3.

the individuals in it. We've seen how the roles played by Colin and David were reversed. Where the semi-son became the outsider, the outsider became the semi-son. That reversal took place because David's input was perceived as more vital to the company's commercial aims. A valuation took place. But such valuations take place in any situation where we bind together with others in a joint endeavour. The endeavour could be trivial, such as assembling a flat-pack wardrobe with a friend, or hold national significance, like starting a political party. No sooner do we find ourselves in such partnerships than a third element comes and stands over the relationship between us, like a master with its back to the sun. This third element is the goal that we're trying to attain. It's this goal that has convened us, and both of us have a duty to fulfil it. No matter how close the bond between the individuals involved, it takes second place to the goal that has brought them together.

As soon as the work begins, however, we become highly sensitive to the level of contribution that we are separately making. In particular, we are attuned to whether our partners are doing their share. We carry a secret measure, like a microscopic, translucent gauge within us, from which we're always taking readings, working out who's showing the greater commitment to the joint goal. I call it the 'contribution sextant'. If, at any moment, we judge that our partner is more distant in his or her heart from that goal, we rate them as less valuable than we are. A draught of estrangement passes between us. To begin with, we ignore it. Generally, we'd rather get on with people than point out their failings, especially if we're supposed equals before the same goal. Over time, however, the tolerance dries up, becomes brittle. Sooner or later it snaps and, with an aggression that's more or less passive, we'll call out the difference between their contribution and ours.

Compare the two triangles below. The first is equilateral, so we see a perfect balance. The distance between my partner and me is the same as the distance between each of us and our shared goal. The shared goal stands above us. We both have a duty to fulfil this goal. Like ladders, our separate efforts lean up towards and converge upon it. Meanwhile, a horizontal line runs between me and my partner, representing the equality that we experience as we labour at our joint task. Neither of us is supposed to give more or less than the other. The horizontal line helps us to feel we are in it together. These two factors, a shared goal and a sense of equality before it, create a bond. It feels right, and because it feels right, it feels good.

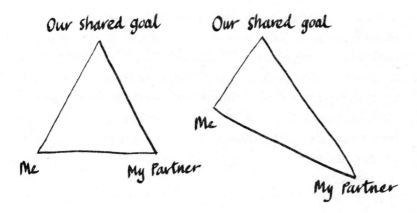

In the second triangle, by contrast, we see a less perfect configuration. Immediately, we sense relative disorder. My line to the shared goal is shorter, and my partner's correspondingly longer. That indicates a greater commitment on my part to the shared goal. The shorter line has the inevitable consequence of lifting me higher up the picture than my partner. This elevated position is in effect the moral high ground. From here I can look down on my partner.

My partner's perspective is altered in proportion. Now he is in a position of inferiority relative both to me and to the shared goal. How will the new configuration affect our relationship? We no longer have the line of equality keeping us in balance. What's more, the distance has grown, and the new angle means we can't see as much of each other. Our relationship suffers from the asymmetry, and we both know it. The disjointing of the triangle leads to an inner knowledge, shared by us both, of damage done.

That second triangle throws light on intimate relationships too. If you replace 'our shared goal' with 'our relationship', and interpret the lines as representing how much each partner is committed to that relationship, you have a triangle where the same dynamics apply as in the work scenario. The question is who feels worse. Is it me because I'm giving more and observing my partner giving less? After all, I'm the one being ripped off, picking up the slack. The diagram suggests that it's actually worse for my partner. Not because she's giving less per se, but because she's located in the inferior position. She is looked down on both by me and by 'the relationship' as a concept. That makes matters less tolerable for her than they are for me. It also means that she's more likely to leave than am I.

Soul knowledge

I believe we all carry such images within us. They might not assume the form of triangles, but we'll have our way of figuring the balance or imbalance in any mutual enterprise. We know when things are off kilter. I call it 'soul knowledge'.

Soul knowledge is deeper but simpler than psychological understanding. In tracking the complexities of human interaction, psychology sometimes loses touch with the underlying realities. Such realities aren't always as complex as we imagine. Sometimes they are so simple that they can indeed be represented by a form as basic as a triangle. The danger, in other words, is that psychology can't see the forest for the trees. Where psychology aims to quantify all sorts of data – tendency to agree or disagree, response to reward, frequency of relapse – soul knowledge measures the essentials. In this case, it takes a reading of the give-and-take in a relationship. Where the give-and-take is skewed, the result is a warping of the system as a whole, like a picture frame ruined by damp. It feels wrong. And because it feels wrong, it feels bad.

In other words, soul knowledge is a form of systemic awareness. It maps the tacit geometry of our connections with other people. We live in systems all the time, be they family systems, work systems or intimate relationship systems – and even fleeting systems like the audience we're part of at a concert, or the queue we stand in at the post office. In all cases, we are switched on to our place in it and the place of others. When the system is in order, it feels right. The soul has an eye for the system as a whole, and unlike the self, which wants to stand out, is always ready to slot into its place.

What's so very challenging about a family business is that two systems have to be reconciled. A family system has to be reconciled with a business system. At Rowland Smith & Son Ltd., the partners in the triangle, Colin and David, were not partners in the way that most colleagues might be, for the simple reason that one belonged to the family and the other did not. Strictly speaking, the former half-belonged to the family and the latter did not belong. I'm not sure it would be possible to chart this system, because Colin stood at once closer to, and further from, the shared goal understood as the family's commercial interests, while also standing above, below and on the same level as David.

Systemically, it was a mess, and I think it had an impact on Colin's soul. All his soul could have known was confusion. It might be pushing it to say that his MS was the direct result of this scrambling of his soul knowledge – being deprived of the chance to see a clear whole – but I find it hard not to draw at least a metaphoric parallel between the neurological misconnections in his body and the eccentric wiring in the system of the family business. In both cases, there's a tragic failure of coherence.

Frenemies

Although David Cooke turned into, or was turned into, Colin's nemesis, I do recall a period when one or two faltering attempts at a friendship were made by my father. It must have been a big deal for Colin, because although he came across as gregarious, handsome and jocular, it wouldn't be an exaggeration to say that he had no friends. Life consisted of his office, our home and the commute between the two termini. I have more fingers on one hand than the number of times I remember my parents going out for the evening, and I have no recollection at all of any friend making a visit. The double bed in the commodious spare bedroom remained cold from 1970 when we moved in, right the way through to 1983 when we moved out.

I say the attempts were faltering, as if they could have been otherwise. But how could they, given that clash of the two systems, family and business? Even without such entanglements as those affecting Rowland Smith & Son Ltd., work friendships are rarely without complications. You don't become friends with somebody through work unless the work was there in the first place to bring you together. The work provided the environment in which you met, and both of you will have gained entry to the organisation on the understanding that you would contribute to the shared goal. Work is the context of your friendship. So when you meet outside work as friends, the most you can do is to put that context in brackets. You can't erase it altogether. Even if you never talk shop, your awareness of each other as co-workers remains in the back of your mind.

Why is that a problem? The presence of a shared goal acts like an alloy, thinning out the friendship's integrity. Obviously, friends often do come together to perform a shared task, like putting up a tent or cooking a meal. The point is that the friendship doesn't depend on such tasks in order to survive. That's how friendships differ from relationships in the workplace, where the lack of a goal leaves people at a loss as to what to do. It is also how friendships resemble family relationships: both are an end in themselves. Friendships should consist in no more than that horizontal line between two people, with no tip of the triangle representing a goal. That horizontal line is also the line of equality. No friendship will be authentic if there's any inkling of one friend feeling superior or inferior to the other. Both positions are bad for the soul.

The test comes when one of the friends quits the organisation. The deeper the friendship, the longer it can survive without the binding of work. We know we were never really friends if we lose touch soon after one of us has moved on. Needless to say, Colin and David did not remain friends in the wake of Colin's sacking. Even when working together, the friendship never got off the ground. Ulterior motive was too much in play. For Colin, befriending David would have been, at least subconsciously, a way of neutralising a potential threat. For David, currying favour with another Rowland Smith could only bolster his position. The most they could have ever been to one another was 'frenemies'.

What's in a name?

The biggest stumbling block, therefore, was the name. Like a bell, my father's surname had a resonance in Rowland Smith & Son Ltd.

that David's did not. Until Colin was removed, that is. Then the roles reversed. David became an honorary Rowland Smith, while Colin – sidelined from business and family alike – effectively forfeited his name. An acquired namelessness, like a reverse baptism, was one of the many facets of his plight.

But we shouldn't let the peculiarities of the Colin/David scenario lead us into thinking that having different names is always a problem in friendships. Quite the reverse. Like marriage, friendship is exogamous. It involves making a bond with somebody outside the family. That requires you to choose a friend with a different surname. I mean by different surname 'coming from a different lineage', even if the actual word – Jones or Patel or Blanc or Diaz or Khan – is the same. If it were really the same family name – the same patronymic or matronymic, to give it its technical title – then you would be making friends with somebody from your family, which is unnecessary. Unnecessary because the bond already exists. If we think of friendship as the reducing of the otherness of other people, or as making the strange familiar, then in a family this labour of familiarisation has been done in advance. It's implicit in the word 'family'. Regardless of how much you like the person, befriending a family member is ever so slightly ingratiating. Ingratiating because superfluous.

It cuts the other way too. The superfluousness of befriending a family member gives us an excuse not to make an effort. With friends there's always a subtle pressure for that effort to be made. I am not saying that one shouldn't bother to be friendly with family. But 'friendly' is different from 'friends'. Family is a blood system, friendship water. Although the two can be mixed, they are intrinsically different. Mixing them evokes a subtle sense of aberration.

So Colin and David did not remain friends after the former left the company. Whether Colin's departure in 1979 really helped the business to recover is debatable. In 1983 Rowland Smith & Son Ltd. was sold to a Dutch enterprise. The following year Colin's father, my grandfather, died.

Incurable souls

Over time, Colin's metaphorical namelessness has become all too real. Now when I visit him, he's not sure what his own name is, let alone mine. Addressing him in his fleece top, sweat pants and Velcro slippers – he hasn't worn shoes for fifteen years – I ask, 'Am I Robert?' Sometimes he shakes his head. Other times he says yes. Or rather he whispers yes, because that's the best his un-exercised larynx can do. His mouth hangs open most of the day, revealing the few teeth that are stuck like plugs of dark sap onto his gums. It's an effort for him to close his mouth in the way that enunciating syllables requires, so the 'y' and the 's' at the beginning and end of the word 'yes' barely have any definition. The lack of consistency in his replies suggests that he just doesn't know who I am. He's guessing. It seems that I, his only son, have become a stranger.

Often he won't reply at all. But then, language consists of more than words. Whenever I appear, his face lights up. After this initial burst, he will zone out, adrift in some time outside time. But during it, he is stirred. He may not be recognising me as Robert; he may not even be recognising me as his son. But that he is recognising somebody is beyond dispute. Only recognition could trigger such elation. I smile back and, for those first few seconds, we are communicating.

We are communicating, but as to what underpins the communication, I cannot say. It's not just he who is unsure about me. To be frank, even though I know rationally that he is my father, being with him is so strange that I feel it like a vertigo. That's partly because I'm in a state of protracted shock, both about his disease and about being related to him as its victim. But it is also because that disease has refashioned him to such an extent that I'm not sure who he is either.

If we can communicate despite having no normal basis for it, it's possible that something else is going on. Not only is the mutual strangeness no bar to communication, it might even be what allows a more immediate form of communication to take place. When two people know each other well, or are each sure of who the other person is, the quality of the communication can actually decrease. How so? The familiarity causes us to rely on our inner picture of that other person, rather than seeing them as they truly are. We become too habituated to properly notice. But, as when a wave recedes and leaves the pebbles on the beach gleaming, when the familiarity recedes and we become strangers once more, we see the other person afresh.

It is more like an encounter between two souls than two selves. Souls don't need to know in the way that selves do, because in the realm of the soul everything essential gets communicated in advance. When two souls come together they 'always already' know each other. That is why, for example, the process of falling in love is instantaneous, and why a new couple will often attest to the uncanny feeling of having known each other before. Their souls arrived at the love-place ahead of their selves.

The key condition for this soul knowledge to occur, therefore, is the dislodging of the mask of the self. In Colin's case, it was knocked from his face for him. He certainly didn't ask for it. Like most of us, his preference would surely have been for a life of presence, identity, connection and value, for the embroidery of the self to weave its threads until it had assumed the form and colour that most people are able to enjoy. And yet it's precisely because his self grew so threadbare that his soul was able to shine through in large smooth patches. Perhaps that's what's so jolting about visiting Colin and seeing the other incurables drooling in their food, or hearing the unidentifiable sounds they make echoing down the long, wide parquet corridors. It's the absence of selves and, in their place, the presence of their naked souls.

Happiness

Given his aphasic state, Colin's medical file lists 'Dementia' next to 'Multiple Sclerosis'. Whilst those categories might work on paper, in the flesh they can't be told apart. The dementia is merely extending the process of effacing Colin's identity begun long ago by the MS, just as the MS itself picked up the work of erasure that had commenced in his psyche at an early age. It is as if the gift of presence, which is what makes life life, was fumbled at his birth. It broke as a glass sphere brimming with light would break. I remember that in the wheelchair period, he would simply sit at home, with the lights and the heating turned off to save money, as if he needed no more sustenance than the objects around him. As if he saw himself as something other than alive.

In this doleful example, we come across perhaps the deepest sense of what it means to be a human. Having a fate, as we all do, means being vulnerable. It calls us away from others and into a future that we can never completely predict. In extreme cases, like that of Colin, it can even separate us from who we are. I say this because Colin's self has come so close to being scrubbed away that there's nothing for him to reflect on. It's as if there is not even an interchange between a conscious and an unconscious self. There's nothing for an unconscious to split off from and no ocean for the shipwreck of his self to sink into.

Is that a good or a bad fate in the end? Perhaps that is the wrong question. It is more a matter of how we play the hand we are dealt. Where others might have reinvented themselves after losing their job, or, as I suggested earlier, summoned their inner resources to keep the MS at bay through diet, exercise and will, my father appeared to let fate take its course. But then, all that he had known from a young age was his life being directed by others. His real tragedy was that he never developed a sense of his own agency. The capacity for self-determinism was always going to be weaker than the forces acting upon him. The final irony, if that is the right word, is that he appears to be happy at last.

> Humans cannot communicate; not even their brains
> can communicate; not even their conscious minds can
> communicate. Only communication can communicate.
>
> Niklas Luhmann

2

The Dream of Three Daughters

But who are these three sisters and why must the choice fall on the third?

Sigmund Freud

In the small hours, the bedside phone is ringing. I am a light sleeper, but on this night of all nights I'm beyond reach. As the calls rain in, I sleep through. Maybe my unconscious is detaining me because it knows that this will be the start of a new life.

What wakes me in the end is not the phone, though it is crouching just inches from my ear. There is a thumping at the door. As my unconscious releases me, I find myself on the edge of a bed in an unlit flat in Oxford, the phone ringing, the door booming, not knowing which to answer first.

Based on some dim argument about presence trumping absence, I opt for the door, for responding to the person who is actually there rather than the remote entity at the other end of the telephone wire. Besides, I know what the phone call is about. As for who's behind the door, I have no idea.

It is a policeman. He is tall and burly, and has a ginger beard. My guilty conscience tells me that he has come to arrest me. But no. He starts saying something about people trying to reach me on the phone. Members of my family have been trying to get hold of me, he repeats, *ringing the receiver off the hook*. As a last resort they have phoned the police station in Oxford, to send a policeman round to wake me up. Is he annoyed or amused? The phone continues to ring. I am still naked.

I head back into the bedroom to pick it up. It is Simone's aunt, Lydia. Simone has gone into labour. It is bang on the due date. We decided it was best to have the baby in London, as there was family near by, while I set up our new flat in Oxford. So Simone is staying with another aunt, Jo, in Primrose Hill. Yesterday evening, when Simone and I spoke on the phone – she in London, I in Oxford – she assured me that no birth-giving was in the offing. Hence perhaps the depth of my sleep. Now Lydia is forcing information at me down the line, and I am trying to drink from the fire hose. Simone is in the obstetrics department at University College Hospital, on Huntley Street, in Bloomsbury, London. Lydia gives detailed instructions on which entrance to use. I can't picture the place or take it in. To me, a suburban boy, central London is a black box.

How to get from Oxford to London at three in the morning? There will be no trains to Paddington station at that hour. I don't have a car. The only alternative is a taxi, but I'm unemployed and have literally no money. The idea of taking a taxi to London is preposterous. I wouldn't take a taxi into town, let alone from city to city. The cost defies calculation.

After due dithering, I decide to call Simone's parents' house. I explain that I can't get to the hospital, and ask to borrow the money. But I call with trepidation. I am the student dropout whom they have met only twice. At the first meeting, almost a year ago, I was just the summer fling. The second meeting was at Waterloo station, where the parents greeted us off the train.

Simone was heavily pregnant with my child, and I was look-ing everywhere except into their eyes. I'm convinced that, to them, I'm the layabout who sponged off their oldest daughter in Perpignan and got her pregnant. My credit rating isn't high. But in this hour of need, as ever, they are gracious. They are active mem-bers of their Catholic church and do good in the community. The money is pledged. I look for my cheque book. I know the cheque will bounce, but that won't come to light for a few days. I fumble through the Yellow Pages, hands now shaking, and call a minicab firm.

As soon as I inform the driver of my mission, he steps on it. He drives like the wind. I have never been driven so fast in a car. He says that if the police stop us, they'll understand. They'll probably put you in the squad car and drive you themselves, he joshes: blue lights flashing, sirens blaring.

With the M40 behind us and the Marylebone flyover bearing us aloft through west London like a toy car on a toy bridge, and now passing Euston station, the driver asks me for directions. I know the name of the hospital. I know the street. But no more. He is from Oxford: London's not his manor either. The well in the driver's-side door has no *A to Z*. Smartphones are yet to be invented. And so, having reached London in about forty minutes, we get mired in the squares and one-ways of Bloomsbury for as long again. It is like being in a maze. He's looking out the driver's side, I'm looking out the passenger window; both of us are scruti-nising the buildings for signs.

At length, we locate the red-brick hospital, gloomy as a castle in the 5 a.m. light. I write out the cheque for forty-three pounds only, slam the door shut, and bound up the stone stairs. Simone is on the bed, pushing hard. The baby comes, a purple and white larva, slippery and warm and as charged with life as a battery. This is the creature we have been referring to as 'Sweet Pea' for all the time that she has been furled up like a fern in the womb. Her very first act in the world is to sneeze, to blow away the prehistoric goo and enter human time.

What does it mean to bring new life into the world? How is the act of birth connected to the act of sex that preceded it? Obviously there is a biochemical chain of cause and effect, but the two events can feel so unrelated that they might as well have occurred on different continents. How can we make sense of taking up a new place in the schema of generations? For at that moment, when Sweet Pea came out of the tunnel and in the light became Anna, Simone was no longer just a daughter but also a mother. I was no longer just a son but also a father. Although Simone and I were both young – just twenty-two – we found ourselves instantly elevated one branch up the family tree, as if on a genealogical ski lift. I felt the sense of being caught in the onward rush of life. That is part of what it means to be a human being, and it is the answer that this chapter will develop.

There is a supplementary question, concerning our relationship to the unknown. I touch on this question because in that room in UCH as the dawn was coming up on an early autumn day in London, with the baby arriving in all its hotness and strangeness as if down a chute from Venus, I felt as if I knew nothing at all. Or rather, the experience was so enveloping that any understanding was blocked.

Down and out in Oxford and Croydon

I had met Simone at a summer job in July 1986, the year before Anna's birth. We were both working at a call centre for British tourists who run into difficulties abroad. We the staff, most of us language students, would liaise with the local services overseas. We would speak French, Spanish or Italian on the tourists' behalf whenever their rental car had a prang or someone broke a leg. Simone had finished her degree and was about to take up a one-year teaching position at the University of Perpignan, in the south of France. I had completed two of the three years of my English degree at Oxford, and was disaffected. I couldn't engage. My plan – my non-plan – was to throw in the towel.

There was another reason for my lowness. Some months earlier, I had broken up with my girlfriend of three years, Astrid. Actually, she had broken up with me, and I was still smarting. In an old Mini, Astrid drove down from Birmingham to Oxford with her identical twin sister to deliver the news. We faced off like actors on set in my high-ceilinged ground-floor room, with me trying to persuade her to stay. While the sister waited in the car, we had the best sex that we had ever had. The sex didn't change her mind. It was a closing ceremony.

I wanted a girlfriend to fill the gap. To redeem myself, in fact. When Astrid left me it felt like I had failed. By finding somebody else, I would prove that I wasn't a failure. I would show Astrid that I was a worthy boyfriend and that she had made a terrible mistake. And so I dated a physiotherapist who had done an ultrasound on my knee after I'd dislocated it, not for the first time, playing cricket. It was the reactivation of a longstanding injury – no pun intended – which, later in life, would make it impossible for me to walk down stairs without pain. I sat in my underwear at the John Radcliffe Infirmary as she smeared the paste around my patella. She pressed the cold metal head against my skin. We caught each other's eye. But when I cooked her dinner, she claimed to have had a big lunch and left most of it. That seemed to stand for something. We didn't see each other again.

Earlier that term there had been a party in the house, in my friend Simon's room next door to mine. I had been dancing with Elizabeth, Simon's supposed girlfriend. After the party had wound down and I had gone back to my room, she knocked on my door and got into my bed. I told her that I couldn't betray Simon. Once I had denied her three times, she walked out and wouldn't speak to me again. She left her sweater in my room, an oversized magenta V-neck by Oscar de la Renta that I kept for years.

That bed was a red futon given to me by Uncle Rowley, my father's half-brother and my godfather. Though he was now living on a farm in remotest Suffolk, we were still close. The futon was a twenty-first birthday present. But it must have been jinxed because every time a girl got in, the prospect of sex got out. There was a chaste American, Sylvia, with whom I'd been flirting. Though she was keen to lose her virginity, I didn't want the responsibility of taking it. There was Poppy, the girl from the library, who spent much of term away from Oxford mucking out horses on her parents' farm. She just wanted to cuddle. There was Bronwen, the dark Welsh beauty, who lived in the house itself, on the top floor, and came downstairs to spend an entire evening on my accursed futon, smiling and twisting her hair, before going back up to bed. And there was Kate, one of my best friends. After going drinking one night, we ended up sleeping in my room, she on the futon, me on the floor. In the dark we started talking about sex. I let my hand brush against her thigh. Our heartbeats quickened briefly before we agreed to remain just friends. Aided by the alcohol, we fell asleep. Once again, the red of the futon had said stop.

So the girl situation was getting me down. But mainly it was Oxford University itself that was sapping me. The freedom it offered opened up like an abyss. Apart from checking in for a one-hour tutorial once a week, we were left to our own devices. Today it would be called 'self-guided learning' but I lacked the maturity to guide myself. I skidded off like a dud missile.

This second year was especially hollow. It was the first time

I had experienced anything close to depression. My thoughts became bleak, my mood saturnine. I lived out of college in a huge and forbidding Victorian mansion on the Woodstock Road, the house where Astrid and I had our valediction. It always seemed empty, even when all twelve study bedrooms were occupied. That house still appears in my dreams, with extra passageways leading into derelict rooms and a basement like a crypt divided into cells, damp and cold.

I spent my days wandering the waterways of Oxford. The evenings found me alone in my room with a treasured Aiwa tape deck, dancing to Marvin Gaye and Talking Heads. I went to bed later and later. I did less and less work. Occasionally I would give in to my weakness for buying clothes, but I was on a student grant which always ran dry before the end of term. For everything else, there was MasterCard.

The lack of money was a background drone and a drain. The previous summer, at the end of my first year in 1985, I had decided to stay on in Oxford for the long vacation or 'vac'. In that era, it was still possible for students to sign on out of term time. The phrase was 'going on the dole'. But my application was refused. I remonstrated with a benefits officer behind a glass screen in the prefab Department of Social Security building on the outskirts of town. To no avail. This was where the government employees received us privileged 'gownies' – as opposed to 'townies' – with the contempt that we probably deserved. It matched perfectly what Kafka describes in his fiction, *The Trial*: faceless administration, baffling paperwork, impenetrable processes. I felt like the Minotaur trapped in the labyrinth.

So for the ten weeks of that long summer, in the year before I met Simone, while I was still with Astrid, I lived on a food budget of a pound a day. I made a few extra quid offering guided tours of Oxford, but not enough to make a difference. One pound equated to a single portion of boiled rice from a Chinese takeaway called Dear Friends – known to us student wits as 'Dead Friends' – and a couple of Snickers bars. That was it. I lost weight. Meanwhile, the credit card bills came through with inexorable regularity, and with interest charged on top like some monstrous dehiscence.

Why didn't I just go home that first Oxford summer and live off my parents, like a normal student, getting my laundry done and having my meals cooked? This was the period after my father had lost his job, when his father, my grandfather, had scraped him like a barnacle off the hull of the ship of the family business, leaving him to bob hopelessly in the waves. To shore up their losses, my parents had moved from the rambling detached house where I had done most of my growing up, into a semi-detached cottage back in south Croydon. The flash cars were sold. My bedroom was a box partitioned out of the master bedroom where my parents slept, with a wall so thin that I could hear them breathe at night. It wasn't home for any of us. On the day we moved in, my mother sat down on the stairs and wept.

Haunting

That wasn't the main reason why I stayed up in Oxford that first summer. Though I too struggled with the comedown in our family fortunes. The loss of social status became all the more acute on going up to Oxford. I could see up close the real-life toffs at Christ Church and Worcester and Magdalen. These were the gilded youth who hailed from old money, had houses in the country, and all knew each other – my peers included David Cameron and Boris Johnson. Before going up, I had assumed that Oxford would be about the scaling of intellectual summits. I soon realised that social altitude mattered more. Being middle class and intellectual was somewhat suspect. Better to be a bit

A short note on cars

The Chrysler in the photo was one of several owned by my grandfather with an 'Oak' licence plate. The registration number refers to 'Ye Olde Oak', the brand name of the tinned ham produced by Rowland Smith & Son Ltd. In the mid 1970s, this vehicle was sold to none other than David Bowie, who was then in his 'plastic soul' phase, and wanted an American car to drive in England. A Chrysler features in his 1975 song 'Young Americans'. Perhaps it was this one. When my father had to give up driving, it represented another break with the Oak dynasty, and a loss of male energy. My own dreams often feature cars. The kind of car I'm driving and the journey I'm on seem to indicate my state of mind at the time.

less bright and a bit more posh. I'd been a keen actor at school and a member of the National Youth Theatre, and Oxford would be a chance for me to take some interesting new roles . . . but the roles were always taken by these chums with skiing holiday tans, liberal allowances and bow ties that needed to be tied.

Admittedly, I had been to a private school myself – the same Dulwich College that my mother aspired to on her son's behalf. But Dulwich was a school for new-money boys from Beckenham or Bromley or, like me, Croydon. By contrast, those bright young things had carved out an elite within the elite, an inner sanctum of privilege cordoned off with a red rope and guarded by a PR team with a list of names from which mine was absent. I wasn't sure if I hated them or wished I was one of them. Probably both.

Ultimately, staying away that summer was a means of avoiding living under the same roof as my father in his castrated state. A state like that of King Lear turfed out of his castle, confined to the outbuildings with the animals. It would have meant seeing his reality first hand. I use the word 'castrated' deliberately. Though the MS would sure enough disable his sexual functioning along with everything else, it was more that the symbolic male energy that should have flowed from father to son, from him to me, had been interrupted. The oil pipeline, the artery of resources, had been blown up by terrorists. Just as I was making my transition from adolescence to the big wide world, and needing male fuel to boost me on, the engine cut out.

More usually the reverse applies: paternal potency induces filial feebleness. There are billionaire fathers with wastrel sons, and celebrity fathers whose male progeny live in their shadow. In those cases, it is an excess rather than an insufficiency of fatherly strength that causes the son to weaken. For me, it was the other way round. And it was as much about timing as anything else. At the point of leaving home I needed a full tank. I had expected my father to fill it up as a parting gift. I got only a few miles down the road before the engine sputtered and died. Why had my father stopped earning money to support me? Why couldn't he have an influential job for me to boast about? Why did he have to crumple into his own despair rather than steer me with gubernatorial ease towards a sure destiny? I felt angry with him, disappointed, cheated.

To tell the awkward truth, I felt it would have been better if he had died. To me he was like a bloodied bull staggering around the bullring, dazed and confused, the picos sticking out from his neck to make a grotesque ruff. A part of me was praying for the matador to put him out of his misery. At least then I would have the opportunity to mourn. In the terms of Sigmund Freud, I would have been able to 'incorporate' him properly. Instead, he was cast into a limbo between life and death. That made it impossible for me as his son to abstract the remaining heat from his corpse, like an electricity thief, and plug it into my own circuit of veins. For Freud, this is one of the chief causes of depression, or what he calls 'melancholia'. Instead of being able to grieve fully for somebody by incorporating them into our memories, we are impeded. They remain only half taken in, and that induces a terrible sadness.

But Freud is talking about people who actually die. He is describing a failure of mourning on the part of those who survive them. My dad did not actually die. Rather, he lived a half life, as if he'd been exposed to radiation. He would stir only to do sums on blotting paper, working out how to eke out his savings, now that no more income was coming in. This half life, half death on his part was the cause of my half mourning. I've effectively remained in this state of half mourning ever since that rupturing of the masculine tract. I think it lies behind the dejection I experienced at Oxford. Freud refers to primitive societies in which the dead king is literally eaten, ingested, as a way of tapping his energy. Not eating leaves you weak. We grow in strength when we consume dead meat. We need the body of the past to sustain us for the future.⬇

The implication is that when you fully incorporate the dead, you won't be haunted by them. They will be satisfactorily swallowed, and you can get on with your business, just as if you'd had a restorative meal. Haunting is less a spectral visitation, in other words, than a failure of mourning. It's not that the dead return, but that the living haven't digested them properly. The living thus keep burping up the dead like a gas which takes human shape, its hologram shimmering before their eyes. And because, with the onset of his two irreversible conditions, MS and unemployment, my father entered a zone that was also neither dead nor alive, it turned him into a kind of ghost that haunted me. It was his ghostly half-presence that spooked me, and I couldn't face living in the little house with it for a whole summer.

But nor could I fight with him. Young adult sons need not only to draw from the male strength of the father, but also to do battle with it. There has to be some alpha wrangle that lets the son believe he has thrown the father over. It's an Oedipal crisis that tightens the relationship between father and son like a screw until the wood splits, and the parts can become individual again. With a damaged father, one mother, two sisters and no brother, I lacked a male adversary to define myself against. My father had become a ghostly gas (the two words are related), and I could punch right through it.

⬆ Freud, like Voltaire before him, makes the link with the cannibalism of the Christian Eucharist, a ceremony in which believers eat the flesh and drink the blood of the father.

The word 'Oedipal', of course, refers to the Oedipus complex as elaborated by Freud. The original version by Sophocles sees Oedipus unwittingly kill his father and marry his mother. Freud recasts the Greek original in psychological terms in order to reveal a general tendency among boys to attack their fathers while idealising their mothers. He says that it is an important phase for a boy to go through. As in, go through and come out the other side. In my attempt here at a Freudian self-analysis, I'm saying that I never quite went through it, or that I might still be stuck in an unresolved version thereof. I couldn't attack my father because he couldn't fight back.

And if I couldn't elbow my way beyond that aggressive phase with my father, does it imply that I remained in a state whereby I idealised my mother in Oedipal fashion? As I pointed out in the Foreword, this book contains disproportionately more material about my father than about my mother. I would answer that writing less about my mother does indeed contain a residual motive to idealise, but in the following sense. Just as my teenage self was squaring up to fight him, I saw that my father was already on the canvas, knocked out by life. With one parent down, and still down to this day – as I write Colin lies in his hospital bed ten miles away – how could I possibly risk damaging the other parent too? Would analysing my mother in the way that I have analysed my father undermine the consolation that I derive from having at least one parent not sitting on death row? Even if any illusions that I hold about my mother serve merely to compensate for the disillusion with my father, that is fine by me. My silence about my mother keeps those illusions about her alive. Those illusions, if they exist, serve a purpose.

Whether or not my self-analysis is valid, it was because of that father–son dynamic that I didn't go home that first Oxford summer. The following year, 1986, I took up the summer job at the call centre and met Simone. Having dropped out of college, I started wondering what I would do with my life.

Sex: more recreation than reproduction

When Freud writes about incorporating those who have passed away, it fits, perhaps surprisingly, with his earlier theory of sexuality. Whether mourning the dead or reaching out to the living, we are bringing the other towards us, overcoming distance, making relationship. Underlying both is an instinct in us to bond with others and get close to them. It is this instinct which for Freud is 'erotic', though in the very broadest sense. He's not talking about sex narrowly defined, but about the wider need in us to discharge our energy. Given that the energy has to go somewhere, our erotic instincts provide a positive channel.

Not that sex is absent from the picture. Our erotic instincts do also take the form of wanting sex with others, that is bringing them into physical intimacy with us. These erotic instincts have an interest not just in the short-term pleasure of the moment, however, but also in the long-term furthering of the species. Sex goes together with life.

Maybe that is a statement of the blindingly obvious. Yet the obvious is recalled more seldom than it might be. Thanks both to the availability of contraception and to a growing acceptance of homosexuality, we make the connection between sex and life less automatically than once we did. Whatever the morals of it, there just is an awful lot of sex that doesn't result in babies being born. That makes sex overall more about recreation than reproduction, as shown in the following diagram. (In the diagram, the size of the circles is a crude indicator of the amount of different kinds of sex that we have.) And whilst the dominance of recreational sex can dull our appreciation of the link between

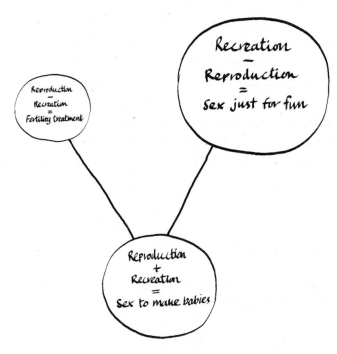

sex and life, our appreciating it less doesn't stop that link from holding.

So how much of the life force is present when we hold erotic feelings for another person? How far is our sexual desire controlled by an unconscious instinct to reproduce? Of course, the question doesn't seem to apply to same sex relationships, where reproduction isn't an option. But does that make the question a bad one? After all, you can still want what's not available. To put it philosophically, impossibility is no constraint on desire. So, oddly enough, we can't be 100 per cent certain that the instinct to reproduce plays no part in homosexual desire, especially if instincts are unconscious, which in Freud they are. That isn't supposed to be an underhand way of averring that gay people are closet heterosexuals. It is just that an unconscious instinct for life might conceivably roam in the background of all erotic feelings.

Unfortunately, it's hard to prove. What we can say is that without reproduction humans would die out, meaning that as a species we need to have sex for our own survival. So although, when we want sex, we might never get any felt sense of the larger imperative, such an imperative could well be there. Maybe that implies that we are rewarded with sexual pleasure by the species as a sop, to ensure its own continuity. But so what? The species isn't different from us, its members. If we are being manipulated, it's we who are doing the manipulating. We win both ways.

Self-sabotage

That summer of 1986, when Simone and I met, turned into autumn. She left to take up her teaching position in Perpignan. I, having checked out of Oxford at the end of my second year, stayed behind in Croydon, in the box room at my parents' house. What was I thinking? I was horrified, revulsed and scared by my father's condition. I had lingered in Oxford during the previous vacation specifically to avoid it. Yet here I was, moving back home. As against the default option, the path of least resistance, which was to complete my final year and claim my degree, I was actively putting the momentum of my life into reverse.

Part of the reason was the fear of sinking further into debt. That fear came with the shame I felt at the prospect of confessing to my financial woes. At home I could live for free, earn some money and covertly get back into the black. And yet the debt really wasn't so large, maybe a grand. Besides, I had a place at Oxford. Imagining a better station in life was difficult. Yet here I was, throwing it away. What was pushing me towards this act of self-sabotage?

I think I felt guilty about driving ahead with my own life when my father had so conspicuously broken down. It would have been like ignoring the fire on the side of the motorway. The point being that it's not how much success you want, it's how much your conscience can tolerate. I didn't formulate it in such terms at the time because I was still saturated with my disappointment in him. All too often that disappointment would come out as hostility. The first time I ever directed the F-word at him was during this period. I remember trembling afterwards, with a mixture of triumph and horror at my crime.

But outer hostility had an inner kernel of love. Or at least a filial concern to tie my fortunes to his, for better or for worse. Even if I longed for him to be different, I was his son, and he my only father. My sabotaging my own prospects was a simple case of a boy wanting to emulate his dad. What made the case unusual was that what was being emulated was catastrophe. When I saw that his car had crashed, I crashed my own.

None of this was conscious. Often, what motivates us at a given point in time is a mystery that becomes clear only with hindsight. I could conceivably come up with a yet truer interpretation of that summer of '86 another thirty years hence, if I'm still around. Big events in life are like dreams in this respect. They spill their secrets slowly, and only after we have forgotten about them for a spell do their meanings achieve transparency. It's not in thinking things through but in leaving them be that the pattern can form which we later discern. Thinking can be a block to understanding. For where thinking wants to *make* meaning, understanding is about receiving it.

And so, with the quotient of hindsight available to me today, I'd argue that, in a way that was obscure to me then, I was seeking to match my fate to my father's. Needless to say, the tragedy points that I scored by dropping out of uni were far lower than those accrued by him. He was suffering from MS, had been ejected from the family business and, still in his forties, had been put out to pasture. Any 'matching' on my part fell far short. In their naïvety, my actions were probably closer to comedy than to tragedy. Nevertheless, I believe the unconscious intention to imitate his story was real.

The conundrum is why I bore that intention at all. What good would it do? The best answer I can give is that I was curbing my own success so as to make Colin's having been deprived of it seem less egregious. Part of me couldn't bear to succeed in case it exposed how far he had been left behind. I suspect such hidden motives might explain many cases where people fail to realise their potential. A secret loyalty is holding them back. I, at least, was nipping in the bud my own prospects for success. It was an intervention designed to exact some parity for Colin, after he had been so outplayed by life and was so many goals down. By breaking my own, I was showing him that a broken life like his was normal. I could thus spare him any sense that he had been singled out for misfortune. I could comfort him that he wasn't alone, and serve as his partner in failure.

Insofar as that intervention involved a sacrifice on my part, however, it was pointless. Maybe copying his downfall helped to absorb the shock it had caused me. Trauma is trauma by virtue of the fact that we repeat it, rather than get over it. But my thriving less could never make him thrive more. Two wrongs don't make a right. If anything, my dropping out would have added to his woes. Indeed, when I first announced that I wasn't going back to sit my finals, he reacted with pure consternation. So pleased was he to have a son at Oxford that he would tell anyone who'd listen. Our local newsagent once reported to me that my father had been in again, buying his paper and talking about his clever charge. 'So proud!' said the newsagent. By quitting Oxford, I was actually taking away one of the few reasons Colin had to be cheerful about the future. His son, so full of promise, was putting his life chances in jeopardy.

I was also allowing my fate to become mixed up with his, like one swimmer helping another swimmer in distress, and causing both to drown. It can be hard for us to accept that fate separates people from each other, especially within a family. Fate undoes the knots that we so readily create as we become entangled with one another. In French, the word for fate is *le sort*, which alludes precisely to this notion of disentanglement, of sorting people onto different tracks. And so, despite my best efforts to subvert myself, to bring my onwards journey to a halt and wait with my father on the hard shoulder, fate had other ideas. A different engine had fired up.

Pomegranate in a shoebox

By the end of that year, 1986, I had tried two further temping jobs. The first was in the accounts department of a computer company located next to the old Croydon Airport. I might have got into Oxford and been a dab hand at English literature, but when it came to numeracy, I was at sixes and sevens. God knows what the auditors made of the books for the period that I was there. The second involved stacking shelves in the food hall at Marks and Spencer, organising the items according to sell-by date. If I was underqualified for the accounting job, I was overqualified for this. With no plan B, I quit on day two.

Meanwhile, Simone in Perpignan and I in Croydon had been writing regularly. We would send each other gifts. In return for a pair of ski pants that I bought her, Simone dispatched a fresh pomegranate. On account of its many seeds, the pomegranate is an ancient symbol of fertility.⬇ The fruit would demonstrate its

---

⬆ The word 'pomegranate' comes from the medieval Latin *pomum granatum*, which means 'apple with many seeds'.

prophetic power in due course, though as a gift it was already suggestive. Simone had wrapped the burnished gourd in news-paper and packed it into a shoebox. With it she had enclosed Baudelaire's poem, 'L'invitation au voyage', which she had written out long-hand in French:

> *Là, tout n'est qu'ordre et beauté,*
> *Luxe, calme et volupté.*

'There is nothing here that is not order and beauty, / Lux-urious, calm and voluptuary'. I lingered over this refrain. Given my context – living with my parents, temping in Croydon – it was beguilingly exotic. Like a siren singing to a sailor all at sea, Simone was calling me to join her.

Again, I would realise it only later, but that wasn't the first time in my family history that such an invitation had been issued. It echoed my father inviting my mother on the transatlantic voyage from England to Canada in 1959 which resulted in their wed-ding. Perhaps that was another reason why I was so amenable to Simone's unwitting reinterpretation of it. My parents' elopement having entered the family folklore, it must have formed a template in my psyche for how romantic events were meant to unfold. The template ran as follows:

> *Out of love, one follows the other across the sea.*

We often play out our lives according to these semi-mythical frameworks implanted in childhood. They work like a fore-shadowing, or the unwitting tracking of ley lines. In both cases, however, accepting the invitation was as foolish as it was roman-tic. By eloping, my parents had been playing fast and loose with their family ties. I was damaging my career prospects still further, for in those days, before the opening up of the European labour market, I had no right to work on the continent. Perhaps it was romantic *because* it was foolish.

A staircase without stairs

Fortunately, Simone had a steady income from her job as *lectrice* at Perpignan's university, which eased the immediate pressure on me to earn money. Perpignan sits in south-west France near the Spanish border. One had only to make the short drive through the slopes of the eastern Pyrenees to see in silhouette against the hills the effigies of bulls that were so talismanic of Spain. The border country also maps onto Catalonia. On Perpignan's labyrinthine streets one would hear Catalan spoken both by old ladies wearing black and old men in flat caps.

A true melting pot of cultures, Perpignan was north African too. Simone had rented digs on the Rue Dugommier in the city's shabby Arab quarter. Our downstairs neighbours were Moroccans. On the one day that it snowed, they congregated in woollen beanies, looking out from the hallway in bemusement. The apartment was on the first floor, above a horse butcher's straightforwardly called A Cheval, with sawdust on the floor to soak up the blood. A few doors down was a bistro, Chez Nicole et Marcel, where they served mussels in piles as high as a wedding cake.

Having a place of our own at that age was wonderful. We had terracotta tiles and red shutters. Not that it was perfect. One day we came back to find that several of the stairs between the first and second floors had crumbled away, leaving a ravine spanned only by the iron of the banister. Whenever the people on the two storeys above us wanted to get into their flat, they had to approach the ascent like mountaineers.

I was to give English lessons. Without a work visa or leave to remain in the country for more than ninety days, however, I'd have to do so on the sly and for cash only. That meant I was nervous of getting caught. It wasn't just paranoia. One night, towards dawn, we were woken by a commotion in the hallway. Doors were banging, people were shouting. '*Ouvrez! Ouvrez! Police des étrangers! Ouvrez!*' The immigration police were conducting a raid. Our Moroccan neighbours in the ground-floor flat were wrenched from their beds. More of them than we ever imagined could live in it were bundled out of the door in their nightwear.

Being on the first floor, Simone and I were next. She was legit, but my number was up. I saw myself thrust into a police cell, questioned and roundly deported. '*Vos papiers!*' barked the gendarme at our door. I fetched my passport from the drawer and proffered it to him as if I were a lamb to the slaughter. No sooner did the officer see the British insignia than he bowed, apologised and moved on. I was as illegal as any of the Moroccans, but the good old racism of the French South had come to my rescue.

In addition to the *grande dame* who hired me to occupy her daughter with English verbs while she had adulterous sex with her lover, one student stood out. For our first lesson, he insisted that we meet at a public venue. I arrived at the Café de la Paix at the appointed hour to be greeted by a Sicilian man called Andrea. He was in his late thirties, stocky, with a broken nose, yellow-tinted sunglasses, a gold chain and greased-back black hair. He said that he was looking for an English-speaking partner in his shoe business. Why he thought a student dropout would fit the bill wasn't clear, but the Oxford connection seemed endorsement enough. I explained that he'd got the wrong end of the stick. I wasn't looking for a business venture, just to earn some francs teaching English.

Andrea and I compromised on a meal at his house, to which

he also invited Simone. In a marble dining room, we feasted on lobster and other *fruits de mer*, accompanied by champagne. The meal was served by his wife, who was coiffed to perfection, dressed to the nines and sparkling with jewellery. Andrea pointed at her as if she were a poodle at Crufts, giving an inventory of each jewel she wore and how much he had laid out for it. Simone and I felt obliged to return the favour, so we had them round to our bijou flatlet. They walked up in their finery, through the hallway that smelled of cat pee. We served trout followed by apple tart. They looked down their noses.

Too much freedom

The disparity in our lifestyles didn't stop Andrea from continuing to court me for my friendship. He would invite me out for *couscous royale* or fillet steak at his expense. He even proposed that I join him on a business trip to Italy. My dual role would be to share the driving and keep him company.

I was far from sure about accepting. That friendship never was quite mutual. I had had my doubts about him from the start. Why did he want to meet in public? What was this notion, exactly, about me being his partner? All I had done was to advertise English lessons in the local classifieds. Out of nowhere loomed this swarthy Sicilian who seemed less interested in learning English than in coercing me into a business scheme. His approach was at best misjudged. At worst, it was sinister. What was his agenda? I wasn't just doubtful; I was also scared. He exuded a dark Mediterranean roughness like that of a Minotaur. With my half-a-degree in English literature, I had only the flimsiest defence. He was unambiguously a man, while at twenty-one I was essentially a boy. It was like the meeting of Innocence and Experience.

In the end, I agreed to go to Italy with Andrea for the feeble reason that I had nothing better to do. When Simone went off to work, I was left to potter around the apartment or mooch about the farmers' market. Apart from a smattering of translation work, there were just my 'little English lessons', as Andrea would disparagingly call them – and not so many of those, frankly. So I was free.

Too free, perhaps, like I had been at Oxford, when I had only to show my face once a week. Because freedom implies the absence of responsibility, it's a close cousin of rootlessness. Pure freedom is bad freedom, in other words. Good freedom comes about when we securely belong. Think of children playing in the garden while their parents make Sunday lunch. The children are all the more free because they are invisibly tethered to the kitchen. It's the feeling of being safely held which, paradoxically, releases them to play.

In my case, there was barely a tether at all. My parents never tried to talk me out of leaving Oxford. After my departure for France, I heard not a peep from them until I dropped the bombshell of Simone's pregnancy. Up to that point, they were content to keep paying out the rope that might have kept me connected, and I was content to keep pulling away. It was all slack. That gave me a strong sense of the arbitrariness of life, of how easy it is to turn onto new paths when there's no firm set of expectations. It lay behind my later decision to make what was, to many people, the bizarre switch from academia to management consultancy. There was never enough glue sticking me to my own track, whatever that was, never any chance of getting stuck in a rut.⬇

⬆ Were it better known, I'd use Scalextric as the metaphor here. Scalextric is a toy car racing game, popular in my boyhood. It's called Scalextric because the *scale* model cars have a rudder that slots into the groove of a metal track, which creates an *electric* connection. The cars are operated by a hand-held throttle. At speed and on bends, they are prone to coming off the track.

The surface over which I moved was as smooth as marble. Freedom and arbitrariness went together. I could slide in any direction.

Red voice, green voice

That trip to Italy in the spring of 1987 began innocuously enough. Andrea and I would take turns at the wheel of his white Audi as we cruised along the Côte d'Azur, while he talked with gusto about sex. He described the positions he favoured for fucking his wife, pausing every now and then to enquire unsuccessfully as to my own proclivities. '*Tu es bien*,' he remarked with sorrow.

Andrea's concupiscence extended to food. He recommended consuming not just the flesh but also the eyes of grilled fish, and sucked the whitened discs from a sea bream. At another restaurant, he returned to his seat having already settled the bill for our five courses – antipasti, pasta, primi, secondi, dolce – so that he could enjoy a second dessert from the trolley, an oozing mille-feuille which he had failed to spot the first time round. He also taught me his method for eating pizza: cut into triangles, roll a triangle up starting with the tip, stab with a fork, then eat from one end, like a wrap.

So far, so good. My doubts on agreeing to the road trip had climbed out of the front seat of my mind and into the back. But they were still in the car. I would describe these doubts as the 'red voice' in my head. If doubt is proactive uncertainty, that is what the red voice was. It said, 'Danger! You are out of your depth!' However, the red voice had competition in the form of a green voice. The green voice was saying, 'It will be fine. Don't be a wimp. It could be an adventure. You've never been to Italy before. What's the worst that could happen?'

Whenever we strike a deal or make an agreement with somebody, we hear these competing red and green voices. The problem arises when we allow the red voice to become stifled. Nearly all difficulties in human affairs stem from poor contracting, that is, when expectations are not surfaced at the outset of whatever the joint effort might be. To take an everyday example that would later happen to me:

> Two couples go out for dinner together for the first time. Couple A declare that they are not drinking alcohol that night, and order tap water. During the course of the evening Couple B consume two bottles of wine. The bill arrives and Couple B pay half the total amount. Couple A pay their half, but they resent doing so. Couple A thought that in announcing that they wouldn't have wine, they had implicitly entered into a verbal contract with Couple B over the division of the bill. But in the social nervousness at the beginning of the meal, that contract wasn't made explicit. The two couples do not go out for dinner again.

In other words, the red voice warns us that the contract has residual ambiguities in it, like undissolved stones that sink to the bottom of a liquid. To mix my metaphors, these stones become the eggs from which poor decisions hatch.

What made me turn the volume down on my red voice was that lack of meaningful work, and a corresponding need to fill it. The mental picture of life in Perpignan that I had painted before leaving Croydon did not feature me as a house husband. A sojourn in the aftershave-drenched company of Andrea's machismo would help to chase away any perceived effeminacy on my part.

In other words, my self-esteem had dropped to a point at which I was more likely to agree to things that I might otherwise have rejected. That's the real danger with low self-esteem: it can draw us into making bad decisions. That sense of my life's arbitrariness, of my being able to slide in any direction, wasn't just about autonomy. It indicated that my life wasn't worth securing.

It was when Andrea and I reached Parma that the atmosphere soured. There had been an intimation of trouble when we crossed the border. Before waving us on, the Italian police had taken a long look at our Palermo licence plates. On our way to the Bologna shoe fair, Andrea and I had checked into a hotel for the night; we shared a room with two single beds. Barely a minute later, the bedroom door was busted open by the cops. They must have been following us all the way from Ventimiglia. It was my second raid in a month. The Armani-wearing carabinieri went through our suitcases. They frogmarched us down to the Audi where Andrea was forced to display his wares. There were just the shoes, as he had protested. That didn't satisfy the police. They lifted the carpets, unscrewed the radio and removed the door panels, questioning Andrea all the while.

They had questions for me too. I was an English student dropout working without a visa in France on a business trip to Italy with a person of interest from Sicily. If those weren't quite grounds for arrest, they were certainly cause for suspicion. My Italian wasn't up to following him, but somehow Andrea managed to blarney his way out of it. The police grudgingly withdrew.

The next day, it all came out. Andrea didn't fess up as such, but he did let me ask questions to which he would supply yes or no answers. Was he laundering money through shoe sales? He nodded. Was it for the Mob? Another nod. The Bologna shoe fair would enable him to close a number of deals, after which he was to report back to his bosses in Milan. Personally, he wanted out. His own brother had been shot down in a helicopter by his mafiosi friends, and Andrea had lost his stomach for it.

A part of Andrea's befriending me, it seemed, was a genuine desire to live a more reputable life. Perhaps that is what he had associated with the Oxford brand. Where I was innocent enough to believe that all experience was good, he, the figure of experience, was hankering after some innocence. He would use this innocence like a cleaning product for wiping his slate: Innocence™. Like the good Catholic that he was, he had an overdeveloped faculty of guilt along with an exaggerated longing for atonement.

We stopped in Milan on the way back, as ordered. Andrea went for his meeting in an anonymous office block, leaving me in the car. Knowing what I by then knew, my wait was tense. What if one of them saw me? Andrea came back half an hour later with new instructions. He was to move his family back to Sicily. After the return drive to Perpignan, I never saw him again.

I arrived home to find Simone in a state. We had been burgled. They took everything, even jeans. My beloved cassette player was gone. In order to unlock the front door from the inside, the bastard had punched a hole through the glass panel next to it, cutting his hand. There was blood everywhere. We were now in 1987, at the high tide of the hysteria around HIV. Would we get infected?

The robbery had a further disquieting aspect. Our apartment was locked and on the first floor. Accessing it required the main door of the building to be breached, as well as that of the apartment itself. Simone herself had been away while I was with Andrea, visiting friends in Provence. We couldn't help wondering whether our Moroccan neighbours were the culprits. Maybe we were being as racist as the immigration police, but who else would have known that we were both away? Apart from Andrea, that is.

The dream

I had arrived in Perpignan with Simone on New Year's Eve, 1986. Simone had been back home for Christmas to visit her parents, and had scooped me up for the return leg. The coach journey from Victoria station took a gruelling twenty-four hours. We pulled into Perpignan's central square just as the restaurants were closing and the floors being swept.

That first night, I had a dream in which I was the father of three daughters. There was little narrative, more a single tableau for me to behold: the three girls and me, as if I were being shown a photograph.

It was rare for me to dream, or at least to remember a dream. Maybe what provoked it was the combination of the travelling, the unfamiliar bed, the first night spent with Simone, and the apprehension induced by having taken this leap into the unknown of another country. More unusual, however, was the fact that the dream featured a family. Of all the fantasies regarding my future that I nurtured at the age of twenty-one, none included children. The very word 'family' freaked me out. It brought up visions of *The Waltons* and other cheesy Americana. The concept of the nuclear family rankled, as it diminished alternative ways of life. Family was so *mammalian*: whither had our human faculties disappeared in this guileless mimicry of the animal world? With a young man's single-mindedness, I also thought that having a family would attenuate my heroic purpose in life. Not that I had one.

What was stoking all this aversion? That lack of tethering to my birth family, no doubt. It was as if, growing up, a centrifugal force had whirred in the house, like the drum in a washing machine, spinning my parents and sisters into different corners. Not to mention the central fact of my father's decline. For me, belonging to a family meant living in a micro-culture that had failed to coalesce around anything much, save for that heart of darkness.

In short, dreaming about having a family should have made me anxious. In fact, it felt benign. By the time I dreamt the dream, on the first morning of 1987, Simone was pregnant.

C'est une fille

It was another three months before we knew. Since we were using birth control, it was a while before it crossed our minds, but eventually Simone went to the doctor. When she came home with the news, I sat on the bed and buried my face in my hands. Here is some of what I thought and felt:

WHAT I THOUGHT	WHAT I FELT
This isn't happening to me	I'm scared
Is it really true?	Phew. It's not really true
It's important to stay in control	I can't cope
We should have an abortion	I'm not ready
We should have the baby	I'm a man
We jointly made this baby	I had nothing to do with it
I know nothing about babies	I'm stupid
This interferes with my life plan	I feel lost
Simone and I will be bound together	I'm not 100% sure about us
She would be a good mother	I would be a bad father
A family is forever	I don't want to be tied down
I don't have enough money	I'm a loser
This should be a joint decision	I want to decide by myself
This should be a joint decision	I don't want to make a decision
This should be a joint decision	Simone should decide
I am being too rational	Simone is feeling lots of emotion
I should take charge	Somebody help me

A few weeks later, Simone went back to the doctor for a scan. This time I accompanied her. Given we were in France, where eating rare red meat was the norm, he warned us about toxoplasmosis, a blood disease carried by undercooked food, and the dangers it held for pregnant women. Simone and I later laughed at how typically French the whole thing was. Other than that, all was routine. The doctor performed the scan. To me, the fuzzy black and white image was as indecipherable as a galaxy. The foetus lay inches beneath the skin yet seemed as remote as an astronaut blurred by cosmic sleet. When we asked about the gender, the doctor suavely replied, '*À mon avis, c'est une fille.*' 'In my opinion, it's a girl.' Sweet Pea was frolicking like a seahorse in her amniotic bath.

Secret motives

The pregnancy came out of the blue. We hadn't planned it, we were using contraception and, for the purposes of bringing up baby, our circumstances were far from ideal. Simone was on a fixed-term contract; I was on no contract at all. Neither of us had a home or a job in the UK to go back to. We'd been together a few short months, and were a long way from committing to each other as life partners. My desire to start a family was zero. To the extent that I had plans, they were as self-oriented as any twenty-one-year-old's plans would be. What's more, the model of fatherhood that I held in my mind was shaped by my own father, Colin. If that was what fatherhood looked like, then thanks but no thanks.

So there were more than a few enemies that the pregnancy needed to defeat. On paper, it shouldn't have won. But despite all those forces lined up in opposition, maybe a part of me wanted what shouldn't have happened to happen – to say nothing of

Simone's own unconscious motives. Was I surreptitiously on the lookout for a chance to become the father whom I wished I had had? It was more than not wanting to be his son. *That* agenda I was already enacting. On my eighteenth birthday I had declared that I would no longer address my father as 'Daddy' (so babyish!), but by his first name, 'Colin'. It felt awkward but I was militant – in the way that a young boy is militant when he runs away from home with a knapsack and a bag of crisps.

Was I now going one step further, by wresting the role of father from Daddy? I did take the first opportunity available: conception occurred within hours of being dropped off from the coach. It was as if I had seen a way to reinstate the figure of thrusting fatherhood which, with Colin's demise, had been swiped away. I was young and healthy, with all my life ahead. If he couldn't do it, then I would. Rather than observing his position as if through binoculars, I would commandeer it. I would lift from Colin the burden of being a father himself, freeing him to slay his own demons and return to vigour.

Who knows. Beneath our stated intentions, the layers ladder down like strata on a cliff face. I would group these layers into four, as in the triangle below:

	MOTIVATION TYPE	BENEFICIARIES	EXAMPLE
LAYER 1	Personal	Me	I don't want a baby, I just want to do my own thing
LAYER 2	Systemic	My family and/or friends	I want to become a father in order to spare my own father
LAYER 3	Societal	My country and/or culture	France wants to up its birth rate
LAYER 4	Biological	The species	We want to reproduce or we'll die

1. We all have a top layer of selfish interests. I was concerned that my own life should go well, without having a baby to worry about.

2. At the next layer down, I was heeding an unconscious call to repair the damage in my family system (hence the 'systemic' label). This I would do by pumping life back into the punctured figure of the father, substituting myself for Colin.

3. Beneath layer two sits that level of motivation which keeps us in line with our society's expectations. Largely without thinking, we will adopt prevailing norms, seeking not to stand out. It takes effort to be different: fitting in is so much easier. Hence the dominance of that nuclear family. On our arrival in France, the government was just launching an initiative to drive up the birth rate. Billboards displayed pictures of cherubic babies, accompanied by cheeky captions inviting the population to go forth and multiply.

4. At the deepest level, our motivations are bestowed on us by the species as a whole. The species is fixated on its own survival. We need life to go on, even if not all of us will serve as its agents.

The further down the triangle we go, the less conscious our motivations become. That doesn't mean they lose power. On the contrary, we find ourselves subject to increasingly puissant forces. By the time we touch the ground floor that marks the species level, we are unlikely to be aware of any 'motivation' at all. Few of us will have children for the sake of preserving the species. But the fact that our minds won't register the needs of the species – except in an abstract way – doesn't mean that our bodies aren't teeming with those needs. That's the life force at work. Whatever else we might be, we are vehicles of life and its indefatigable drive to keep driving. Some of us create children; none of us created life. Although we can suppress life through contraception, abortion, and even acts of killing, we are only holding back a force that is stronger than we are.

Up to a point, this force fits with what the nineteenth-century German philosopher Arthur Schopenhauer refers to as 'will'. For Schopenhauer, 'will' is a striving in all things – animal, plant and mineral – to continue being themselves. It has an invisible but surging energy. Schopenhauer doesn't focus on the transferring of this presence from one generation to the next, yet the quality of 'will' that he describes seems close to what I mean by 'life force'. It is that which compels all things to be what they are. It also stops them, for as long as they exist, from becoming nothing. Human beings are no less subject to this law than are the animal and plant kingdoms, and even the realm of the inanimate. If my guiding question for this book is 'What does it mean to be a human being?', then one answer is that human beings, like everything else, are saturated with will.

The future of the past

Each one of us represents a bet placed by the species in the interests of multiplying itself. Not all the bets will come off: that's what makes them bets. And yet every one of us is living proof of a bet that did. We leave behind a cloud of countless lives that never came to be, like a trillion soap bubbles popping in the air. We, the few, got life. They, the many, did not. For as long as we are alive, we keep life itself alive. That is perhaps the deepest vocation that we can follow. Without our lives to bear it like a flame, human life itself would expire. Say we achieve little success personally; or fail to love our family as much as we could; or make a negligible contribution to society. Nevertheless we will have kept life alive, and that is not nothing.

As far as furthering the human race is concerned, the brute fact is that those of us without children represent an end-stop.

But we can look down the telescope the other way. To be here implies having come from somewhere. The life force has flowed into everyone, regardless of whether it flows out into the next generation. We are ancestral creatures one and all. Typically, we will look back as far as our grandparents or great-grandparents; we will hold three or four generations in mind. Our ancestors are active in us from roughly a hundred years back. They animate our memories even if they no longer move in the world. They enjoy an afterlife during which their name, whenever it is recalled, will swivel like a weathervane in the minds of those who survive them. In this sense, our ancestors don't finally die until the fourth or fifth generation after them has arrived.

That sounds like a stretch, although in ancestral terms it's nary a dot on the timeline. Our ancestors extend back for hundreds if not thousands of generations. There isn't one of us who is not descended from real people who lived in the eighteenth century, the eleventh, the fifth. We have hind-parents from the time of Muhammad, Jesus, Buddha, the Pharaohs, the builders of Stonehenge and before. Hind-parents are people who lived at the same time as those iconic figures, and who placed their children on a serpentine line that eventually found its way to us. Before they were people, they were apes; before they were apes, they were birds; before they were birds, they were fish; and so on, back to the flickering origin of life itself. Thanks to the DNA that was passed down, we hold that line in our bodies. We are the past from which we have come.

The majority that do have children are prolonging the being of their remotest ancestors. It works like an ancient yeast, this thing called 'being', a germ with the miraculous power of regeneration. Not that this wonder-culture is any vaccine against death. Even as our children keep a trace of us going, we die. Their arrival signals our departure, no matter how drawn out. Obviously, people without children are mortal too. It's just that, with an extra generational layer beneath them, parents may find their mortality more clearly framed. The clock doesn't tick any faster for parents than for non-parents, but perhaps it ticks louder.

In my case, there was a twist. Let us run with the hypothesis that, by becoming a father, I was replacing my own father. In doing so, I was also giving life to my own future replacement, in other words the baby. I made myself both vital and redundant at a stroke. Hardly the action of a genius. Really, all I needed to do was to love my father for who he was, rather than wishing he were someone else. Trying to change their parents is one of the most futile pastimes in which children can indulge. If only I had learned that lesson earlier. I might have spared myself those psychological contortions.

But had I done so, there might never have been any Anna, the daughter who began life in the womb as Sweet Pea. Not to mention my second daughter, Ruby, and my third daughter, Greta. They arrived in 1991 and 2006 respectively, as if fulfilling a prophecy.

The dream revealed nothing, however, about that fifteen-year gap, nor the fact that the daughters would have different mothers. In this respect, the dream was a riddle, not unlike the witches' prophecy in Shakespeare's *Macbeth*.⬇ In Act One, the witches tell Macbeth that he will never be killed by a man 'of woman born'. From this information, Macbeth quite reasonably infers that he is invulnerable to murder. In Act Five, Macbeth is stabbed by Macduff. It turns out that as a baby Macduff was delivered by Caesarian section. He was never 'born'

⬆ As well as *Macbeth*, Shakespeare's *King Lear* comes to mind, a play in which the eponymous king divides his estate among three daughters.

in the technical sense. The prophecy was playing with Macbeth's assumptions, just as my dream had tricked me into assuming that all three daughters would share the same mother.

The importance of doing nothing

Trying to stand in for my father spoke to an urge on my part that was immature. Or premature, rather. Because I couldn't bear to spectate on his life, I was trying to hasten his death. Doing so would turn me prematurely into a father in my own right. As a precocious essay at adulthood, that fitted with acts of far lesser import, such as the calling of my parents by their first names, which was supposed to prove how grown-up I was. It fitted with starting to shave before I really needed to, as I had done at fifteen. It fitted with lying about my age to my first girlfriend, Emma. I told her I was doing my A levels like an eighteen-year-old, when at sixteen I was only doing my Os. In all cases, I was jumping the gun. Maybe it was a response to having an older sister, showing that I wasn't lagging behind. Whatever the cause, the natural – and unhurried – process of maturation caused me stress. I was forever trying to catalyse it.

Knowing *when* to act is at least as important as knowing what to do. Ripeness is all. And sometimes the best course is to do nothing. Broadly speaking, that is the Taoist approach. It's not about inertia, however. The advantage of minimising our own activity is that it maximises the effect of powers larger than we are. We get out of our own way. That allows us to be carried instead by a knowing tide. We recognise that there are wider forces ready to disport themselves, forces such as that species imperative. If being human means standing in the flow of life, then perhaps we should allow that flow to happen, and accept that life is stronger than any of us. Let us stop trying too hard.

Because we in the West live in a culture that believes in making rather than letting things happen, that approach might be unpalatable.⬇ We favour action, looking down on inaction with disdain. Yet it was exactly at the point where I was no longer calling the shots that I was rewarded with a daughter.

When I decided to drop out of Oxford, I believed I was taking my life into my own hands. I was exhibiting, even flaunting, my agency. As I've said, there was a powerful enough default option, in the form of carrying on with my degree. Interrupting that momentum took effort. But as the thunderbolt of Simone's pregnancy proves, I could direct events only so much. My interruption was interrupted. The result, however, was a daughter whom I love. That raises the question of what other powers were at large, powers operating a level deeper even than the species. Might there be a fifth layer to our triangle, a wider base?

That I was prematurely made a father might have been chance. Except that 'chance' is such a non-answer. Given that Anna's appearance in the world was so positive, was there a benign will that made it happen? In pop terms, was this 'the universe' doing me a favour? The practical benefit of Simone's pregnancy was that it made me realise I should go back to Oxford and finish my degree. It forced me to sober up. If I was to be a father, I should give us as a family the best foundation. An Oxford degree, which luckily enough I was two-thirds of the way to completing, was exactly that. At the very least, I would be pulled out of the hole I had dug. Whether it was chance or the machinations of a spirit, some goodness was abroad, some benefit being dispensed like overnight dew.

⬆ I was once asked by an interviewer how to let things happen. The problem with the question is that it's trying to ascertain how to *make* letting things happen happen.

Again, it's hard to know. Powers such as chance or 'the universe' are inscrutable. That is partly what it means to be human. We never know for sure the balance of our own agency versus all the other forces operating upon us. The lesson that I draw from Simone falling pregnant is that sometimes it is better to take one's own hands off the steering wheel. Trust that you'll be delivered safely to the right destination, even though that destination might not be the one that you punched into the SatNav.

A pint of Guinness

Put another way, knowing can be the enemy of being. Although it is human to want to know, the fact that our knowledge has limits is what keeps us open to experiences we can't fully understand. That is possibly the moral of the Garden of Eden. In warning Adam and Eve against eating from the tree, God is imparting general advice to us all: keep your knowledge in check, so that you can enjoy the benefit of forces beyond your ken, forces working for your good. Yes, that sounds paternalistic; but then we are talking about God.

The experience of Anna's birth was one I will never fully know or understand, no matter how many the hindsight miles by which I overtake it. Too many thoughts, feelings and prior events had converged at that point for me to make sense of them. But that is exactly what allowed it to make such an impression. My reasoning couldn't block out the experience. Some fragments: the grey light filtering in from the courtyard; Simone squeezing my hand to the point of crushing it; the crowning of the baby's head as slick as an otter's; the rapidity with which the body slithered out once the shoulders were through; the whole scrunched-up baby held aloft by the midwife, with the umbilicus attached, as though she were lifting an oversized telephone with its cable; the placing of this rubbery alien on Simone's breast.

Later that day, my oldest friend from school, Charlie, came to visit. He was at the same stage as me, about to start his third year at university. He insisted that we wet the baby's head. We went for a swift pint of Guinness at a nearby pub. It was there that he told me his girlfriend had fallen pregnant by accident, and that they were going to keep it.

> Now the family is rejoined. In a
> gold circlet they weep of old fears.
> It is warm here, the sycamore
> pales at last. His to keep. Amass.
>
> J. H. Prynne

3

The Keys to the Tower

If you want to identify me, ask me not where I live, or what I like to eat, or how I comb my hair, but ask me what I am living for, in detail, ask me what I think is keeping me from living fully for the thing I want to live for.

Thomas Merton

Michaelmas Term 1987 began two weeks after Anna was born. By now, the three of us were ensconced in a breezeblock-lined, one-bedroom flat, in a university accommodation complex several leagues north of central Oxford, far up the Banbury Road. This was the very flat where, a fortnight previously, I had received that late-night phone call from Simone's Aunt Lydia, urging me to make haste to London for the birth. Anna slept in the living room, snug in a Moses basket perched on my red futon, which was now doing respectable duty as a sofa.

It was the first term of my last year. With a new baby in the mix, I approached it like a job. Where my fellow students were getting up when they fancied, shaking off hangovers, smoking roll-ups, playing snooker in the common room, and putting off work until the essay deadline was upon them and they were forced to pull an all-nighter, I was a picture of orderliness. I arrived at the library when the doors opened, did my research, wrote my essays, reported for my tutorials, and in the afternoon relieved Simone of baby care. I cycled back not just with books in my basket but bumper packs of nappies dangling from the handlebars.

In the evenings we'd stay in, watching *EastEnders* on a portable black and white TV with a dodgy picture, while Anna fed or snoozed. When she was doing neither, and just crying, we would take turns swinging the Moses basket and humming lullabies until she dropped off. When even that didn't work, we'd turn on the vacuum cleaner. No, not to suck the bawling infant out of our lives. It's not unusual for babies to find 'non-periodic' noise soothing, and for Anna it did the trick.

That model of 'lots of time, few responsibilities', which was the model by which most arts students lived, was supposed to empower them. Free from the quotidian constraints that were to shackle them after college, they would not only satisfy their academic requirements, but would naturally read around their subject and generally improve their minds.

That was the theory. In practice, the absence of pressure caused a reduction in drive. They grew lazy. At least, that had been my experience before dropping out. Now that my third year had come around, the time available to me for studying, shortened by family commitments, meant that I had no choice but to be efficient. I would argue that the constraints actually improved the quality of my work, in that I saw my studying time as precious. I focused. No doubt there is a general rule in that: we work best under a certain amount of stress. A bell curve applies, as in the diagram opposite. Maybe all students should have a young family.

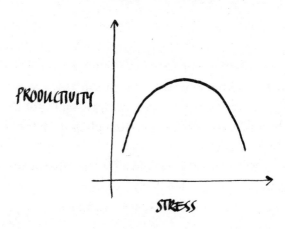

On purpose

The overarching question that guides this book is, 'What does it mean to be human?' While tracking a life, in this case mine, along a more or less straight line, each chapter offers a different tangent to that question. The tangent suggested in the last chapter was that of *standing in the flow of life*. As if planting one's feet in a river, being human means feeling the past of the species surge up behind us, while sensing its urge to flow onwards. None of us is more than a boulder in the onward mission of the life force.

In this new chapter, I shall crop that trans-generational view down to an individual life span. How do we make our allotted time on earth meaningful? We do so, I believe, by identifying and pursuing a purpose. By 'purpose' I mean more than doing what we have to do to survive. One of the elements that makes us human is that we are capable of going beyond meeting our immediate needs for survival. Of course, we don't always have the luxury of doing that. Sometimes survival is the best that we can hope for. Think of refugees or people living on the breadline. Once our basic needs have been met, however, we naturally want to optimise our lives, to make them go as well as possible.

That we can do in one of two ways. Either we try to make our lives more comfortable or we try to make them more meaningful. In reality, the choice isn't black and white: we'll make trade-offs between the two. To use an obvious example, we might take a job with a charity that doesn't pay so well because we want to make a difference; but we stop short of giving away all our earnings in order to maintain a standard of living. Thus we strike the balance between meaning and comfort that feels right for us. Often we find that balance intuitively, without explicitly posing the question. It's an intuition that we all possess, this knowing whether we are driven more by meaning or by comfort.

The lucky few manage to square the circle. A human rights lawyer will have meaningful work while enjoying a pretty decent lifestyle. A smaller minority still will pursue personal comfort with no regard for meaning at all. To use another obvious example: bankers. For such groups, there is perhaps a hidden cost to be paid, however. Not only can gaining money go together with losing meaning, but in the process the conscience may become restive. In the blinkered pursuit of wealth, the desires of the self eclipse the needs of the soul to such a degree that, in the darkness, doubts about one's very goodness as a human being may arise. An excess of comfort can feel uncomfortable. The thicker the mattress, the greater the chance of a pea.

I was given my own sense of purpose through those twin occupations of studying for my finals and being a parent. They filled the crater that had opened up when I dropped out and went to live in France with no life-plan to speak of. As it turned out, my studies provided a purpose that would sustain me beyond the immediate challenge of preparing for my exams.

French intellectuals

I had gone up to read English at Oxford in October 1984. There had recently formed a group calling itself 'Oxford English Limited' (OEL). The name was a pun: OEL's mission was to expose the limitations of the English Literature syllabus. Its high-minded members claimed that the study of English at Oxford had been reduced to whimsical musings about novels and the lives of their authors. Made up largely of Marxists, OEL insisted that literature be examined in its political context. Rather than extolling *Pride and Prejudice* for its marvellous characters and charming plot, we should be looking at the way in which class differences were reinforced by its author. Through this lens, which was the opposite of rose-tinted, it appeared that Jane Austen was doing little more than condoning the bourgeois way of life. She was thereby perpetuating capitalism rather than disrupting it – disruption being the Marxist protocol.

The early 1980s was the era of Margaret Thatcher. Discontent with her brand of Conservatism infected not just those on the far Left but also those of more moderate kidney. That Marxist approach to literature fitted with an anti-authoritarianism that was in the air. Yet to me it came as a jolt. At school I had been taught to judge literature purely on its aesthetic merits. Did the novel achieve a satisfying unity or did it feel fragmented? Were the characters 'flat' or 'round'? How successfully did the language used by the author express his or her intentions? Here was a much more abrasive approach. According to OEL, a novel was less a work of art than a battleground upon which ideologies were fought out. Like many of my peers, I was forced to rethink my assumptions.

The OEL call to politicise the study of literature went together with a wider attempt by progressive dons in the English faculty to bring continental thinking to bear upon literary studies. Of especial interest were the ideas of Parisian intellectuals such as Michel Foucault, Julia Kristeva, Hélène Cixous, Roland Barthes, Jean-François Lyotard, Gilles Deleuze, Luce Irigaray and Jacques Derrida. Though the differences between these thinkers were as great as the similarities, their output was often taken *en bloc*. This block went by the moniker of 'Post-Structuralism'. It combined a depth of analysis with a width of reference that made the Oxford way of doing things seem to me parochial and lightweight.

From that list of thinkers, it was the last, Jacques Derrida, to whom I felt the greatest draw. There was a book of Derrida's called *Writing and Difference* – my paperback translation had an avocado green cover – over which I pored as if it were the oracle. I'm not sure that I understood a word to begin with. But that didn't matter. I became mesmerised by the intricacy of the sentence structure, the elegance of the argumentation, the intensity of the analysis, the boldness of the conclusions.

This too was disruptive but in a way which, to my mind, was far more fundamental than that of the Marxists. Derrida was systematically deconstructing the cornerstones of Western philosophy, all the way from Plato through to his own contemporaries. Those cornerstones weren't merely academic. They were the ideas on which Western society as a whole was built – ideas like democracy, truth, justice and freedom. Derrida was showing how many of these ideas just didn't stand up under scrutiny, and that it was time to start again from scratch. To me, it was thrilling.

The very word 'deconstruction', which has since entered common parlance, comes to us from Derrida; although strictly speaking it originates with his precursor, Martin Heidegger. Derrida sought to distance himself from the term, however, on account of its negative connotations. In fact, his work had both a negative and a positive mode, both brake and accelerator. The brake involved taking a fine-toothed comb to the texts of leading thinkers in order to expose biases, point out contradictions, and highlight apparently marginal remarks that undermined the central thesis. The accelerator saw Derrida blending disciplines usually held apart, such as psychoanalysis and philosophy, in order to produce fresh insight. Ever inventive, he created a host of new concepts as well as reinventing the old. Even when debunking the arguments of another philosopher, he would generally do so in a highly respectful manner, helping the reader to understand that other philosopher's reasoning. Through Derrida, one could learn about the entire history of ideas. One also saw how these ideas could be renewed.

Not everybody appreciated both sides. The innate conservatism of Oxford led many academics to denounce Derrida as an intellectual terrorist, bent on detonating the achievements of Western civilisation. They claimed that he was a nihilist. They said that the prolixity of his prose served to mask a lack of clear thinking. To quote a phrase of the times, they belittled his writings as 'intellectual masturbation'.

Jacques Derrida was a divisive figure. In Oxford, the majority took against him, especially the philosophers, although he enjoyed support among a group of Literature dons and assorted mavericks. In many British universities he was reviled, but still there were pro-Derrida camps, especially at Sussex University, in Brighton, which after all was closer to France. At Cambridge – always more international in its tastes than Oxford – the controversy reached a head when a motion was submitted to award the contrarian an honorary doctorate. It threw the academy into turmoil, and the story made the nationals. After measured oration and bitter wrangling, the proposal squeaked through.

The purpose star

Like other Derrida fans, I felt that his detractors had jumped to their conclusions. When I probed as to which particular aspects of his thinking they eschewed, I would be met by generalisations. It turned out that they hadn't read Derrida first hand, and were going on hearsay from their academic friends. It seemed that an uninformed view expressed by a trusted peer counted for more than unfiltered data from the primary source.

Perhaps that's not surprising. One cannot form an opinion without excluding some of the facts. Moreover, one makes that exclusion for the sake of affirming identity. Opinions are first and foremost expressions of our belonging. The content comes a distant second. Whenever we opine on a given subject, our underlying motive is to indicate the tribe to which we belong, and affirm our membership of it. It's one of the reasons why people so rarely change their minds. Changing your mind involves changing the group to which you feel you belong. That takes courage. Change more broadly follows the same rule: many people attest to wanting to change, but precious few are willing to disturb their identity.

I tired of defending Derrida. My leaning was towards the philosophy itself. Before long, it became my passion. I began collecting the master's books, in English and in French, taking especial delight when I stumbled upon a bilingual edition. I ordered copies direct from Paris. To celebrate the end of my third year, I shelled out forty-seven pounds – a king's ransom – for a hardback copy of Derrida's signature work, called *Glas*.

But why did I latch on so? Why Derrida and not Marx? What's happening when we make such attachments? For many if not all of us, there is a time in our lives, usually in our teens or twenties, when we hit upon the thing that is going to guide us in our work life. At that point – and it often is a point – we see the thing, like an apparition, to which we are going to pledge our time. It might be training as a doctor, setting up a business, working for a politician, joining the navy, making ceramics, coding software, looking after children. Sometimes we make a false start, studying as an accountant before becoming a teacher, or taking up nursing only to leave for the theatre. But nearly always there is a moment – or at least a period – when we identify our guiding purpose and attach to it. It is like noticing a star that you had never seen before and deciding to follow. I call it the 'purpose star'.

Finding the purpose star seems to occur when three conditions are met:

1. There has been an interim beforehand of uncertainty, lack of direction, or sheer purposelessness. It is virtually impossible to make an instant transition from one strong sense of purpose to another. Fallow periods play a vital role in preparing for fertility. Before our purpose can be known, first it must be unknown. Time spent feeling uncertain, therefore, is not invariably unproductive. It could represent a precondition of certainty, a prelude that allows the mind to sift its junk and make space for purpose's arrival.

2. The purpose has to fit with our context. I wouldn't have latched on to Derrida had I not been a student. I wouldn't have latched on had Derrida's work not been a hot topic. I wouldn't have latched on had the study of English literature at Oxford not been in a state of torpor, needing rejuvenation. Realistically, my purpose could never have been to become a fisherman or a miner: such possibilities were too remote from the world that I inhabited.

3. Our purpose has to align with whom we want to be. It is an expression of our ideal selves. I adopted Derrida because I saw him as clever, innovative and cool. If I am candid, these attributes

were exactly the three that I would have picked to describe my ideal self. They were how I wished to be seen. That's not quite the same as identification, which is the process of identifying with somebody else, whereby my hero and I share an identity, or there is an existing affinity. It's rather that a fantasy about oneself is embodied by another person. Jacques Derrida and I were not the same. Between his identity and mine, there lay a gap. What filled that gap was my aspiration to be like him. He might not have been clever, innovative and cool at all. The point is that I valued those three attributes, and then attributed the attributes to him. That made him an ideal version of myself. If he was my hero, he was a proxy for me as my own hero. I then aspired to become this ideal version of myself.

Interestingly, finding our purpose in life has much in common with falling in love. In both cases, we discover an ideal. It lifts our heart and eyes. We experience a delectable sensation of pleasure and meaning combined. There is nowhere else we should be, so it feels as right as it feels good. Falling in love also involves an exclusive attachment to the one person. While it might be possible to love two people at the same time, it's very hard to be *in* love with both. Finding our purpose has the same quality of singling out a unique object, that individual star. We might have several responsibilities, and even more tasks, but we can commit to only one purpose at a time. Put simply, we know we have found our true purpose in life when we have fallen in love with it. Liking is not enough.

The golden arch

My infatuation with Derrida continued through the end of my third year, after coming back from Perpignan. In the early summer of 1988, I sat my finals. I donned my 'subfusc' – dark suit, white shirt, white bow tie, academic gown and mortar board – and went to sit in the examination hall for a full eighteen hours of written tests. When finally I had put the last full stop to the last sentence of the last paragraph of the last essay of my last paper, I stepped out into the lunchtime sun.

The atmosphere resembled VE Day. War was over. Students tossed their headgear into the air and embraced. An Oxford tradition involved the tipping of flour over the examinees, although year on year the ritual was becoming more extreme. By the time I exited onto the cobbles of Merton Lane, we were being doused in takeaway vindaloo from aluminium foil containers. Actually, I was spared. While others clustered in groups and were festooned in varieties of masala, I made a beeline for Simone. She was waiting with eight-month-old Anna in her arms. The three of us had a picnic on the lawn at my college, sauntered through the University Parks, then went home for tea.

The mixture of euphoria and relief that day was heady. But in the days that followed, I and many of my fellow students – fellow ex-students – experienced a fatigue like nothing before. There were tales of people sleeping through until the morning after the morning after. Fatigue subsequently gave way to flatness. This was the low that followed the high. It was as if, walking out of the exam hall that day, we had all passed beneath a huge golden arch; but that now, a week or two later, our steps had carried us away from its glow, onto land that was less bright and warm. What's more, where the arch had pressed us all together through its hoop, we were now in open country, fanning out onto divergent tracks.

When, an agonising six weeks after the last paper, the exam results were posted, the question of our destination became acute. Thanks to that enforced work regime of mine, I had earned the option of staying on in Oxford to 'do research'. Doing research meant another three years of reading and writing, in order to acquire a doctorate.

The yes on my part wasn't automatic, however. For some time, I had harboured the desire to become an architect. While awaiting my results, I'd gone so far as to secure a place at the Architectural Association in London. I had even lined up a junior part-time job with an architectural practice to fund it. But when it came to the crunch, the offer to immerse myself properly in Derrida's work was one that I couldn't refuse. As an undergraduate, my attention to Derrida had been diluted by the other authors whom we were obliged to study. I felt that my understanding was both patchy and thin. Here was a chance to go into depth.

And so, having prematurely escaped from Oxford and come back, I was now signing up for more. Instead of cutting down the amount of time that a student would normally spend among the dreaming spires, I was doubling it. Three years became six. That six would double again, like a roll of the dice.

The shape of a trilby

My purpose was now as clear as it would ever be. I read Derrida's substantial oeuvre in its entirety, first in English, then in French, then in English again. I learned ancient Greek so that I could check out his references to Plato in the original. I enlisted for a refresher course in German so that I could research background material by Heidegger, Kant and Hegel. When quoting Derrida in English, I would work out my own translations from the French rather than relying on the version in print. I even negotiated two supervisors, instead of the customary one. Alan Montefiore's role was to challenge me on my knowledge of

philosophy.⬇ Ann Wordsworth held my feet to the fire on psychoanalytic theory, which was central to the aspect of Derrida that I
was tackling.

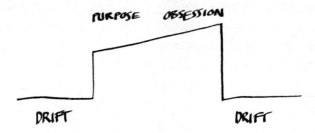

All of which raises the question of when a sense of purpose
mutates into obsession. There's always a chance of following the
trilby shape in the diagram above, from left to right. Before we
find our purpose, there comes that period of uncertainty which
I mentioned before, labelled here as 'Drift'. Then, if we are lucky,
we take a sharp step up to a new level whereupon we reach
our purpose. Should the drive to pursue our purpose become
excessive, however, its character morphs: purpose ramps up
into obsession. And obsession, because so intense, cannot be
sustained. Sooner or later it arrives at a cliff edge. When the obsession burns out, we tumble down into a new state of drift – richer
for the experience, perhaps, but with our energy reset to 'Low'.
Notice that purpose doesn't provide a purely horizontal surface: it
tilts, so that there is always the risk of falling backwards. We need
a little bit of that obsessive energy to keep us pepped up, but not
so much that it turns into obsession proper, which nudges us
towards tripping off the higher end.

In this play between purpose and obsession, there is again an

⬆ Alan Montefiore makes a cameo appearance, on the lawn at Balliol College, in Derrida's book *The Post Card*, which is partly autobiographical. The
two were friends.

analogy with falling in love. I devoted as much time and effort to thinking about my project as I would have spent mooning over a beloved. That sounds sweet enough, but this cerebral romance brought with it a shadow. With the tunnel vision of an entrepreneur, I focused on my project to the near exclusion of everything else. Partly I was driven by the need to complete the thesis within the three-year envelope of my funding. But that doesn't explain the obsessiveness. Simone was now working part time, and we were sharing the childcare. But much as I loved Anna, I was happy when my shift was over, so that I could get back to my research. I began to live in my own head.

If by dropping out I had mimicked my father's loss of purpose, I had now swung to the other pole. All work and no play, I was a dull boy. Maybe I was trying to do double duty: compensating for, rather than imitating, Colin's chronic underemployment. Whatever the cause, it was an addiction. An addiction with two facets. One was that compulsive need to be left alone with my project as much as possible. The other was the sense, common to all addictions, of a rapidly draining tank. There was a celerity on my part in feeling empty, along with a corresponding need to be topped up. Just as an alcoholic finds it hard to register when they have had enough to drink, so I felt that, even after long hours of work, I had barely added to my personal GDP, and needed to heap on more.

Like that alcoholic, however, I was still taking pleasure from it. So although I say that I was 'all work and no play', rarely did it feel like a labour. Or rather, the boundary between work and play dissolved to such an extent that neither word adequately describes my state of absorption. My purpose took me out of myself. And yet it allowed me to be completely present. It was as if I had seen a further golden arch in the distance and was walking fixedly towards it, bathed in its light.

AutoBioPhilosophy

For the title of my doctoral thesis, I chose the words *Derrida and Autobiography*. I wouldn't mention this fact were it not for its bearing on this very book. My research explored the connection between the philosophical and the personal, which is precisely my aim today. This book is a work of philosophy which, in order to illustrate its propositions, draws on life. My nickname for it is 'AutoBioPhilosophy'.

That link is more than a curiosity. It shines a light on the nature of purpose. A year into the planning of the present book had to pass before I made the connection with the thesis written nearly thirty years before. In my fifties, I was reprising a theme that in my twenties had so preoccupied me. Does that imply that purpose stays within us, but alternates between dormancy and activity? Maybe purpose is less like a star and more like a volcano.

So my purpose, then as now, was 'autobiophilosophical'. As if there were always a mirror, we are capable of living our lives and reflecting on them simultaneously. Even if our bodies can't, our minds can stop time, pausing to think about who and why and what we are. We have two selves. There is a bodily self caught irresistibly in the onrushing current of a stream. And there is a mental self, which can step out of the stream at any point, shake itself dry, and look back at its bodily avatar in the water. We all have a wet and a dry mode.

The dry philosopher will spend more time reflecting than most. That on the one hand is an advantage. Time given to reflection allows for perspective. On the other hand, it means living life at one remove, as if behind glass. It can also mean not being present in the moment. It has occasionally given me the troubling sensation that my life is a laboratory: an experiment as much as an experience. The following chapters will tell the story of how

I continued to make shifts as the years progressed. In part, those shifts were no more than a rational response to changing circumstances. However, I might have been reorienting my life simply to provide me with a new angle on it, thus becoming my own case study. Was I, like a diamond-cutter, hewing more surfaces merely to enhance the stone's lustre?

There is a philosophical as well as a psychological aspect to this. Philosophy had seen itself as an objective discipline, undistorted by the subjectivity of the philosopher. Derrida was showing how absolute purity could never be achieved. The philosopher will always colour the philosophy. That renders the cherished ideal of 'pure reason' a fallacy. After all, if people who use reason can disagree, it suggests there is no universal thing called reason. Subjective interests will be in play. Derrida was implicitly admonishing Heidegger, whose assessment of intellectual biographies was summed up in the phrase, 'He was born, he thought, he died.' In Heidegger's mind, the legacy trumped the life.

But not in Derrida's. For Derrida, life and work were inextricably linked. During an interview for a documentary about his own life, Derrida revealed that what he would most like to know about the lives of other philosophers was *'leur vie sexuelle'* – their sex life. Inspired by Derrida, some fellow enthusiasts and I would go on to devise a documentary called 'Sex Lives of the Philosophers'. We got so far as filming a trailer on Brighton beach. The subject matter was never prurient, however. Derrida was making the simple point that philosophers are human beings. They have sex lives too. They aren't brains on sticks. Indeed Derrida's own sex life became a subject of national interest when he fathered a child with Sylviane Agacinski, the wife of Prime Minister Lionel Jospin.

At the very time that I was writing *Derrida and Autobiography*, Derrida was drafting his actual autobiography. Bearing in mind the point about cross-contamination, however, Derrida's text was as much a work of philosophy as a memoir. The title was *Circumfession* – a *confession* beginning with a philosophical reflection on his own *circumcision* as an infant Jewish boy. Although that caused a headache as far as the timing of my research was concerned – having to rein back my work until he had published his – *Circumfession* furnished me, when it arrived, with the perfect material. Up to a point, it was the inspiration for the book that I am writing today.

Praying for all the souls of the Hundred Years' War

In 1990, with two of the three years of my doctoral funding burned through, the time for thinking about next steps had again arrived. Being an academic doctor was worthless unless you planned on being an academic. Of the university jobs that were going, one stood out: Prize Fellow at All Souls College. It wasn't so much a job as a living accolade, somewhat like a knighthood. Only one or two such Fellowships were offered each year. In the world of academe, they enjoyed a giddying prestige.

That prestige was reinforced by the college's wealth. It was rumoured that All Souls had been reprimanded by English Heritage for restoring its chapel to an excessively high standard, spreading on the gold leaf like butter. Though the story may be apocryphal, the wealth was real. All Souls College owned whole villages in England, and boasted a wine cellar second only to that of Buckingham Palace. Not to mention the chief practical benefit of the college's bank balance as it concerned the academic job-seeker: the Prize Fellowship was funded for seven whole years, whereas most colleges could at best afford three.

Wealth bought the college independence. In the University of Oxford, all colleges are sovereign in the sense that they can broadly make up their own rules. But All Souls enjoyed special latitude. It felt under little pressure to demonstrate its 'added value'. That said, the university did once venture to suggest that the college might consider spending more on academic pursuits and less on wining and dining. All Souls' sole mission, handed down from its foundation in the 1430s, was to pray for the souls of all the faithful departed of the Hundred Years' War. Once you'd said your prayers, as a Fellow of the college you could in theory take the rest of the day off.

As a guiding purpose, praying for dead souls sounds antiquated. Compare it with the current mission statement of, say, Unilever:

> Our purpose is to make sustainable living commonplace.
> We work to create a better future every day, with brands and services that help people feel good, look good, and get more out of life.

That could hardly be more modern. But it is no more relevant to its times than the 'mission statement' of All Souls would have been in the 1430s. I would go further and say that praying for the souls of the dead represents a purpose that is evergreen. Like deciduous leaves, the words of the Unilever statement will turn brown and fall to the ground, to be refreshed with a new set the following year.

The 'mission statement' of All Souls demands nothing from its academics in terms of work, but work is a given. I ask in all seriousness, what higher purpose can there be than praying for the souls of the dead? No doubt that question comes across as hyperbolic, but it does make us raise our sights. Furthermore it draws attention to a modern fixation with the living, the present and the future, a fixation that leaves the dead behind. Along with an appetite for isms such as relativism and individualism, an abhorrence of death seems defining of the modern Western world. Because modernity defines itself *against* nature and *with* technology, death, which is natural, doesn't compute. One might add that modernity is that which makes progress to the precise extent that it causes damage, so it is always cancelling itself out.

Me, I had a purpose in completing my doctorate, but by comparison that was trivial. It was less of a purpose and more of a task. Inspired by the All Souls example, I offer the following checklist to assess the validity of one's purpose. Only when you can answer yes to all three items can you say that you have found the real thing:

1. Am I in love with it?
2. Will it sustain me for the rest of my life?
3. Will it benefit others as well as myself?

Perhaps those questions still set the bar too high. Yet all three can be answered in the affirmative quite easily. It only takes choosing a purpose such as 'taking care of my family', which is humble enough. In reverse order: to take care of one's family benefits others; will probably sustain you for life; and, as a vision to fall in love with, is more than credible.

Parfit nominat Smith R. R.

Before going up to Oxford, I hadn't heard of All Souls. That in itself is telling. The college was then, and today remains, a virtual secret. It hides in plain view, plumb in the centre of town, with an entrance on the High Street and a western elevation running along Radcliffe Square. The main reason why it's such a mystery is that, uniquely, it admits no undergraduates, so no undergraduates can report on it. All Souls is purely a research institution.

And yet – another idiosyncrasy – not all of its seventy Fellows are researchers. A handful are barristers, politicians, financiers, or the equivalent. In the college vernacular, they are the 'London Fellows'. One of the college's many contradictions is that it is both the most ivory-like and tower-like of all ivory towers, and yet it keeps one foot in the real world. I do not mean the real world of the coal face, patently, but of the Establishment. When I was elected in 1990, my colleagues numbered several lords, including Lord Hailsham, Lord Waldegrave, Lord Wilberforce, Lord Neill and the subsequent Lord Pannick. That level of public distinction carried across to the academics themselves. On my first night at dinner, I had on my right Isaiah Berlin and on my left Leszek Kolakowski, two of the world's most honoured thinkers.

Access to this temple was tightly controlled. You had either to be a world-class intellectual or demonstrate the promise of becoming one. The Prize Fellowship was aimed at the latter category. Candidates without a first class degree from Oxford or Cambridge – or Harvard at a stretch – needed not apply. Assuming that you met that criterion, and that you were under the somewhat arbitrary age of twenty-six, the application procedure involved:

1. Writing to the Warden, expressing a desire to join the college.
2. Being interviewed by the same Warden, one to one – though this was more a character assessment than an intelligence test.
3. Sitting six exams of three hours each:
   a. Two papers on your specialist subject (mine was English Literature).
   b. Two general papers. General meant politics.
   c. One translation paper. That involved being given a booklet

containing passages of text in about twenty different languages. You had to translate as many as you could. You could also request a specific language, say Basque or Swahili.

    d. One essay paper, requiring all candidates, regardless of specialism, to write on one topic for three hours. In my year, the topic was 'Memory'.

4. Being called out during one of these papers for an 'informal' interview with about twenty of the Fellows, in the mahogany-panelled Common Room.

5. Attending a drinks reception after the last paper.

6. Waiting to hear if you had been shortlisted.

During that celebration of finals two summers before, one of the phrases hit about like a beach ball had been, 'No more exams!' Now here I was, taking another turn on the rack. As if the process wasn't torturous enough, it became more so after the shortlisting. I was summoned for the formal interview on the morning of 27 October 1990, a Saturday. I breakfasted with Simone and Anna, put on a green cotton suit, draped my gown over my arm, and set off, trying to master my nerves. After waiting for the previous candidate to be released from his ordeal, I was called in to the Wharton Room. Upon entering, I was confronted by the full battalion of seventy Fellows, sixty-seven of them men, all begowned so that they looked like vultures, and lined in serried ranks around a huge table decked in baize. Hailsham, Berlin, Kolakowski et al. surveyed me from beneath foreheads lined like text.

There was a lead examiner – or cross-examiner, given the resemblance of the proceedings to a court of law. It was he who conducted the investigation into my intellectual soundness, requiring me to defend the arguments put forth in my papers. His role did not, however, debar his peers from intervening. Having come across a defence of feminism in my exam script, one of these free-range interrogators asked, 'Perhaps you write about feminism in order to impress your female friends?' With a presence of mind that I have seldom been able to recreate, I replied that I found his question offensive. That set off a murmuring among the Fellowship. The Warden himself, chairing the inquisition, proffered an apology. That moment caused a stir that was to last for some time.

It wasn't the only reason why an air of controversy clung to my name. Along with, say, the Reform Club and Balmoral, All Souls College was counted among the most conservative institutions in the country. I do mean conservative with a small 'c', although guests would sometimes include members of the Conservative inner circle such as Douglas Hurd (charming) and Keith Joseph (scary). William Waldegrave and John Redwood, also Tory big cheeses, were Fellows anyway.⬇ I am referring rather to a conservatism of the academic kind. The college's strong suits were history and law, and in all matters it favoured empirical research in the English tradition. In me, the Fellows had before them an intellectual arriviste proposing to spend seven years' worth of their money, office space and food on the work of Jacques Derrida. Derrida of all people! Continental, theoretical and provocative – the associations triggered by the name Derrida could not have run more counter to the All Souls culture. Were the Fellows seriously prepared to garland a card-carrying Derridean with their finest laurels?

Well, no, not quite. They were split. In the end, support for

⬆ As for the presence at All Souls of senior figures from the Labour Party, two Prime Ministers come to mind. At dinner I once sat next to Jim Callaghan. To my embarrassment, I didn't recognise him, and asked what he did. 'I dabble in politics,' came the reply. Only then did I read his name card on the table. Famously, Harold Wilson put in for the Prize Fellowship twice in the 1930s, but was turned down on both occasions.

my cause arrived from an unlikely source in the shape of a world-renowned philosopher very much in that English tradition: the late, great Derek Parfit. His word was influential. The All Souls election process is such that, even when the vote fails to deliver a unanimous verdict, every Fellow is obliged to endorse the person chosen by the majority. This is done by writing one's name on a chit of paper, followed by the Latin word *nominat*, followed by the name of the preferred candidate. Thus '*Parfit nominat Smith R. R.*', 'Parfit nominates Smith R. R.' Every chit is placed in a silver urn. The urn is then emptied, and the senior ranking Fellow declares the result. So it was that on All Souls Day in November 1990, I was 'unanimously' elected to a Prize Fellowship.

How a cat can be an angel

On my walk home after the big interview in the Wharton Room, the Saturday before the Fellows assembled for their final deliberations, I turned over and over in my mind the answers that I had given. I was polishing them to remove the flaws in what I had actually said, flaws which I now recalled with flinch-inducing clarity. I kept going back to the feminism incident, fretting that my response had overstepped the mark. Again and again, I saw the look of confidence on the face of the candidate before me as he came out of the interview room. I convinced myself that I had blown it, and resolved to apply for other jobs as soon as Monday morning came round. As the adrenalin ebbed, I began to feel cold and hungry, resigned to my failure.

All at once I stopped. In front of me was a black cat. I would say that it was the cat who stopped me. It stared up from the pavement on Linton Road, fixing me with its green eyes. I have never been particularly superstitious, but from its gaze I knew that I would be accepted by All Souls. I have rarely been so sure of anything. It was simply a fact, as plain as the road down which I was walking.

That cat was a kind of angel – an angel in the etymological sense of a bearer of news. The word 'angel' comes from the Greek for 'messenger'. As was the case with the prediction of my having three daughters, which was relayed via a dream, messages of special import will sometimes come to us from outside the normal channels. Which is not to say that such angelic messages can't arrive in more conventional forms too. We might fall into casual conversation with a fellow passenger on a plane or a fellow patient in a waiting room, only for them to utter a sentence or two that touches our own situation with uncanny relevance. It is like receiving the answer to a question which has been obscurely burdening us. The stranger's words provide the answer. Equally uncanny is that the stranger appears unaware of the significance of their words. It is as if they were but the passive vehicle of a message from elsewhere.

It follows that what goes for strangers also goes for us, insofar as we all serve as strangers to other people. Without us necessarily knowing, we will, even if just once in our lives, carry such a message to someone we scarcely know. For that person, the message will have a profound resonance, while leaving us unmoved. For example, I once received this tweet from a follower, referring to a book that I would later write, called *Driving with Plato*:

Thank you. Your book gave me the answer I was looking for.

I had no idea who the follower was, nor to which section of my book she was referring. I guess I felt pleased that my book had had the effect it had had, but the feeling was mild at most. Between the two of us, the impact was perfectly asymmetric.

What's critical about the receiving of such angelic messages is that we should be ready for them. There needs to be an openness on our part. To be precise, we need to be open to both the content of the message and the possibility that it will arrive from an origin capable of flying under our radar, bypassing our habitual cognitive frequency. What I mean by 'habitual cognitive frequency' is that our thoughts tend to run up and down a familiar scale, a process which gradually inures us to it. Messages of deep significance need to be met by receptors in us at a level beneath or behind or beyond that cognitive frequency, because the latter can't field them. Such messages enter us not through the brain, but via another conduit: possibly the heart, possibly the gut, or possibly an affective centre as yet unidentified.

What is the connection between angelic messages and purpose, which is the theme of this chapter? Only that purpose is sometimes revealed in such angelic fashion. The classic example would be the epiphany, that moment when somebody hears an inner voice from God calling them. Whereas a standard message is delivered from the front, presented for interpretation by its recipient, the angelic message concerning one's ultimate purpose is felt within. It requires little, if any, interpretation, because it is free from all ambiguity. Once again, there is an analogy with falling in love. We don't so much fall in love as realise that we already have. As soon as we realise that we have realised, as it were, scant room remains for doubt. Doubt gives way to gratitude and wonder.

The Lord Mallard

To my surprise, the Prize Fellowship at All Souls began from the instant I was elected. When the Warden telephoned me with the good news, he implied that my attendance at dinner the next day, Sunday night, was non-negotiable.

As if I'd been dropped off by helicopter amongst an Amazonian tribe, I found myself in a new world of codes, taboos, traditions and rules, all of which I rapidly had to learn. You wore a suit and gown to dinner on week nights, but a dinner jacket on Saturdays and Sundays; and you took the gown off after dinner, passing it to your own and not somebody else's scout (a kind of valet), before proceeding to dessert in the Common Room; although you had to keep hold of your napkin. Whichever nights you chose, you had to attend at least twenty-eight dinners per year. This requirement was known as 'pernoctating'. Once the company had adjourned to the Common Room, the port had to be passed to the left, though the drinking of port was considered nouveau-riche compared with the imbibing of claret. The latter was served below room temperature: allowing it to become 'chambré' was equally gauche. Both alcohols were shunted in their decanters, like liquid gems, along the wax-polished table, using 'Bathurst's claws'. This was a wooden stick with a vice, custom made for a long-deceased Fellow with a withered arm. French and English cheese, exotic fruit, and snuff in a silver box could be passed in any direction. As the most junior Fellow, I had to serve as 'Mr Screw'. When I first heard the term, my mind flew to boarding-school prefects sodomising their fags. But no. In return for free wine, it was the duty of Mr Screw to get up and press a button by the fireplace whenever the claret ran out. The button rang a bell in the pantry. The bell summoned the butler, whom I would commission for more. Nobody could leave the table before the most senior Fellow had left; and I had to leave last. The Warden technically was a guest of the Fellows.

The presence of other guests was strictly monitored. You could bring in the same guest for a maximum of three nights per term, although partners were limited to Special Guest Nights – nights which made some of the more traditional Fellows nervous because of the potential for disruption. Special though such nights were, the presence of outsiders meant that a certain thickness of culture was lost. To get the undiluted experience, you had to attend the Gaudy. This was held on the feast of All Souls in November, on the very night of the meeting at which the award of the Prize Fellowship was agreed. For this climax of the college calendar, all categories of Fellow would gather – Prize Fellows, London Fellows, 'Fifty Pounders', Quondams, the Regius Professor of This, the Chichele Professor of That. It was the academic version of the Mad Hatter's Tea Party, a wonderland parade of the fat and the thin, the bloodless and the sanguine, the hale and the lame, the marrieds and the confirmed bachelors.⬇ This motley troupe reported in black tie for a champagne reception that lasted until the butler banged a gong like a prop from *Carry On Up the Khyber*, inviting us to proceed through to the candlelit hall. The usual three courses expanded to five; the flight of wine was so sublime that it had wings; the satisfaction of belonging to the only club that mattered was immense. Dinner was followed by a speech in Latin, larded with puns, marking the highlights of the year gone by.

After the speech came a hearty rendition of the college song, led by the Lord Mallard. 'Mallard' because the song commemorated the legendary discovery of a duck in the college drains, in the fifteenth century, when the building was still under construction. In my time, the Lord Mallard was the musicologist Alan Tyson. Despite his eccentricity, he was my idol. He had known Sigmund Freud personally and had worked on the landmark translations of the Viennese doctor's writings into English. In a frail but pitch-perfect tenor, the Lord Mallard projected his song from

---

⬆ It was precisely the strange gallery of individuals at High Table in Oxford that inspired Lewis Carroll to come up with the Mad Hatter's Tea Party.

the dais, and we the assembled company lustily repeated the chorus:

> *Oh, by the blood of King Edward,*
> *Oh, by the blood of King Edward,*
> *It was a swapping, swapping mallard!* ⬇

The 'loving cup' – like a football trophy, only filled with wine – was then passed up and down the banqueting tables, for us to take a sip from, as in some druidic communion. After dessert, there was brandy from the grog tray and a box of cigars that Isaiah Berlin claimed were a gift from Fidel Castro. The evening was rounded off with fireworks. These were skewered into an oval lawn as flat, green and close-cropped as the baize on the Wharton Room table. The fuses were lit by the scouts, sent out into the dark like infantrymen by their officers in the Great War: black figures scurrying between the orange sparks. The rockets boomed like heavy artillery, echoing off the cloistered walls of the quadrangle, all beneath the vault of a starry sky.

I loved it. I loved the ritual, the tradition, the food, the wine, the prestige, the secrecy, the costume, the theatre of it all. I loved the architecture. The north quadrangle, where the fireworks were held, had been designed in the early eighteenth century by Nicholas Hawksmoor, with towers almost literally ivory in colour. To reach the top from inside there were narrow stairs followed by a series of ladders. For all the glory of the towers from the outside, climbing up those claustral shafts was like being trapped in one of Piranesi's imaginary prisons. The one time I went up I almost lost my footing and fell.

If you examine the photograph, you can see where I had my

⬆ 'Swapping' is an archaic term for 'prodigiously large'.

study. Look at the tower on your left. Now find the second window up from the door at ground level. Then move your eye two windows to the left, to the window nearest the left edge of the picture. My study lay behind that window. I loved that study, refurbished according to instructions which, to my amazement and joy, I had been asked to provide: blue carpet, yellow walls, blue velvet curtains, and a pair of armchairs in blue ticking from Habitat. The Wharton Room – the interview chamber – is two windows beneath, on the ground floor, extending left out of the picture.

All Souls College, Oxford

With few exceptions, I loved my colleagues too. Derek Parfit, my unlikely champion, was a model of fair-mindedness. Richard Smith, an historian of medicine, was appointed as my mentor despite the yawning gulf between our fields of interest: his patience with my intellectual efforts knew no bounds. And Malcolm Bowie, long since one of the faithfully departed, was the Maréchal Foch Professor of French. Bowie had written on Jacques Lacan, another Parisian intellectual who caused panic and/or disdain in Oxford. The two of us would occasionally conspire like an embattled minority. I also loved a certain older Fellow. It turned out that he loved me too. He whispered it into my ear one night over dessert in the Common Room.

Integration

Along with Simone, I hadn't ceased being a jobbing parent through all this: ferrying Anna to nursery on the back of the bicycle in all weathers, wiping her nose, making her tea. It was a schizophrenic existence. In hall, I tucked into *tournedos de boeuf* and quaffed Château Margaux; at home, we had lentil stew and tins of Carlsberg. In college I rubbed elbows with the world's luminaries at dinner; Sunday lunch was served on a trestle table we carried out from the shed, and shared with the in-laws. To get to work, I passed among the finials, architraves and Corinthian columns of colleges; on my way back, these were replaced by the satellite dishes that spread like postmodern fungi across the rooftops of New Marston, where we were now living. Through the arched window of my study, I could hear rehearsals for Mozart operettas in the gardens of New College; in our front room, with its three-bar electric fire, we had Tracy Chapman on the red plastic replacement tape-player. By day, I worked through Derrida's finely wrought text, and would come home wanting to discuss my thoughts with Simone, who'd spent her own work day dealing with the public, and was rightfully tired. When Anna's sister, Ruby, was born in 1991, and again there were nappies to change, teething pains to soothe and sleepless nights to endure, the contrast between family life and the shining bauble that was All Souls only intensified. These were parallel universes.

That gap between universes was extreme but perhaps not anomalous. Many will know about having a work life and a home life that run on parallel tracks; or, analogously, keeping a social life separate from time with one's parents. Balancing the various worlds we inhabit probably counts as another fundamental aspect of being human. I say 'probably' rather than 'definitely' because in certain small communities and so-called primitive societies, where everybody knows everybody else, the overlap between family, friends and 'colleagues' can be so large that they merge into one. Even in modern cities, the overlaps are probably on the increase, thanks to technology. Thus a smartphone corrals messages from all our contacts onto a single screen.

And yet for many Westerners, the pattern of belonging resembles a corkscrew, as depicted in the following diagram. It will vary from person to person, but as a rule there will be distinct boundaries between groups, as well as overlaps. Probably the greatest separation exists between colleagues and birth family, insofar as encounters between our parents and our work associates will be rare. The least separation exists between our birth family and

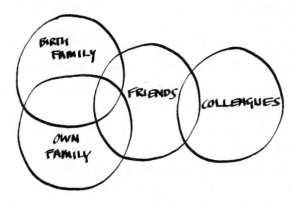

any family of our own that we go on to have, not least because grandparents will want to see their grandchildren. Hence the biggest of the overlaps.

For the most part, we weave easily among the links of the chain. With colleagues, we are professional; with friends, relaxed; and with family, we tend to behave according to our place in the genealogy. Why is it so easy to adapt? Because we tacitly accept that each group requires us to follow its own rules. We stick to these rules in order to belong. Also, each group is largely indifferent to our behaviour elsewhere. Within limits, colleagues don't mind how you are at home; and your family doesn't mind how you are at work.

That is the way the world turns. But it does raise the question of whether we remain the same person across the different situations. Identity is supposed to be about consistency. So what if you are restrained with your colleagues yet raucous with your friends? or a tyrant with your children but submissive with your parents? Is there:

(a) an underpinning, essential you, of which these different
    behaviours are merely alternative manifestations? Or could
    there be:
(b) no essential you, but different persons on different occasions?

Option (a) implies a hub-and-spoke model, where the hub is the true self and the spokes are the behaviours that we display in different situations. Option (b) is like the rim of the wheel, with no hub or spokes at all.

Westerners tend to choose (a) over (b). We believe in an underlying essential identity, or a true self. We might accept that we behave differently with friends and colleagues, but we say that's just a matter of context. Which is precisely why the notion of 'behaviour' is so critical. It allows us to talk about our outer actions while exempting our inner self. Just because I behaved like an idiot last night, it doesn't mean that I am an idiot intrinsically. I was having a bad day.

And yet we are never not behaving. Our behaviour simply adapts to the context. When it doesn't, we risk being ostracised. Turn up to a board meeting in swimwear with a cocktail, and you'll be putting your job on the line. The reason we never do is that context is stronger than identity. So strong is it that our identity will perforce adjust from context to context without pause, like water striving for equilibrium. At no point is our identity ever stripped bare. Even when we're on our own – taking a shower, say, or sitting on a park bench – we're behaving in an 'alone' kind of way, driven by the circumstance. Although it goes against the grain to say it, perhaps *where* we are beats *who* we are. If it were a game of 'rock, paper, scissors', context would be the paper to the rock of identity. It smothers a force that we took to be indomitable.

The difficulty arises when two contexts collide. All of a sudden we have to reconcile competing types of behaviour. Simone once brought Anna into All Souls for tea in my study. Anna rode her tricycle round the gravel path encircling the lawn in the Hawksmoor quad. As I went to meet them, my home and my work identities were brought into tension with each other. That caused me to feel conflicting emotions. On the one hand, I was happy. Seeing the blonde toddler in the pink dress, her legs spinning with the pedals against the neoclassical backdrop, made me smile. On the other hand, I was nervous of the reaction of certain Fellows. I could sense the tutting from behind the windows overlooking the quad – no different in its quality than that of a dyspeptic neighbour twitching their net curtains. They were judging me, I thought, and I was scared of losing their approval.

How could I maintain my belonging to both groups? I knew that my priority lay with my family but I was on All Souls turf. That context was powerful, like the pull of the moon. My hamfisted solution was to embrace the girls quickly, then hurry them out of sight. The opposing forces tugging at the perforation down the centre of my life would only grow.

This question of identity and context, of who we are versus where our allegiances lie, has a big impact on our sense of purpose. That is because we tend to conflate 'following your true purpose' with 'being who you are'. The trouble is that *who* you are can change according to *where* you are. Put another way, what drives our choice of purpose is often the desire to conform with the ethos of a particular group. The most vivid example would be that of young men enlisting as jihadis. Purpose and belonging go hand in hand. Sometimes finding a mission and finding approval are one and the same.

Paternal and maternal purpose

In my case, there was an additional factor. If my father was proud of me for getting into Oxford in the first place, he was in seventh heaven when I was elected to All Souls. Yet it hadn't always been thus. When I was sixteen he actively tried to stop me from going on to do A levels, on the grounds that I should get out to work and start earning. He was a businessman through and through. It took a summit meeting with my teachers to persuade him that I had academic potential.

Besides my teachers, the other countervailing voice was that of my mother. She had always valued education more highly than had my father, who had had the (mis)fortune to attend a boarding school. Since she grew up as a girl in the 1940s, education wasn't something that my mother could easily access, so she tended to idealise it. Her younger brother, born after the war, had been sent to a grammar, and even went on to university, the first in the family to do so. Her father – my grandfather, Leslie – had been something of an intellectual. Sadly, the war robbed him of the chance to develop his interests. In fact it turned him to the bottle, and the bottle lured him to an early grave.

All three of those considerations must have gone into my mother's support for my continuing education. First, it offered her the opportunity to have a vicarious education of her own; second, the gap would thereby be closed on her younger brother, who had enjoyed advantages not available to her; and third, it would allow her to see me fulfil her own father's academic promise.

The point is that, for me, following an academic path meant obeying the maternal imperative. That wouldn't be so interesting were it not for the fact that when my Prize Fellowship came to an end, I went into business. That is, I jumped over to the paternal path. I did so, I am sure, not least because my father was no longer able to walk down a path himself, either metaphorically or literally. One of the many reasons why I so wished he had carried on as a businessman was that it would have allowed me to continue an academic career in parallel. I wouldn't have seen myself as needing to come onto the pitch again as his substitute.

Those circumstances were particular to me and yet the question applies, I think, to everyone. Is it the mother's or the father's path that we are following? We know that parents will often influence the career choice of the children, but typically they do so at a conscious level: 'I think you should be an engineer,' they might say. But what about these silent imperatives that children hear, even when a parent has not spoken them, to choose a career with the unconscious intention of rescuing, healing or atoning for their mother or father?

Human lefts

That switch into business sounds terribly abrupt. But it wasn't as if I worked and worked on Derrida until one day I flipped over to become a businessman. Before the switch came another period of 'drift', as was illustrated in the trilby diagram on page 85.

I finished my thesis just one year into my All Souls fellowship. With a contract to turn the thesis into a book, I spent another year making revisions. When *Derrida and Autobiography* was eventually published in 1995, I sent a copy to the man himself. A few weeks later, I found a package waiting for me in the Porter's Lodge at All Souls. It was a bundle of books personally signed by Jacques Derrida. One of these was *Politiques de l'Amitié* (*The Politics of Friendship*). The title hinted at a warm response. On the inside, the esteemed author, my hero, had scrawled the following words in a cursive as hard to decipher as that of a doctor:

Pour Robert Smith, en signe de profonde gratitude, J. Derrida.
('For Robert Smith, as a sign of profound gratitude, J. Derrida'.)

And there was better to come. This was a copy of *Mal d'Archive* (*Archive Fever*). The handwriting was even more impenetrable. I found the magnifying glass that came with my *Oxford English Dictionary*, turned the book this way and that, wrote Derrida's message out for myself in French, and then made a literal translation:

For Robert Smith, as a sign of very admiring recognition,
J. Derrida.

He had then added in what read to me like a surge of enthusiasm:

Your book is a superb work of generosity and rigour! An immense success. I hope to have the chance to thank you and to meet you soon. J. D. 25 March, 1995

Not only had J.D. read my book, he rated it. The saying 'to burst with pride' can sound like an exaggeration, but when I finally deciphered those words, I practically exploded.

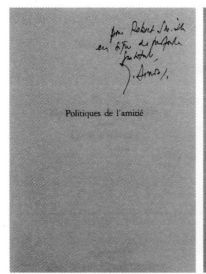

Politiques de l'amitié

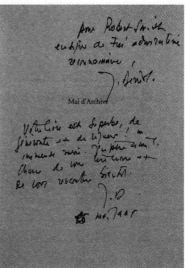

Mal d'Archive

Not long afterwards, buoyed up by Derrida's approval, I took the Eurostar from Waterloo to Paris. I sat in on his famous weekly seminar at the École des Hautes Études en Sciences Sociales, on Boulevard Raspail. Since I planned to introduce myself to him afterwards, my heart thumped and my palms sweated through-out. When the seminar was over, I joined the queue of admirers eager to quiz the master further on his thoughts. On telling him who I was, Professor Derrida looked taken aback and replied, 'But you are so young!' He invited me for a drink.

We went to a brasserie over the road. There we were joined by Derrida's wife, Marguerite, a psychoanalyst. My nerves caused me to speak the worst French that I have ever uttered. To spare my blushes, my hosts reverted to English. At one point, Jacques (first-name terms!) went to the bathroom while Marguerite reiterated how much her husband admired my book. Again my pride exploded. After another drink, we parted company, agreeing to stay in touch. Jacques also offered any support that I might need, academically speaking. *'Comptez sur moi,'* he wrote, after I had broached the subject. *Count on me.* He became my referee.

Renault 5 Campus

What was the great man like in person? Affectionate, vulnerable and self-deprecating. Playful too. A couple of years later, I would pick him up from Heathrow to drive to an event in Oxford on human rights. My car at the time was a red Renault 5 Campus, procured for me by my old friend Charlie, who had gone to work for the car maker. In that it epitomised France and that the 'Campus' brand had all the right connotations, the car was perfect. But I did worry that a three-door hatchback was inappropriate for so distinguished a visitor. Should I have hired a Mercedes?

As I pulled into the short-term parking at Terminal 2, I was struck by the responsibility that I had taken on in conveying my cargo back to Oxford. If I crashed, I'd be altering the course of Western philosophy.⬇ Fortunately, Professor Derrida was relaxed. Coming from the continent, he tried to get in on the driver's side, the right. When corrected, he quipped that he was in England to speak about human lefts. In other words, Jacques Derrida was nothing like the stereotype of the French intellectual, who takes himself too seriously, is socially overbearing and feels it necessary to talk heavy-duty concepts twenty-four hours a day (although, very Frenchly, he did complain about English food). Nor was he the hot-headed militant, intent on acts of intellectual vandalism, portrayed by his detractors. With me, at least, he was never anything but charming and kind.

Disintegration

That meeting with Jacques Derrida after his seminar in Paris represented the high-water mark of my university career. It came much earlier than anticipated. With the book done, I found myself unexpectedly adrift. After working so assiduously on Derrida's output for a good four years, there was nothing else I wanted to say. That's not because I had exhausted his oeuvre. It was rather that it had exhausted me.

I had thought that this purpose of working on Derrida would sustain me indefinitely. Or that I would find a subject that was equally compelling and continue with my academic vocation. I doodled ideas for a number of new projects but none caught

⬆ Ironically, the possibility of not arriving at one's destination is a key theme in Derrida's philosophy. Perhaps this is also the moment to point out that the 'auto' part of the word 'autobiophilosophy' is a reference to cars.

my imagination. I published some articles, mainly on Freud, and continued to lecture in Oxford and overseas – including a speaking tour to Romania, where I was spied on by the Stasi, the only partially disbanded secret police from the era of the Communist dictator, Nicolae Ceausescu. But I had lost my mojo. Embarrassingly, I still had a few years of my fellowship to run, years that others would have broken down the door to use in my stead.

And yet one obsession was already giving way to another. At that drink with Jacques and Marguerite Derrida, there was a fourth person around the table.

> the proof, the living proof precisely, that a letter can always not arrive at its destination, and that therefore it never arrives.
>
> Jacques Derrida

4

A Love Quadrangle

Our days are a kaleidoscope. Every instant a change
takes place. New harmonies, new contrasts, new
combinations of every sort. The most familiar people
stand each moment in some new relation to each other,
to their work, to surrounding objects.

Henry Ward Beecher

With his tweed suit, short back and sides, passion for Miles Davis, knowledge of Hitchcock, taste for malt whisky and succession of vintage cars, Cameron Taylor was a throwback to a bygone age. The academic version of Cary Grant, perhaps, he was handsome, witty and raffish. I was beguiled.

In many ways, we were opposites. When I met Cameron in 1992 and we were both twenty-seven, I was a parent and he was a bachelor. My love life was stable; he was repeatedly enmeshed in transient liaisons with girls. Where I was smugly set up in my fellowship at All Souls, Cameron was having to scratch around for undergraduate tutorials to teach on a freelance basis. What with my partner and daughters, family life to me was an all-female affair. Cameron was one of five brothers. He lived in a man's world.

On the subject of brothers, I would go so far as to say that Cameron stood in for the brother I never had. At least I felt a brotherly love for him. As to which of us was the elder and which the younger, it would alternate. Sometimes I looked up to him as the worldly big brother who had ventured out into the stormy weather of contingency and chance whilst I, cosseted in my ivory tower, was writing poems and drinking tea. At other times he looked up to me as the mature one with the family and the steady job.

The role of surrogate brother wasn't the only gap that Cameron filled. Through him I could vicariously enjoy the sowing of wild oats on which I, having had a family so young, had missed out. I was captivated by his stories of assignations, frustrations, indiscretions and conquests. I would listen as if sitting at the feet of an intellectual Don Juan.

Indeed Cameron's talent for storytelling filled another gap. As a philosopher, my mental landscape was populated with abstract concepts, as motionless and virginal as modernist sculptures in a park. For all their perfection, however, concepts don't move in a way that characters move. Immobile, they can't act out a story. Cameron, whose research was in the field of biography, saw the world as a caravan of human drama.

He enabled me to see the world like that too. I can feel his influence even now as I attempt to combine concept with narrative, philosophy with autobiography. I picture that coming together of the two as the bisecting of a horizontal line by a number of verticals, as in the diagram opposite. The horizontal represents 'narrative flow' or the unfolding of events. At intervals this forward-moving horizontal is punctuated by static concepts, concepts that frame what's going on in the narrative. When such understanding occurs, the result is a moment of insight.

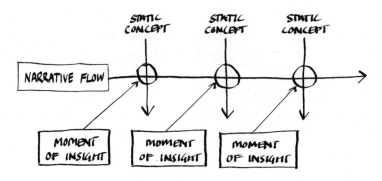

Take *Romeo and Juliet.* The key moments in the story are that two young people meet, fall in love and die. That is the horizontal line, the narrative flow. This narrative flow is intersected by a number of concepts. Perhaps the most important concept is that of 'ancient enmity' – the historic feud between the two lovers' families. By adding the horizontal of love to the vertical of war, we generate a third element. That third element is the moment of insight, so pithily expressed by Juliet herself in the words, 'My only love sprung from my only hate!' It is the insight that her fate is tragic.

When it comes to the balancing of narrative with concept, Shakespeare is a master. Ordinary mortals will tend to be stronger at one than the other. There are the narrators and there are the reflectors. Broadly, these categories overlap with those of extrovert and introvert. Where the narrators like to entertain, the introverts prefer to absorb. The rarest breeds are the hybrids: the introverted storytellers, like the very English Alan Bennett, say, and the extrovert reflectors, such as Barack Obama. They are the outliers, as in the following diagram. The narrowing to a tip is supposed to signal, however, that extrovert reflectors are still a bit less extrovert than most extroverts, and that introvert storytellers are less introvert than they might appear. This very book would probably fit into the left wingtip of the diagram.

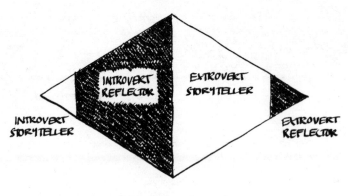

Miteinandersein

Our lives are also stories. As if snorkelling, we dip our faces into that narrative flow and become transfixed by the colours. Then, after a while, we come up to make sense of what's going on. And while each person's story will be unique – as it was, say, for my father – one element runs through them all. Our life stories feature other people. We exist in relation to others. Indeed, the idea of relating one's life *without* reference to one's relationships seems absurd.

If the question guiding this book is 'What does it mean to be human?', then part of the answer has to be that we don't exist in isolation. Even if we live like hermits, cut off from outside contact, we still have a relationship with people in our minds, and the world continues to be populated. So fundamental is this fact of coexistence that Martin Heidegger coined a term for it. The word in German is *Miteinandersein*. In English, it would translate as 'Beingwithothers'. Although it is not uncommon in German to do so, Heidegger's reason for running three words into one was to emphasise that without that 'with' and 'others', being makes no sense. 'Being alone' would amount to an oxymoron. Being human means being among other human beings. No one is an island.

Holding this notion of *Miteinandersein* in mind, I want in this chapter to explore what it's actually like for us to be among others. Where, in the chapter before last, I looked at how we stand in the flow of generational *time*, here I'm investigating how we stand in *space*. Space as in the network of relationships to which we belong.

To the image of a network, however, I prefer that of a kaleidoscope.⬇ 'Network' sounds a little too fixed to capture the changing pattern of our relationships. We exist among other people, yes. But it's not always the same other people whom we exist among. People come and go. We lose contact with some, even as others become permanent fixtures. Were we to take a snapshot of our relationships at the age of five, it would differ drastically from a snapshot taken at thirty-five. We progress from configuration to configuration. The shapes dissolve and re-form like clouds in the sky. Sometimes a picture will hold for a decent length of time: say while we are at secondary school and hang on to the same classmates as we step up through the years. Other times the picture will be ephemeral, as when we attend a residential course for a week. During those days sequestered together, the relationships that we form can feel like some of our most proximate. Then the final day arrives, we say our goodbyes, and the elements of the pattern disperse. Like a kaleidoscope, our *Miteinandersein* – our 'beingwithothers' – is constantly changing.

⬆ The dictionary defines a kaleidoscope as '1. a toy consisting of a tube containing mirrors and pieces of coloured glass or paper, whose reflections produce changing patterns when the tube is rotated. 2. a constantly changing pattern or sequence of elements: *the dancers moved in a kaleidoscope of colour.*'

The curious Maddison

Generally, I construed Cameron's adventures with women as being more about sex than love. But that was before Maddison Clarke. An American university alumna, she had enrolled at Oxford for a postgraduate degree. Cameron was smitten. He would buy her flowers, send her *billets-doux* and take her out to dinner. A knock on the door of my study and he would come in to rhapsodise over 'TGM' – which stood for 'The Gorgeous Maddison'.

One day, Cameron persuaded TGM to accompany him to one of my lectures. It was in the Wharton Room at All Souls, in the Hawksmoor quadrangle, where I had had my grilling. On identifying her in the audience, I was surprised. Cameron's old-fashioned aesthetic had led me to assume that he would go for a woman of similar style. With her long, straight, sun-bleached hair, round blue eyes, perfect teeth and denim jacket, this calcium-rich twenty-two-year-old looked like a Californian who'd come to maturity in the 1980s. Which is exactly what she was. Gorgeous? Absolutely. An aesthetic fit with Cameron? Pass.

For Cameron it wasn't the mismatch in styles that was the problem. It was the mismatch in attraction. Much as Maddison was entertained by Cameron's brilliance, she never felt the chemistry necessary for taking things to the next level. Besides, she was already in a relationship. Her boyfriend was an Oxford Blue named Ed, a university sportsman to whom she referred, in her American college patois, as a 'jock'. Jock, beefcake or stud, Ed was far more the standard-issue boyfriend than clever Cameron could ever be.

And yet Maddison's appetite for the conventional went only so far. While going out with Ed, it seemed that Maddison was semi-seeing a woman. This was Lana, another American at

Oxford. In my first proper conversation with Maddison, I asked her to name the three things that I should know about her. Her response was: 'I'm bisexual. I'm from San Francisco. And my steady state is purple.'

That third statement left me perplexed. The second I simply logged; though it wasn't long before I found out that Maddison wasn't from San Francisco but Los Angeles. Under the influence of college friends, she had come to see LA as 'lame' and was trying to distance herself from it. It was, and still is, common for northern Californians to be snobbish about their southern neighbours. Maddison was 'from' San Francisco in the sense that she had attended university in the Bay Area, but it was in LA that she had been born and raised.

Like the San Francisco answer, Maddison's claim to be bisexual lay in the grey area – or Bay Area – between the true and the false. Certainly, where Maddison led, Lana followed. Maddison would take Lana to Trade, for example, a nightclub for gay women in London. Between the two there was clearly an attachment, plus a curiosity about lesbian culture. But how *sexual* their 'bisexual' relationship was remained to me obscure. Also, this was the early 1990s, when some mystique still applied to the notion of bisexuality. Today, it is just another life choice. And there was Ed. He too was a Maddison follower, although no equivalent sexual mystery surrounded his relationship with her. In every respect, all appeared pretty straight.

If Maddison was bisexual, I reasoned, it wasn't that she was equally attracted to women and to men. Fundamentally Maddison was heterosexual, but the idea of being bisexual appealed to her and she was thick enough with Lana to make the idea plausible. It represented her ideal rather than her true identity. That's no indictment: Maddison was still young and figuring out who she was. Her youthful experiments included introducing herself in Oxford as 'Maddison', whereas back home she was known as 'Maddy'. At some point during the flight over the Atlantic, heterosexual Maddy had transformed into bisexual Maddison, as if she'd switched outfits in the onboard toilet. But outfits is all they were. Straight Maddy was just trying identities on.

Not that any of this was consolation to Cameron. Whatever heterosexuality Maddison did possess, too little was irrigated his way. I wondered if what really mattered to Maddison was not the gender anyway but the number. Maybe she just preferred being in a three to a two, regardless of boy or girl? Supporting my theory was the following fact. Back in the Bay Area, while Maddison had been going steady with a man named Kyle, she was also half going out with Kyle's best friend, Marcus. So if Maddison, Ed and Lana constituted a semi-threesome, it was a repeat, to my mind, of the Californian trio. Maddison had form.

Three: that's the magic number

Meanwhile I was caught in a love mathematic of my own. Before Ruby was born in 1991, Simone, Anna and I had made up a three. We were a triangle, and by and large that triangle was robust. Although Simone and I had never planned on starting a family, when it happened, we made it work. We made it work *because* we hadn't planned it. It was as if the bones of our relationship hadn't set before we learned that we were to be parents. Because those bones were still soft, they could be manipulated into the triangular shape needed to accommodate the baby.

Couples sometimes find that when a baby arrives, the little one comes between them. That didn't happen in our case. But nor did the baby bring us closer. It was rather that Anna provided Simone and me with a focus outside the couple that we were.

As such, we were living out exactly the dynamic recommended by Hegel in his philosophy of the family. Rather than rebounding claustrophobically between the two members of the couple, like a tennis ball between two walls, the love has a third wall to bounce off. The third wall provides love with the extra dimension that it needs in order to express itself fully.

But there was a catch. The very factor that made us strong as a family made us weak as a couple. Precisely because it was barely a few months into our relationship before Simone and I knew that we were going to be parents, we hadn't had long enough to bond as a pair. What gave the bones of our relationship the malleability to be shaped into a family was also what made them insufficiently rigid to support us as a couple.

That structural weakness was exposed when Ruby was born. Naturally, that was through no fault of the baby. The decision to have children lies not with the children. It is the responsibility of the parents. But what parents tend to underestimate is the degree to which numerics play a part. Simone and I became a three before we had properly become a two – we were just two ones. But the two ones could be added to the one of Anna to make a triangular three. So we were a strong family because we were a weak couple. As a four, however, we were a *weak* family because we were a weak couple.

The underlying reason for such a kink in the logic was that the triangle had changed into a square. The engineering was different. In a triangle each line is connected to the other two lines, creating interdependency. Not so with a square. Although each line in a

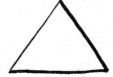

square is also connected to two other lines, there is a third line, opposite, to which it has no connection at all. The level of interdependency in a square is therefore lower than that in a triangle.

That lower level of interdependency means that a square generates the option for any one of the four lines to become detached. Which is exactly what happened with the four that we, as a family, had become. One of us got separated from the rest. We divided along gender lines. There were the girls and there was me. A new triangle formed, but with one piece left over.

It's not that I was excluded. Far from it. It would be truer to say that I took the opportunity of being in a four to exclude myself. And why would I want to do that? First, because I had an inveterate tendency to retreat into my own head. The reality of life with two young children sometimes made that inner cave beckon like a refuge. Second, the masonic world of All Souls was still there to lure me away. It too was a refuge, even if, as refuges go, it lay at the premium end.

A hopelessly brief word on the future of the human sciences

In the last chapter, I made a plea for the significance of *where* we are relative to *who* we are – the paper of context smothering the rock of identity. Now I'm saying that *how many* we are is just as vital to our guiding question of what it means to be a human being. It's not simply that we will always find ourselves in a kaleidoscope with other people. It's that these other people can be added up. Having added them up, we adjust. We behave in notably different ways with one other person than we do with two, three, four and so on. As if sitting in a boat, we shift our position ➡

← when somebody gets in or out, to prevent capsizing. It's a question of equilibrium.

Up to about seven, we count fairly precisely. Thereafter, we take a quick reading of whether a group is small, medium, large or very large. In all cases, the point of the calculation is to adapt our behaviour to that number, because the number is an instruction on how to behave. The number demands that we respect the size of the group. The size of the group dictates the shape of the group, and the shape of the group can only be preserved if we fit into it.

In answering the question of what it means to be a human being, our default as denizens of the twenty-first century will be to draw on psychology or philosophy or sociology. But perhaps they are all too sophisticated. Perhaps the number of people around us and the shape that they make is as significant a factor as anything. Is there a new human science to be developed on the numerics of human interaction and how the geometry affects us?

Big Brother

Obviously it is with the benefit of hindsight that I offer this account of my time with Simone. But does hindsight invariably make a history more accurate? Is my analysis *now* of the situation *then* the best that it could ever be? At what point exactly does hindsight reach its sharpest? It all seems highly friable.

Having said that, certain parameters apply:

- Interpret an event too soon after it took place and you won't have enough perspective. *Under-ripe apple.*

- Wait too long and the memory will degrade. *Over-ripe apple.*
- Longer still and you might unwittingly start to doctor the original, inserting features that don't belong. *Apple rotten with worms.*
- At that point you run the risk of believing in your own false memory instead of recalling what actually happened. *Perfect, shiny apple that is mainly fantasy.*

When it comes to looking back specifically on romantic relationships gone awry, that risk of distortion only goes up. *And* the process starts earlier. No sooner is the relationship finished – long before the memory has ripened – than we turn to modifying the account. We start to tamper. That sounds wicked, but it is only human. What tempts us into such altering of the record, or at least into a redacting of the painful parts, is a basic need to make ourselves feel better. For, having experienced both the joy of love and the sorrow of its loss, there *will be* painful parts. It hurts. We take to revising the relationship as we might reach for an aspirin.

I am reminded of Winston Smith in George Orwell's *Nineteen Eighty Four*. Winston is the hero of Orwell's novel, a bureaucrat working for a totalitarian regime known simply as The Party. That regime, loosely based on the Soviet Union, is committed to the production of what today we might call 'alternative facts'. Winston's job at the Ministry of Truth requires him literally to rewrite history on behalf of the state. The past has to be made consistent with present policy. 'Oceania was at war with Eurasia; therefore Oceania had always been at war with Eurasia,' mouths Winston as he is being brainwashed. He knows that Oceania and Eurasia were previously allies, but his knowledge is made to seem like a delusion.

What goes for Orwellian ideologies also goes for relationships. We just need to replace Eurasia and Oceania with 'you' and 'I'. Put at its starkest, the formula would then read as follows:

I used to love you, but now that I hate you, I always hated you.

If we allow ourselves to see beyond its chilling quality, that phrase also lets us in on an aspect of hate that we might otherwise miss. For we tend to think of hate as the opposite of love. Love stands on one side and hate on the other, in positions that appear fixed in space. But what if, as that phrase implies, love and hate are related not by space but by time? The hate springs up only *after* the love has died down, like a parasite that feeds on ashes. It is secondary.

Such a separating-out of love and hate over time would fit with our development as infants, where love comes first. For no baby *begins* with a hatred of its mother, even if, after only a few weeks, the same baby might experience flashes of hatred when it is not fed or picked up on demand (as argued by the psychoanalyst Melanie Klein). In our adult relationships, we rarely *start out* by hating the other person. There needs to be a cause. Unlike love, which is a primary feeling, hatred is a reaction. Love and hate are less like twins, coeval and symmetric, and more like older and younger siblings.

My theorem, therefore, is that the true nature of hate is one of revenge on aborted love. The energy in hate, which counterintuitively can exceed the energy in love, comes from the urge to overturn a loss suffered by the heart. Hate emerges only when an incipient love that we felt, even momentarily, for another person, has been cut short and we want reparation. We cleave to hatred to save us from our disappointment in love. All of which could be condensed into the following, alternative formula:

I hate you because I loved you.

At the source, there is love. It wants to flow and to keep on flowing. But from time to time it crashes into a hate-shaped bend. That bend alters love's character as well as its course, turning the fresh water brackish. So hate is love perverted rather than love opposed. We hate people when the price of loving them is too high.

Occasionally the revising of a relationship will begin *before* the end. *Revision* becomes *pre*-revision. Such pre-revision serves to hasten the relationship's demise, especially if you are the leaver rather than the person being left (it's never completely mutual, despite what people say). You add a dark gloss to the history of your relationship in order to justify your role as its executioner. It's as if you were sorting through the joint photographs, keeping only the most flattering pictures of you and the least flattering ones of your partner. You then show the edited selection to your partner, silently saying, 'See? I was better than you. Good riddance.'

But we do ourselves no favours in the process. If we are to find the truth of what went wrong in a relationship, first we have to empty all the reality, rubbish included, onto the carpet. The less we tip out, the smaller the chance that the truth will lie among it. What a slow and dirty business. And the results aren't always so consoling either. For one of the truths we are bound to turn over is that *both* partners were innocent *and* guilty. In contrast to our conviction that there was a clear victim plus a clear perpetrator – end of story – the truth presents us with an ambiguous picture. That's because a relationship is a *relationship*, the product of a relating. Try as we might to amplify our innocence, the fact that we co-created the relationship means that we can never be guilt free. By the same token, the supposed villain won't be entirely devoid of innocence, much as we'd like to shovel all the blame their way. As if we had been painting a house together, neither party will come out with totally spotless hands.

It is not solely the need to preserve our innocence that makes us resist such ambiguity and revert to seeing the past in black and white. We are led into such a binary view by the language that we use, borrowed as it is from systems that are themselves binary. I am referring to the systems of law and of morality. In the law, you are innocent *or* guilty; in morality, you are right *or* wrong. We carry this *either/or* language over into the parsing of our relationships, where it is too imprecise for the task. It's like sewing in boxing gloves.

World-forms

As I look back now on the final phase of my relationship with Simone, it is impossible to tell how corrupted my hindsight has become. With that caveat in mind, I believe that it was the afore-mentioned changeover from triangle to square which launched the endgame. Unless, that is, presenting the relationship in such depersonalised terms is a way of shirking my responsibility for its failure? All this ethereal talk of triangles could be a smokescreen. It could be a means of projecting my innocence or concealing my guilt in just the fashion that I was deploring a moment ago. For the truth is that it was I and only I who saw in that square the possibility of an exit. If one of the square's four sides could be opened like a door, then I was the one to open it. I slipped out.

When I write about threes and fours, or when I liken us as a family to a triangle or a square, it would seem that I'm doing so in a purely metaphorical fashion. It is a writer's fancy, apparently. Surely Simone, Anna and I were not *literally* a triangle? Surely he doesn't mean that the family *literally* became a square with Ruby's birth? 'Triangle' and 'square' must be metaphorical ways of describing the situation. All true. And yet the use of geometrical terminology is more than subterfuge on my part. The experience of being in a three was very much one of a felt interdependency. It was as if we really were a triangle. When it was just Simone, Anna and I, my feeling was that we were bound to each other. When we added Ruby, that feeling palpably changed – again through no fault of the baby, as I insist. You might think that a larger family would create a tighter bond, but not necessarily. Although there was one more child, a child whom I loved with all my heart, I felt less connected to the whole.

I have observed a similar dynamic played out in other families. In a family of four, Mum takes child A to dance class, while Dad takes child B to football, and nobody feels any the worse. The unity of the family is intact. But if, in a family of three, Mum takes the only child swimming while Dad stays at home, the family's unity is brought into question, if only faintly. A triangle seems to demand from its three members a loyalty to the code of 'all for one and one for all' in a way that a square does not.

The rule applies outside families too. When you go for a drink with friends, it's usually easier to get up and leave when there are four than when there are three. When you are in a meeting of four people, the departure of one person feels less of a blow than when, in a meeting of three, one person bows out. Why is that? The smaller the group, the more valuable each member becomes. One person leaving a group of a hundred barely registers. It is also because a group of three produces the sensation of a tensile balance, a balance to which each person is contributing equally. Being cruder, a four doesn't have the same quality of balanced tension. It's as if a square recognises that it has more constituent parts and so is more accepting of being broken up. A triangle knows that it is perfect and does not appreciate its integrity being messed with.

Triangle and square might not be the literal shapes that we make when we gather in groups of three or four, but nor are they mere metaphors. They occupy the middle distance between the world out there and our minds, that luminescent zone between reality and thought. They are the frames through which we process the real. I call them *world-forms*. Such world-forms are not optional. We can't experience reality without them. At some level we know that when we are in a group of three, we are in a triangle. Our sense of that triangle produces a world-form, rather as a window-frame helps us to comprehend the view that it carves out. It is thanks to this frame that we make sense of the experience. Were we to have no such frame, we would be lost.

The logic of emotion

With no romance on the cards, Cameron and Maddison settled into a friendship. Because I was friends with Cameron, I became friends with Maddison too. The three of us would socialise together, though I wouldn't see Maddison on her own. Because Maddison was with Lana – in whatever way it was that Maddison was with Lana – I also became friends with Lana, though to a much lesser degree. I never saw her independently either. Ed remained in the background. Possibly to spare Cameron from having to witness her with another man, or possibly to spare Ed himself from laceration by Cameron's superior wit, Maddison kept Ed out of sight. I was still with my family but now at one remove. My view of the distribution of characters is shown in Kaleidoscope 1.

As in the reading of tea leaves, there are a thousand ways of interpreting that kaleidoscope. My own position in the firmament, at roughly the midpoint between Simone and Maddison, can be seen not only as a move away from the former but also as a transition towards the latter. Such an interpretation would be both wrong and right. It is wrong insofar as, at the beginning, I

had no romantic interest in Maddison. I looked upon her mat-ter-of-factly as the woman with whom my closest friend was enamoured, and stood off accordingly.

If anything I was slightly wary. Perhaps it was because Maddison was still working out her identity. Perhaps it was the Californian *laissez-faire* that contrasted a little shockingly with the formality of Oxford. Perhaps it was her wandering across relationship boundaries that others might have patrolled more strictly. Whatever the cause, I detected something unsettled in her, a lability that unsettled me in turn.⬇ The result was that on the first day that Maddison came to visit me at All Souls on her own, I firmly told myself, 'Don't ever get involved with this woman!'

That was a pretty allergic reaction on my part, considering. Maddison had only popped in for tea. Her part was in Cam-eron's story, not mine. She had a whole boyfriend plus a quarter of a girlfriend too, sort of. I was with Simone, and although she and I were drifting apart, there was no exit strategy coalescing in my head. What I'm asking is why, if the prospect of my getting together with Maddison was nil, did I feel the need to repudiate it so vehemently? Either there wasn't a risk of such an eventuality, in which case the pep talk to myself was superfluous; or there was a risk, and my pep talk was an inside-out way of admitting it.

⬆ Lability is a key word for me in thinking about Maddison. A close cousin of 'volatility', lability is defined as 'liable to change; easily altered'.

Given that Maddison and I would end up married, it's pretty clear which of those two options it was. I was telling myself not to get on the train, but I was already on it and the wheels were in motion. I wouldn't call it *denial*. The attraction wasn't yet strong enough for me to need to deny it. It was more that I was registering the danger of *becoming* attracted. Moreover, I was sensing *the attractiveness of the danger*. That lability which I saw in Maddison was a quality I both feared and desired. It sent the signal box in my brain into overdrive, the switchboard lights blinking, the wires becoming hot.

While that signal box was beginning to crackle and smoke, a slower, cooler process had been triggered in tandem. This was a strategic will on my part to face the anxiety that Maddison induced in me and find a way of subduing it. It wasn't that I wished to suppress her lability. I found it gripping in the way that an action movie can be gripping. No. It was rather that I needed to dampen what it was in me that her lability provoked. If Maddison made me anxious, my stratagem would not be to run away but to get closer. Only through proximity to Maddison could I conjure my anxiety into life, as if rubbing a lamp to release a genie. Once it was released, I would hold the little demon in view, come to understand it, tame it, and, when it wasn't looking, stick a pin through its invidious heart, making it vanish for good.

Those are the reasons why interpreting my position in Kaleidoscope 1 as a move towards Maddison is at least as right as it is wrong. Had it been simply a matter of moving away from Simone, other tangents were available. The course that I set was the only one that put Maddison directly in my sightline. My purpose in doing so was what psychiatrists call 'anxiolytic', that is, aimed at reducing anxiety.

Strictly speaking, though, I was hoping not to reduce but to *increase* the anxiety, so as to make the target bigger. I could then shoot and stand a better chance of hitting it. In Maddison I had found somebody to host the anxiety about losing control that had plagued me since I was young. Her free-spiritedness was something that I, with my overly ordered character, envied. But instead of learning from her example and just chilling out, I responded as if there were a psychic emergency. In stealing towards Maddison, I was focusing on a condition of my own that I hoped to disarm. It was like approaching a bomb from a distance, with the intention of defusing it.

Such febrile calculations are probably what make emotion emotion rather than reason. For emotion does have a logic to it, although it is not rational. It was only by getting close to Maddison that I could deactivate the bomb that was my anxiety. That sounds reasonable-ish. And yet I wouldn't have become anxious had I not got close. That sounds a bit mad. It didn't occur to me to walk on by, ignoring both the anxiety and its accompanying need to be quelled. Or rather it *did* occur to me, very clearly: it happened at that moment when, over tea with Maddison, I told myself never to get involved with her. But by then it was too late.

The splitting of the ice sheet and the end of the Ice Age

Kaleidoscope 1 didn't last, hence its label as Kaleidoscope '1'. It was just the first. Before long it was given an almighty shake. As well as the existing *dramatis personae* changing position, new actors entered the scene. Some of the movements took place in parallel, others in sequence. What follows is a loosely chronological account. The warning I would issue is that my version remains as subject to those memory-distortions as anyone else's. The version is also somewhat compromised in that my drive for honesty has a rival in my reluctance to condemn myself completely. My

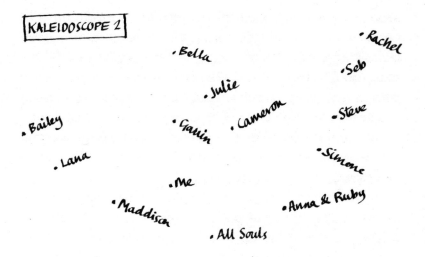

KALEIDOSCOPE 2

• Bella

• Rachel

• Seb

• Julie

• Cameron

• Bailey

• Gavin

• Steve

• Lana

• Simone

• Me

• Maddison

• Anna & Ruby

• All Souls

story is to reality, perhaps, as a Tube map is to the geographic terrain.

Cameron and Maddison had settled into that friendship. Whether he was heartbroken, I cannot say. Maybe he remembered that there were other fish to fry – he did continue to fry a few – and was phlegmatic. The reason why I don't know is that the ice sheet on which he and I had stood together was splitting right between us. A separation that would never end had got under way. It is conceivable that, even before I had, Cameron had picked up on a frisson between Maddison and me. When the three of us hung out together, did he notice Maddison's eye twinkling in my direction? If so, was this favouring of me by her – on top of my academic success and the arrogance it assuredly brought out in me – a tad too much for him? I have some photos of the three of us larking about in an Oxford college garden. Maddison's smile is ebullient; Cameron's a little quizzical.

Nor do I know if it was the experience of being slighted which changed him. But a change there was. The next thing I really did know was that he was in a relationship with a man. If I was taken aback, it wasn't because of the homosexuality *per se*. This was Oxford: there was a lot of it about. Rather it was the incongruity. For as long as I'd known Cameron, he'd been not merely heterosexual but promiscuously so. When you thought about Cameron, you thought about his dalliances. What's more, the man's world that he inhabited lent him a particularly 'male' feel, whatever that means. Or, to throw in another flimsy bit of evidence, Cameron was the least camp person one could imagine.

It wasn't any male lover that he chose either. Many are the adjectives to describe Gavin – urbane, funny, accomplished, melodramatic, connected, cultured, shrewd – but the key fact is that he was another mutual friend. Actually, I was the one to introduce Cameron to Gavin. To that extent, I believed that Gavin and I were more friends than Gavin and Cameron. In his infinitesimally subtle way – so subtle, that is, as to have deniability pre-wired into it – Gavin had even tried to seduce me one night, after cheese and wine at his house. So when I learned of the Gavin–Cameron nexus, I felt both jealous and blindsided. Just because I wasn't gay and didn't want Gavin in the same way that he at one point wanted me, it didn't mean that I was okay with him having Cameron. Even less did I like it going on behind my back.

It is tempting to read Cameron's love affair with Gavin as a preemptive strike against me for my impending betrayal of him with Maddison. Having got himself into a triangle with me and Maddison in which I won and he lost, Cameron set out to construct an alternative triangle with me and Gavin in which I would lose and he could win. But just as that reading understates Cameron's humanity, it overstates my importance. Cameron's world didn't revolve around me.

Even if Cameron wasn't trying to hurt me – and I honestly don't think he was – I was hurt nevertheless. Nor did I hide my feelings. Whatever it was that I said in response to Cameron's disclosure about Gavin – and to my shame I suspect that it wasn't very kind – it seemed for him to be one of the last straws in our friendship. The exchange took place while Cameron was round for dinner with Simone and me. In the middle of the main course, he stood up and left.

That wasn't the last time I saw Cameron, despite his pique. But the next time I did see him, some months later, the rope that had once looped us together was now stretched out between us, taut and fraying, as he and I tugged, he to get away, I to bring him back. By now Cameron had moved on from Gavin. He was with a woman again. This was a French-Canadian archaeologist named Julie. Insofar as Julie was yet to extricate herself from a relationship with a female partner, however, a few questions about sexual orientation were left hanging. Was Julie basically gay? Was leaving Bella, her girlfriend, a way of denying it? Was Cameron basically gay? Had the relationship with Gavin brought him out? Were they both bisexual – bisexual in a more credible way than Maddison might have been? Were Cameron and Julie using each other to present a heterosexual front while continuing to enjoy homosexual lives behind closed doors?

In the context of the recent relationship history of both Cameron and Julie, all those questions were valid. And yet none hit the mark. The pair seemed genuinely in love. There was even talk of marriage. Partly, that talk was driven by Julie's need to secure her immigration status, much easier to do as the spouse of a Brit. But it was more than pragmatism. Committing to the partnership as a going concern, both Cameron and Julie exuded delight.

The side effect of Cameron's brace of relationships – first Gavin, then Julie – was that it diverted him from Maddison. Before then, my access to her had been blocked by Cameron's aspirations. Now the stone was rolled away. Yet it wasn't as if I had been waiting. I had Simone and we had our children. My cranium still reverberated with the commandment to 'never get involved with this woman!' There was also Ed, Maddison's official squeeze. He wasn't quite the donkey that he had been cast as. Maddison always spoke about Ed with fondness and respect. Not to mention Lana. Without Maddison's lead, where would she go? Of the several hurdles between Maddison and me, only one – Cameron – had been removed.

And yet it proved decisive. With Cameron having chicaned away from Maddison, a great unfreezing followed. It was like the end of the Ice Age. Warmth returned to the planet. Love-birds chirped at the coming together of Cameron and Julie. Maddison and I fell in love. Simone also fell in love, with a man from work called Steve. With him she would go on to have a third daughter: that dream of three daughters could have been her dream that I was hosting. Lana met a man named Bailey who became her fiancé.

Fallout

The new sunshine produced new shadows. Not everybody basked in its warmth.

When Julie left Bella for Cameron, Bella was not happy. Or so I heard.

When I left Simone for Maddison the same year, Simone was not happy. Although we had been coming apart over many years, there was that historic bond fused in Perpignan. Together we had gone through a unique and binding experience. We had never married but compared to sharing children, marrying is nothing. Simone cried.

Anna was six. She was not happy. We were close. I was her daddy. I had been an equal carer of her with Simone. I loved her. She cried when I told her I was leaving. I picked her up in my arms.

Ruby was two and seemed too young to understand. But it entered her psyche.

When Maddison left Ed for me, I cannot say if he was heartbroken either. But I am sure that he was not happy.

When Maddison 'left' Lana for me, Lana lost some of her access to Maddison and wasn't happy. She had yet to meet Bailey.

When Steve left Rachel for Simone a while later, he also left his son, Sebastian. Sebastian was about the same age as Ruby, a toddler. I don't know how he felt. I heard that Rachel was not happy.

There were those in the sun and those in the shade. The happiness of a few came at a cost to several others. The backing track to it all was Alanis Morissette's 1994 hit, 'You Oughta Know', with its molten chorus:

> *I'm here to remind you*
> *Of the mess you left*
> *When you went away.*

Guilt is good

The concept of 'delayed shock' has become commonplace. An event takes place that is too intense for the psyche to compute at the time. Like an acid whose vapours curl off from its meniscus in menacing ribbons, the event has to be kept in a safety bottle, and the bottle in a cellar. Only when the liquid has lost its lethality – and it might take years – do we dare to unscrew it again. Well, delayed shock has a less famous cousin in the form of a syndrome that I would label as 'postponed guilt'. We adopt a course of action in the knowledge that it will hurt other people, but we bottle that knowledge up until we can face opening it. Even then, we don't drink it down in one draught. We begin with quarter-teaspoonfuls, increasing the dose by only the tiniest increments.

That is partly what happened when I left the family home. I didn't want to turn and see the guilt. It pulled at my sleeve, stumbling along beside me like a disabled younger brother whom I was trying to disown, while I pressed on. Indeed it was only by ignoring the guilt that I was able to take the action that I took. Had I given due regard to its beseeching countenance, I would have been stopped in my tracks. How could I have kept on going in the face of its suffering?

My point is that whatever its moral profile, guilt is an inhibitor. Just as our veins are starting to fill up with the intention to act, guilt reaches in and turns off the taps. Its aim in so doing is to restore the *status quo ante*. For guilt doesn't like change. It is a deeply conservative force, trained on keeping things as they were. Its aim is to terrorise us into inertia. That is why it is favoured by authoritarian regimes such as The Party in *Nineteen Eighty Four*. Deployed like the Thought Police, guilt is a weapon for ensuring compliance with prevailing norms.

So if guilt is the enemy of action, action needs to push back against guilt. To act is to break away from those prevailing norms. Of course, not all action requires such an existential level of intent. The action of brushing one's teeth or parking a car is scarcely going to involve wrestling with one's guilty conscience. In this context, 'action' refers to big decisions only – decisions like leaving one's family, defying the state, switching careers or emigrating overseas. Action on this scale means putting a foot outside the circle in which you hitherto belonged and accepting, even welcoming, the guilty effects of so doing. The two go together. As action gets to its feet, its shadow in the form of guilt arises too. The challenge for action is to see guilt precisely as a shadow. Investing it with too much reality will cause action to shrink back down again.

The German psychologist Bert Hellinger goes further. He argues that guilt is no moral force at all but simply a measure of our belonging. We feel guilty when we make a move away from our belonging-group and correspondingly innocent when we stay. Our so-called 'moral conscience', which we took to be so lofty, is little more than a way of indicating how secure we are in our tribe.

Hellinger uses this argument to explain perhaps the darkest paradox of the twentieth century. Namely, how it was that thousands of ordinary German men were transformed into sadistic Nazis. According to Hellinger, their primary intent was not ethnic cleansing *per se*, as though they were lieutenants of Satan to a man. Rather they were driven to such atrocities by the wish to secure their belonging to the Nazi movement. The more they expunged the other – Jews, intellectuals, liberals – the more they strengthened the coherence of Nazism and their identification with it. From a moral and legal perspective, that is patently no defence. From their point of view, however, they were murdering in all innocence. For innocence = the feeling of belonging. No doubt Hellinger's equation is provocative, but how else do we resolve that paradox?

Action produces guilt, in other words, not because it is Wrong with a capital *W*, but because it undermines our sense of belonging. Which implies that authentic action, on the scale described, has to involve feeling guilty. You are not acting in any meaningful way if there is no guilt at all. Only when the Guilt Police begin to stir do you know that you are finally doing something to wake them up. Instead of complying with the rules obeyed by the mass to which you belong, you are breaking away. It is a sign of independence. In which respect, guilt is good. To use a phrase from Hellinger's great predecessor, Friedrich Nietzsche, guilt would be the strange sensation that accompanies 'becoming who you are'. All true individuals are guilty.

Fortunately, or unfortunately – depending how you look at it

– I experienced no such rush of Nietzschean heroism at the time that I broke away from the family. The non-rational logic of emotion in my case ran as follows:

1. I didn't feel guilty when I left the family home. It is axiomatic that I didn't. For had I felt guilty, I wouldn't have left. The guilt, were it *bona fide*, would have numbed my faculties of action.
2. More precisely, I didn't feel guilty *enough* for it to stop me from leaving. There wasn't sufficient active ingredient in the guilt injection that pierced my skin to prevent my departure.
3. More precisely still, I felt *more than* guilty enough. *Because* I was taking drastic action, I felt guilty. So guilty that at the time I couldn't handle it. I therefore commuted that guilt to a later date. That later date is today, the day on which the deferred guilt has begun to vest, like a malignant dividend. Hence the concept of *postponed guilt*, a homologue of delayed shock.

Lovesick

By now – 1995 – Maddison and I were holed up in a maisonette that an estate agent might describe as 'in need of modernisation'. It hadn't been touched since the 1960s, a fact reflected in the peppercorn rent. What it lacked in mod cons, however, it made up for in location. This was Park Town, the most sought-after address in the most sought-after district of north Oxford. The 'street', in the shape of a wine glass, boasted an eighteenth-century oval in Headington limestone; free-standing Palladian villas; a locked *hortus conclusus* or inner garden; a raised terrace; a hidden lane through to the park; a Victorian pillar box topped with original acanthus bud; and its very own arboretum made up of pine trees – the 'pinetum' – by which means it screened off the reality beyond.

If Oxford was a bubble to start with, then north Oxford was a bubble within that bubble, Park Town was a bubble within north Oxford, and our garret under the eaves was a bubble within Park Town. There was a final, innermost bubble, like the baby stashed within a Russian doll. This was the relationship forged by Maddison and me. We spent every hour together, talking, walking, sleeping and eating, as if we were conjoined twins.

Park Town, Oxford

Such closeness was predicated on the state of 'drift' described in the last chapter. What allowed Maddison and me to find a vocation in each other was the lack, in her case as much as mine, of an external purpose. Maddison had extended her postgrad degree into a doctorate. A glib professor had misled her into believing that it was a simple matter of bulking up her Master's thesis, like sprinkling on bran. In reality, the doctoral research demanded going back to square one, widening and deepening the approach in a properly scholarly fashion. When Maddison – who academically was more of a sprinter than a marathon runner – took in the scope of the task, she lost her appetite for it. She barely got going.

Her drift coincided with mine. This was the phase after finishing my Derrida book, when I was casting around for a replacement project. With the dawning of each day, I would come up with a new idea. But on none of them could I settle. So although I tried to maintain my work routine, I had nothing in which to ground it. My discipline began unravelling like the 'sleeve of care' described by Shakespeare. The result was a vicious circle, as shown in the following diagram. Dutifully I would go off to my study. Having sat down at my desk, I was confronted by blankness. I was still giving lectures and teaching tutorials, but all I could think of was Maddison. So I went back home to her. Immediately, I felt bad for neglecting my non-existent project. I returned to my study. Repeat *ad infinitum.*

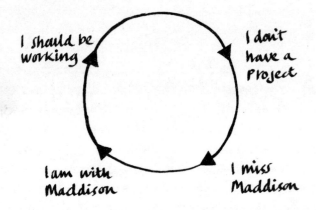

My work rate dwindled, levelling out to match Maddison's. That made room for the one thing on our minds. Not sex necessarily, but love. Love was the narcotic that we craved and that we could score only from each other. Like sailors on an opium boat, addicted to their own export, we would languish in our flat, becalmed on our bed, as the daylight beyond our attic window widened towards noon and narrowed into the evening. We would continue there in our crepuscular state through the night.

If I was able to defer the pain that I might have felt at the pain of others, it was also because of this, the opiate of love. While releasing drops of exquisite pleasure, it dulled me, like an analgesic, to any noise of suffering elsewhere in the universe. Reality receded. As if we had opened a portal in time, we uncovered in each other's presence an infinity that made the outside world seem all too bounded. In a profane simulacrum of the sacred, we submerged our individual identities into the One.

Even when Maddison and I did bestir ourselves to see people, we kept the electric fence around us switched on. Not surprisingly, others found that it had a repelling effect. On the rare occasions that Maddison and I double-dated with Cameron and Julie, for instance, and didn't refrain from kissing during dinner, they understandably winced. Lana complained that between Maddison and me there was no daylight to be seen. She resented not being able to spend time with her friend alone.

But to us such objections were as nought. Our cocoon made the voices around us sound muffled, the faces appear blurred. All we needed was each other. Even at that much-anticipated encounter with Jacques Derrida after his Paris seminar, I chased the meeting to a close so that I could be alone with Maddison again. It was she who was the fourth person at the table. There is no way that I would have gone to Paris or anywhere else without her. As if huddling by a radio aerial for a transmission from outer space, I was so attuned to her that all other phenomena were a distraction.

As well as the state of drift common to the both of us, there were extra factors that enabled our free fall into such a delirium of co-dependence. Maddison was six thousand miles from home. In Oxford she had none of her network around her, so life with me became all points on her compass. That wasn't always easy for her. From time to time she would attest to an existential panic at having lost touch with who she was. For my part, I felt under pressure to ensure that the relationship with Maddison was the *grand amour* that I had advertised it as. That was the only way that I could justify having left my family. How foolish would it have been to go through all that upheaval, only to return to the house in New Marston a few months later with a suitcase and with my tail between my legs?

Not that it was forced. Having lived in a triangle with Simone and Anna, and then a square with Simone, Anna and Ruby, but never properly in a dyad with Simone by herself, I now gorged on the one-to-one intimacy with Maddison. We both did. The problem was that, like any gorging, it led to nausea. We fell sick with love. If Hegel says that the love between a couple needs a third dimension in order to express itself, then a third dimension is exactly what Maddison and I had renounced. The tennis ball had only the two walls between which to bounce. Spending twenty-four hours a day in each other's company, we became hyper-sensitised to every look and word that passed between us. We over-analysed each micro-moment. Our conversations became about our conversations. In our maisonette, paranoia flowered like a strange orchid.

Pause before re-beginning

To flee the stale air, Maddison at one point called the whole thing off. She flew back to Los Angeles. She had to reconnect with who she was. She needed to gulp down the oxygen of normalcy. Which was understandable, except that as she inhaled I crumpled like a lifeless lung. Having my conjoined twin leave so abruptly meant that my vital system began to fail.

At first I sublimated my sense of loss into exercise. From Park Town I would run to a gym on the far side of town, do an intensive workout and run back. It was a form of self-castigation for losing hold of love. Where my soul had fallen short, I would perfect my body. Then one day I came out of the front door in my trainers and stopped. I tried to run but couldn't move.

Looking at my test results, the doctor probed as to my immune status. Toxoplasmosis was rare. In the UK, it was contracted mainly by those who were HIV positive. The only other cause was eating undercooked meat, as Simone and I had been warned by the gynaecologist in France. Since I fitted into neither category, the cause of the toxoplasmosis was never discovered. For the first time I appreciated the meaning of a term that I had previously dismissed: 'psychosomatic'. With Maddison gone, my life force had waned. The doctor prescribed amitriptyline, an anti-depressant. I took one dose, hated the wooziness, and tossed the rest into a bin on Brasenose Lane.

Second-hand news

Six months later Maddison returned. She too had suffered the symptoms of withdrawal from the obsession machine that we had jointly assembled, and that had begun rusting in a corner of the flat. We plugged back in and it whirred into life. The future that had been curtailed by Maddison's departure clicked back into view as if beamed onto the wall by a vintage projector. In that future I saw us at play on the West Coast, gambolling along the yellow sands, cruising in a convertible, greeting friends at a pool party.

By now the kaleidoscope's glass fragments had thinned out markedly. It was as if a tray of iron filings had been shaken, leaving just a few. Even with those remaining, the relationships became more remote. Although I was seeing Anna and Ruby regularly, the three and a half miles between their house and Park Town felt a galaxy away. That house, in any case, was the new one that Simone had set up with Steve, in east Oxford. It was not my territory. All Souls, once the sparkling hub of my world, had become a faded tapestry on the wall. My locus there had also weakened. Lana was by now with Bailey and they were forging a coupledom of their own, out of sight.

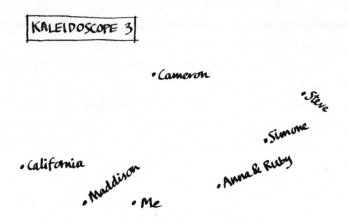

As for Cameron, he too moved further out of orbit, like Major Tom. I tried several times to get in touch but with no joy. Any information that I did glean came to me on the grapevine. He and Julie got married, though neither I nor Maddison were invited to the ceremony. The marriage didn't last long. Julie's need for a work visa was too big a motive. They divorced. I heard that Cameron had found a new girlfriend. I learned that he had moved to an outer part of the city. Somebody told me that he had a bad dose of the blues. Second-hand though such reports were, I used them to tell myself that Cameron wasn't deliberately shunning me. He was just dealing with his own troubles.

Our friendship lapsed, then expired. We didn't even become enemies. At least with enemies, a bond connects the two parties. It was rather that Cameron and I lost more and more substance and colour in each other's eyes, in a slow transformation like a deathly bleaching. Finally we were nothing but a memory to each other. My clever, handsome stand-in brother had been washed away.

> The apparition of these faces in the crowd;
> Petals on a wet, black bough.
>
> Ezra Pound

5

Going to California: a case of *aller-retour*

The question of what it is to be a human being – the question that is the lodestar of the present book – is considered by Prince Hamlet in the following poetical terms:

> What is a man
> If his chief good and market of his time
> Be but to sleep and feed? A beast, no more.
> Sure, he that made us with such large discourse,
> Looking before and after, gave us not
> That capability and godlike reason
> To fust in us unused.

Hamlet is drawing a distinction between mankind's lowest and highest faculties. The lowest make us nothing more than animals. We sleep and feed like beasts. The highest involve the use of 'godlike reason'. Our mental abilities elevate us not just above animal level but above the realm of the human altogether. At this dizzy height we may even scrape the heavens. What it means to be a human being, therefore, is facing a choice between two extremes. We can be bestial or we can be divine.

It is clear which way Hamlet leans. Since we have been blessed with a godlike gift for reasoning, we should make the most of it. It is too precious to let it 'fust in us unused'. That is, we mustn't allow our brains to become mouldy with idleness. Hamlet is vocalising the received wisdom of the late Renaissance. Through our faculties of reason, human beings have the potential to become perfect. If God made man in his own image, it's our duty to keep up to the mark.

Easier said than done, of course. Even if we could rise above our animal status to become godlike, we would still be prey to our emotions. Which is Hamlet's problem. Try as he might to puzzle out his predicament using the resources of reason alone, his feelings – of jealousy, doubt and betrayal – keep getting the better of him. His behaviour turns eccentric. He starts making poor decisions. So poor that he winds up dead.

It is tragic and yet all too human. Tragic *because* all too human. All right, we have godlike potential. But the word 'potential' implies that it's just as possible for us to fall short of that potential as it is to fulfil it. We fluctuate between high and low. It's this rise and fall that is so typical of us. Sometimes we make excellent choices and things go well. Other times we screw up. We can't help but make mistakes.

That is what this chapter is about. It's about the fact that we are prone to error. It's about things going wrong. It's about making plans that don't work out.

At the Randolph Hotel

In the summer of 1997, before leaving for Los Angeles, Maddy and I held a tea party at a hotel in Oxford to say goodbye. I picture the scene as if it were an Impressionist painting from a hundred years before. The painting has a classic title such as *At the Randolph Hotel*. Guests converse on upholstered chairs; a piano bears sheet music by Erik Satie; staff in uniforms bring Viennoiserie on cake stands; newspapers drape over a mahogany rack; and all is reflected in the gilt-framed mirrors punctuating the salon walls.

On that late afternoon, with the sun slanting in through arched windows, my happy assumptions were that:

1. Maddy and I would stay together for ever. The fact that we had taken up again after being apart implied a renewed and irreversible commitment. Our relationship was now destined for longevity, as if it had been written thus in a fortune cookie.
2. I would find a job as easily as falling off a log. Once they had taken note of my Oxford credentials, American employers would beat a path to my door. The only difficulty would be choosing from among the surfeit of offers coming my way.
3. On the back of the above, I would get a visa to work in the United States. My application would be fast-tracked and any bureaucratic snags would fall away like knots undone.

Maddy and I made our farewells in the belief that we were leaving for a better life.

Twinkle, twinkle

Our descent into LAX carried us over the vast jewelled carpet made up by the night lights of the San Fernando valley. It was as if all the stars had fallen to the floor. Along with the drone of the aircraft, and the miracle of its whale bulk banking on nothing but air, that mixture of darkness and glitter was deeply soothing. In our long-haul funk, we were held in the sky as in an artificial cradle.

If, according to Walter Benjamin, Paris was the 'capital of the nineteenth century', Los Angeles was the capital of the late twentieth. Specifically LA was the apogee of Postmodernism. Owing to its location on the Pacific Rim, which made it seem as open to possibility as it was to the sea and the sky, the former Hispanic pueblo was poised to welcome the New. It was as if, like the weather, innovation could arrive only from the west.

The signature of Postmodernism was inscribed throughout the city. Not far from Maddy's father's condo in Santa Monica stood the building that first made architect Frank Gehry famous.⬇ This was the headquarters of Chiat/Day, an advertising agency. The edifice took the form of a giant pair of black binoculars. I interpreted the shape as a reference to the dominance in LA of the image, and how the image was magnified in both senses: made bigger and venerated. What made Gehry's structure *postmodern* was that the design had won out over more practical considerations. In the language of architectural aesthetics, form had beaten function.

The fact that it housed an ad agency only bolstered the building's postmodern credentials. Of course by the 1990s the advertising industry in America was mature enough. There was

---

⬆ That condo had been purchased by Maddy's father from songwriter Burt Bacharach. As the creator of perhaps my favourite song – 'Walk on By', recorded by Dionne Warwick – Bacharach was my hero. When Bradley, Maddy and I went to view his property, the maestro, silver-haired and wearing a single diamond stud earring, was improvising at an electric piano. Grammy awards and platinum discs lined the staircase. On a yellow Post-it next to the phone in the kitchen was a handwritten note to 'call Elvis back'. This was the period of Bacharach's collaboration with Elvis Costello, another hero of mine, which resulted in the album *Painted from Memory*. Bacharach's next-door neighbour was actor Jean-Claude van Damme, who kept a fearsome Hummer parked outside like an Alsatian. Just across the road was another actor, Mickey Rourke, who in his obsession with boxing was fearsome enough in his own right.

nothing especially postmodern about it. The difference in the 1990s was that the advertising mindset was creeping well beyond the profession's confines. Everything had become an image intent on selling itself, people included.

The standout example was a TV series called *Baywatch*. Filming took place on the beach a stone's throw from the Chiat/Day offices. Each episode featured Pamela Anderson and other nubile actresses, clad in scarlet bathing suits designed to accentuate their curves, sashaying along the seashore. When the sequences were dialled down to slow motion, as sometimes they were, the atmosphere produced was that of a shampoo commercial. Was it a drama? Was it an advertisement? So long as it was easy on the eye, it didn't matter.

Another example of the Californian taste for blurring image with reality was represented by Ronald Reagan, who had set the tone for the twentieth century's final acts. In postmodern style, he had been an actor before becoming California's governor and then Commander-in-Chief. He appeared to construe the very office of President as a role and was determined to put on a good show. It was in the year of his landslide victory in the presidential campaign, 1984, that the LA Olympics had been held. The Games seemed to be less about sport than about pageantry.

By the late 1990s, when Maddy and I arrived, that twinkle of American confidence had only brightened. The Berlin Wall had been bulldozed and Soviet communism as a whole was discredited. There was talk of the 'end of history'. It was just a matter of time before all four corners of the world bowed to the American model of liberal democracy, and perpetual peace broke out. The dotcom companies of Silicon Valley were on the rise. Their forecasts were of a brave new 'knowledge economy', whereby unprecedented levels of wealth would be generated from the intangible. The GDP of California alone already made it richer than most nations. The attacks of 9/11 had yet to take place. Worries about global warming were confined to a lunatic fringe. The sub-prime mortgage bubble was blissfully inflating, unnoticed. The only concern was Y2K, the chiliastic threat of a wipe-out of all electronic data. That turned out to be a false alarm.

Not that this wider context impinged much on the consciousness of Angelenos. What mattered in LA was LA. The only thing that could possibly matter more was the self. That made for a stark contrast with the European cities that I knew, designed as they were around the citizen rather than the private individual. By and large, Europeans think of themselves as being in a relationship of mutual responsibility with the state and its institutions. In LA the public good comes a distant second behind personal fulfilment. But that is just one in a series of contrasts between the Europe whose door I had closed and the California whose door I had opened. Instead of a focus on meaning, there was a preoccupation with happiness. Of course, happiness is a blessing, but the *idea* of happiness is a curse, and in LA it was the idea that prevailed. Instead of the European need for things to be interesting, Angelenos valued things that were easy. Instead of irony, niceness. Instead of the past, the future.

The absence of a centripetal pull into a civic centre was made manifest topographically. Packets of private living squeezed out any possibility of a commons. Indeed an Italian friend of Maddy's arrived in LA for the first time only to exclaim, 'Where is the piazza!' The city was, and remains, a quilt of districts – Westwood, Los Feliz, Culver City, Koreatown, Compton, Pacific Palisades, Venice, Silver Lake. The effect is one of dispersal. Of Oakland in northern California, Gertrude Stein famously wrote that 'there is no there there'. But the phrase applies equally to its southern counterpart, Los Angeles. There, there is no there, for the very good reason that 'there' is a place for everybody. In LA there is only 'here' – that is, the place where I am.

Perhaps that is why, as our plane shuddered to a halt on the runway, I felt that LAX marked the spot where I should have always been. I was here now, so this was home. At least that was the illusion on my arrival.

Fish, water

In Oxford Maddy had been a fish out of water. Like the Romans who elected not to settle it, she reacted against the city's bone-chilling mists and pewter sky. Habituated to California cuisine with its arugula salads and wheatgrass smoothies, Maddy would look aghast at the watery cabbage and jam roly-polys that were dished up in Oxford colleges. From the beach volleyball culture of Malibu, she had, as if through a looking-glass, landed among the ermine-clad protocols of academe and found herself bewildered. Against Oxford's backdrop of Gothic stone, Maddy's presence appeared as oneiric and evanescent as a coloured cellophane cartoon flexing in the air.

Back on her home turf of Los Angeles, that all changed. Maddy came into her own. Where she had been foxed by Oxford as by a flying machine improvised from catgut and balsa wood, she breezed into LA and flicked on all the switches as if settling into the cockpit of a Boeing 747. At her touch, all the lights came on.

And she knew how to navigate. When it came to scouting out an apartment for us to live in, her instincts never erred. On account of the cooling breezes, our quarters had to lie on the slopes north of Sunset Boulevard. Not so far north, however, that we would find ourselves in the Valley. In every respect that would be uncool. It was sweltering on the flats; the appellation of 'Valley Girl' was beyond the pale; and to forfeit the treasured 310 dialling code was social suicide. So Mulholland Drive became the northern boundary. There were eastern and western borders too. One had to go east of Beverly Hills, which was outmoded; yet no further than Hancock Park, which was veering dangerously close to the then dead zone of Downtown. Hollywood might be okay were it not for all the failed actors nesting together in shared houses, like doves in a columbarium.

Holding fast to these desiderata, Maddy found us a place in West Hollywood. Being the city's gay district, it had an edge that attracted her. Our local gym, The Sports Connection, was known locally as 'The Sports Erection' and sometimes more wickedly as 'The Sports Infection'. The apartment itself was just off Sunset. Our street ran north from the junction where 1960s music club the Whisky a Go-Go still kept a-going. In a city built around the car, we were within walking distance of hipster landmarks that included Tower Records, Book Soup and Johnny Depp's Viper Room.⬇

Maddy's return to her native town seemed to call an entire social scene into action, like a field of small animals waking out of hibernation. First among equals was Briony, an exuberant, kind-hearted, goofy and beautiful friend from Maddy's school-days. Briony had achieved appreciable fame and fortune as a child movie star, but had never fully leveraged her early success. She had been forced to eke out the lump sum of cash that she had earned in childhood. Like a tycoon in possession of a prodigious ice sculpture, she kept it in the basement, to slow the ineluctable melting of its capital.

The rest of Maddy's network was made up of other friends

⬆ A few months later I would meet Johnny Depp in person. I was with Maddy and her friend in the Bodhi Tree, a bookshop on Melrose Avenue, and so was Johnny. Maddy's friend knew him from the film business, and introduced us.

from high school along with their siblings and/or boyfriends. What they had in common was wealth, whiteness and a kind of conservatism that I had never previously encountered. Although a few of them self-identified as Democrat rather than Republican, that was mainly the 'narcissism of minor differences', to quote a phrase of Freud. With the goal of asserting their individuality, they might have expressed differences of opinion but, compared with the underlying conservatism of outlook that the friends shared, these were marginal.

When I describe Maddy's circle as 'conservative', it wasn't that her friends were forever trumpeting views from the right of centre. They were apolitical. In this section of LA society, to mention politics at all was to commit a gaffe. It implied a coarseness that might snag on the silky fabric of affluence. Whenever I ventured into that subject area, people would either look embarrassed or laugh it off as British eccentricity. I learned to keep my mouth shut. Why in any case would one wish to draw attention to defects in a system that served one so well? Being apolitical was a way of passively endorsing a status quo from which they derived benefit. That was tantamount to actively feeding it.

Take domestic services. Every morning, a phalanx of Hispanic maids, nannies, handymen and gardeners would drive in from El Este in battered Toyotas, to earn their daily bread among the mansions of Brentwood. In the dawn light they were dropped off like dark ghosts. Just as the automatic sprinklers began jetting their artificial rain over the ground, these obsequious figures would creep through the tennis courts, swimming pools and landscaped gardens to take up their tasks.

When, awake early because of jet lag, I first observed this phenomenon, I was as entranced as if witnessing fairies at work among the flowers. A midsummer night's dream. But in the light of day I was shocked. Shocked by the sheer disparity between the lives of this underclass and those of their masters. Hispanics were considered second-class citizens in ways reminiscent to me of the treatment of blacks in the Deep South. In the minds of the elite among whom I now circulated, such a comparison was incomprehensible. Here was no question of politics or civil rights. Here was simply the service economy at work. It was a given, like electricity. Besides, many of the Hispanic workforce were illegal immigrants, and were lucky to be earning dollar at all. We were doing them a favour.

Respect vs. engagement vs. control

As well as Maddy's friends, there was her family. At its crown sat her long-widowed grandmother. A cross between Miss Havisham and Gloria Swanson, she whiled away her days on a bed that dwarfed her, among cushions, magazines, tissues and chocolates. Her golden days had been those of Busby Berkeley musicals, lush double chords, sweeping staircases and champagne served in coupes. The pink velour tracksuit that was her daily attire did nothing to spoil the aura of glamour past: it was just an updated version.⬇

Her residence, which could have been a wing of Jay Gatsby's, was supported by her millionaire son, Bradley, Maddy's father. Bradley had divorced his wife and had a girlfriend whom he endlessly demurred over marrying, despite her heavy hints. He preferred to spend his puppyish energy on his mother. Whenever he was in town he would be round to check on her. When he was away he would ring. Throughout, he was keen to prove himself over his older brother as the better son.

⬆ It was around Maddy's grandmother's kitchen table that *Baywatch* was first thought up, by family friends.

But Bradley was no less devoted to Maddy, his only child. Even when we were in Oxford, I had been surprised – and a little peeved – at the frequency of his long-distance phone calls. I had also been appalled by the depth of his involvement in Maddy's life, on all fronts from money to medicine. The calls only increased when we were back in LA. I wondered whether what had prepared Maddy for symbiosis with me was a prior experience of the same with her father.

Bradley's dual focus on mother and daughter suggested to me that while he knew how to value vertical human connections – mother above, daughter below – he struggled to afford similar status to the horizontal – the girlfriend and brother to his side. Perhaps that raises a question for us all. Do we pay more heed to those people above and below us than to those on our flanks? What does it say about who we are?

In the diagram below, the left-hand side, shaded more lightly, represents family relationships. The darker right-hand side shows

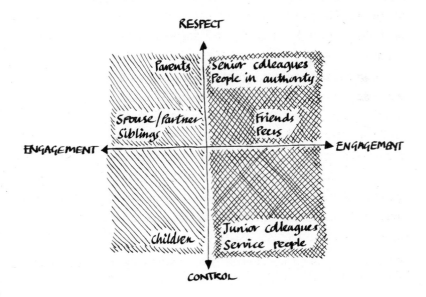

relationships outside the family. In both cases there is a vertical and a horizontal axis. The question is which axis we privilege. Attention upwards suggests respect. Attention downwards suggests an attitude of paternalism/maternalism, or even control. Attention on either side implies an attitude of engagement. With which of those three – respect, control or engagement – are we most at home?

It is all too possible to pervert the order in the diagram. One might control one's partner, thereby twisting a properly horizontal relationship into an unnaturally vertical arrangement. One might engage one's elders in a chummy fashion, thus flipping what should be a vertical through 180 degrees, and shedding the appropriate deference towards them in the process. Treating a friend with excessive respect is to turn that friendship into a seesaw of inequality. That is anathema to friendship because friends should be equal. When such 'perversions' – if that is not too strong a word – occur, it feels awry for all concerned.

It is tempting to conclude that the horizontal axis is the more progressive. It feels democratic and so fits more naturally with modern values. It is likely to be the axis with which those of a liberal mindset feel most comfortable. Conservative types are more likely to appreciate the vertical axis, as it betokens order and probity. Yet there is a place for both. Indeed, any difficulty we have in recognising that there is a place for both will show us where our ideological and psychological biases lie.

Bradley's clear orientation was towards the vertical. As far as his mother was concerned, that was dandy. She had a faithful son to look out for her. For Maddy, however, it was nettling. She resented being reliant on her father as it made her weak. Already in her late twenties, she was seeking to establish her independence. But Bradley's girlfriend hadn't quite filled the hole left by his ex-wife, and that led him to pull Maddy into the space left over. Also, Bradley was forever offering to do things for Maddy, like buy her dinner, sort out her taxes or get her car fixed. Such favours were understandably hard for Maddy to refuse. And so her attempts at escape were thwarted as if she were a bird with one leg tied to a string.

Capital

Whatever the entanglements produced by that father–daughter dialectic, Bradley's support for Maddy went to reinforce her base in Los Angeles. That caused me to feel weak in turn. The power balance between the two of us shifted. Where in Oxford Maddy had been the fish out of water, in LA it was she who was in her element. Like a fuse in an electric circuit, she appeared embedded, active and connected. Energy flowed from, through and around her. Now I was the one six thousand miles from home, struggling to make sense of a new environment and fit in. The casket of assets from which I had drawn in Oxford – a glamorous job, a familiar home and a network – I had abruptly relinquished like a king in a revolution who has fled his realm.

That reversal of power was more than symbolic. It played out in everyday life. When the phone rang it would always be for Maddy. After a while I refused to answer it, as it made me feel like a secretary. When we got in the car, it was always Maddy who took the wheel, as I didn't have a California driver's licence. When we socialised, it would always be with Maddy's friends. I would go along in tow like the spouse of a diplomat.

Then there was money. My All Souls fellowship had petered out and I hadn't found American employ to replace it. That meant turning to my feeble savings account. So feeble that it was like taking a lighter to a cone of sawdust. Dabbling as she did in part-time jobs, Maddy had scarcely more income than I, but there was that safety net strung tightly beneath her by her father. Money could be accessed on Maddy's mother's side too. They were landowners whose holdings included a vast cattle ranch in the Midwest, where many of them lived. So when Maddy's personal finances wobbled, it wasn't a disaster. She was underwritten by substantial capital. That capital created in me the impression of a financial fortress, a granite citadel hulking in the bluish background of a pastoral landscape. In its long shadow I felt small.

I felt small too because Bradley's wealth, combined with his energy and optimism, was such that I couldn't help but make comparisons with my own father. Bradley would go jogging every morning. Afterwards he would meet up with his girlfriend for fat-free blueberry muffins and decaf coffee. He'd keep abreast of the latest gadgets and was among the first to own a Palm Pilot, forerunner of the smartphone. He'd book impromptu skiing trips to Aspen, inviting friends or family to join him. In all, I saw him as bounding forward into the Pacific air of the future that rushed to embrace him in turn. Why couldn't my dad have been like him? Everything about Bradley suggested positivity and resilience and reaching-out and earning power. Everything about my father was derelict.

So if I associated Maddy and her family with capital, really I was identifying a force that was as psychological as it was monetary. 'Capital' was shorthand for 'the power of the father'. Specifically, it denoted the power of the father, thanks to his abundant resources, to dispel the anxieties of the child. In a way, my idea of capital was nothing more than a reverie about travelling back in time, to a period in boyhood when everything felt safe. In LA, my lack of collateral set off the feeling in me that every form of resource had gone missing. I felt under-powered and over-exposed.

With Maddy and her family's finances in mind, I wrote a poem at the time about that idea of capital:

Rests upon capital:
the headland,
the deposit,
the mineral wealth
& after a time
acculturation.
Flowers appear
on metal & stone,
the sense of
interest changes.

The poem is trying to say that capital is the 'headland' on which everything rests. Capital produces a sense of security for those fortunate enough to enjoy it. Once such capital is in place, culture can proceed. Hence the image of flowers carved onto metal and stone. Under such conditions, 'interest' changes its meaning. Instead of referring solely to financial interest, whereby capital produces a return, interest becomes about cultural diversions. It represents the luxury of taking an interest in things less fundamental than economics, such as the arts.

1 August 1997: Day one

I wake up to a halcyon sky. If only we had known, back in old northern Europe, that the source of our dolours was neither the oppressiveness of tradition nor the legacy of warfare nor even the death of God. It was the lack of vitamin D. The sun makes everything better, as if flooding the ether with a rosy-gold dye. I step out onto our balcony that looks over lemon trees. The breakfast temperature has already touched the upper seventies. 1997 being an El Niño year, the mercury will later climb to a hundred, like a metal tongue reaching up for rain.

This is no holiday, however. My mission is to find a job. The rub is that coming to LA with the intention of pursuing employment puts me on the wrong side of the law. I am in the USA on a tourist visa waiver. As was the case in Perpignan ten years ago, I can stay in the country for up to ninety days, for the purposes of sightseeing or visiting friends, but I am barred from looking for work. Being my girlfriend rather than my wife, Maddy provides no channel through which any rights can flow my way. A Green Card, that icon of immigrant hope, shimmers out of reach like a gold coin in a digital game.

And so I become trapped in a maze. I can't obtain a work visa without an employer to sponsor it, but employers won't look at me unless I have a work visa. I try to discuss the issue with the Immigration and Naturalisation Service (INS). Despite multiple attempts, I fail to break out of the automated phone system, all in Spanish, to speak with somebody in person. When I request certain forms on the punch pad, the wrong ones arrive in the mail. Hiring an immigration lawyer is beyond my means. My visa status means that I can't claim a Social Security Number (SSN), which also prevents me from applying for jobs. It also means that I can't get a driver's licence, so I am not able to legally drive. I am snookered.

Beneficial harm

Dodging or fudging questions about my eligibility, I approached employers regardless. Was that immoral? No doubt. But what alternative was there? It was either lie or go back to England.

At first, it was universities that I targeted. That was the obvious sector for a person with my skill set. But I did so half-heartedly. Leaving Oxford had been very much about quitting the academy, not just escaping from a provincial town that had become over-familiar. At thirty-two, I had already resided in Oxford for thirteen years. I had been lecturing for ten. Life in the Senior Common Room, with its subscriptions to journals, its standing jugs of over-brewed coffee, its academic gossip and its anti-fashion parade of corduroy and Clark's shoes, had become stifling. That was no culture for young men.

I also saw the long-term effects of an academic existence on certain of my colleagues. Their intellectual refinement had been achieved at a cost. One day in Sainsbury's I glimpsed a middle-aged fellow scholar in the same aisle. His jacket was stained, dandruff powdered his shoulders, and there were holes in his jumper. His hair was unkempt. His back was stooped. His skin was pasty. Standing by the frozen food section, he appeared baffled. One might have mistaken him for a tramp. Back on campus, just a couple of miles away, this was a man whose intellectual prowess commanded awe. Admirers would fawn over him and the attention had made him vain. When he arrived at the check-out, he treated the female assistant with the condescension that was his wont. Not a vision that I found appealing.

Hamlet argues that we should develop our 'godlike reason'. But what if, like that Oxford don, you have developed your godlike reason to an impressive extent, but let other faculties – from personal hygiene to emotional intelligence – slacken off? Realising our potential must surely involve expanding on all fronts. I am thinking of the British psychoanalyst Donald Winnicott. Were he alive to answer our overarching question of what it means to be a human being, I believe his reply would run along the following lines:

Our earliest experience in the world is as babies. That experience is largely one of dependence and helplessness. Therefore there is an imperative on us to develop. But we develop not just for the sake of survival. It's not enough for us to be stewards of our existence. Being human means that we have a need to develop creatively and emotionally too. This creative and emotional development is vital because it is the expression of our essence.

The state of becoming that is familiar to us from childhood, the process of unfolding like a crocus bulb, should not cease when we turn into adults. Just because we are done with growing up, it doesn't mean we are done growing. For the sake of what Winnicott calls our 'true self', it is incumbent upon us to move forward. Otherwise we die, in the sense of allowing our emotional and creative faculties to wither.

Although I didn't frame it in those terms at the time, I realise now that the urge to grow was my deeper motive for saying goodbye to the life academic. As its name half suggests, Oxford was a box. Unless I opened the lid and climbed out, I would never flourish as a person. In the humid dark I would keep cranking the academic handle – writing articles, running seminars and attending dinners. Not an unattractive life in itself. One day I might even become as revered as the professor from the supermarket. But I would be like a piston moving repeatedly through a single plane rather than pushing into other dimensions. I would be going through the motions.

But how exactly does growth occur? No doubt there are better metaphors, but growth is generally activated by pruning, as in the cutting back of plants in order to stimulate growth. What's key about pruning is that although it represents a staple of the gardener's trade, there is nothing natural about it. To prune a plant is to make an intervention; it interrupts the organic process. The first lesson, of three, being that if we want to grow, we *have to act*. It's no good carrying on doing what we have always done. Pruning also involves the removal of the previous season's matter.

That is the second lesson: *out with the old.* If you want the new to arrive, you have to make space for it, as would any good host. The third lesson is that of what I would call *beneficial harm.* By lacerating the branches, pruning acts as a stressor. It causes the plant to put on a spurt, in a kind of deliberate panic. With a combination of urgency and control, the plant shoots up with renewed vigour. But it does so only through being shocked into action.

So when, like birds of ill omen, the university rejection letters began flocking to our mailbox there was, despite some bruising to my ego, relief. The dead wood was being scythed off, and space for change uncovered. I also gained the benefit of simplification. We tend to think that the more options at our fingertips, the better. But having an option taken away can be clarifying. It is like the moment when, at a card game, your opponent removes a valuable card from your hand. At once, the frustration flares up, but often it is followed by a tiny, inappropriate waft of pleasure. What we lose in possibility, we gain in focus. Fate didn't want me to be an academic? Fine. An academic I would no longer be. With that particular destiny blacked out, I could swivel my telescope towards other galaxies.

Maybe it wasn't fate at all. Maybe my half-heartedness about taking another university job came through in the applications that I sent off. At an energetic level, my lack of enthusiasm was being picked up. The reason why those employers didn't want me was that I didn't want them. Not fundamentally. Nor could I dissemble keenness. What I am insinuating is that 'fate' might still have been at work, though in another guise. Fate was perhaps an alternative name for what I inwardly hoped would happen. Rather than being a steering wheel in the sky, twisting me this way and that, regardless of my will, fate was externalising my own dubiety. It had glimpsed in the wings my instinct not to get an academic job. Now it was working to make that anti-wish come true, pushing it centre stage. It was doing me a favour, in effect.

The moral is that what happens to us in life is what, most deeply, we want to happen. That sentence isn't intended to reassure, however. What we most deeply want to happen is not always good for us. To believe that would be sentimental. Even when we suffer, it is sometimes because, down in what W. B. Yeats called 'the foul rag-and-bone shop of the heart', we want to suffer. While we are justly declaring a wish to thrive, it is possible that, behind the scenes, a Mephistophelean presence is busy decocting a less medicinal result.

28 October 1997

My three-month visa period runs out. I am obliged to leave the country. My job search has come to nought. I return to Oxford. All my stuff is in storage. I can't ship it to the US until I know I have a job there and won't be returning permanently to England. A week later, I fly back to LA. Again, I'm on a tourist visa waiver, which buys me another ninety days. I still have no entitlement to work, no Social Security Number and no driver's licence.

White space, yellow pages

Despite the initial setback, the white space left by the university rejections, blended with that coastal air of infinity, filled me with the helium-headed belief that I could now apply for just about anything. Where better to start, in that case, than with the *carte blanche* of the Yellow Pages? I could get an instant read on the jobs that people actually did.

Riffling through the local directory, I was struck by the prevalence of attorneys, private detectives, escort agencies and realtors. It read like the casting list for a Hollywood film noir. The city's occupations were a window on its *pre*occupations: litigation, paranoia, sex and property. But that only reinforced my sense of myself in LA as being a square peg in a round hole. Within a matter of minutes, I realised not only how narrow was my expertise but how irrelevant. The demand in Los Angeles for British philosophers was somewhat lower than the supply; and the supply totalled one.

Discouraging though it was, the Yellow Pages exercise had its merits. By displaying the gamut of human endeavour, it defined my own limits, and so delivered an object lesson in humility. I was chastened. Finding what was relevant to me was like trying to tune in to a pirate station amid the hundreds on an analogue radio. If I was to have any chance, I would have to change my frequency. That meant exploring careers loosely contiguous with mine. Namely, advertising, communications, law, policy and management consultancy. I thought about psychoanalysis but was put off by the length and cost of the training. Ditto architecture.

So began a second round of applications. While awaiting the replies, I devised a screenplay. If that sounds random, doing so in those parts was practically *de rigueur*. If you weren't writing a screenplay or engaged in at least one of the following activities – seeing a shrink, cutting out carbs, moaning about the maid, taking meds, worrying over your investments, or employing a personal trainer – you weren't normal. My film script did not make it to the silver screen.

The rejections this time were even balder. At least the universities had understood what they were turning down. To these new prospects I simply wasn't legible. Although impressed by the Oxford brand, they couldn't assign it a value in their own world. It was as if a docent in a museum had drawn their attention to a significant artefact. They nodded with respect before walking on, unable to make any link to their own reality. No question, I was an asset, but an asset that couldn't be exchanged for dollars.

Adaptive fantasy

I was experiencing what I would come to know as the 'Double S' or 'seahorse' model of change, as in the following diagram. Back in the Randolph Hotel I had assumed that the transition from Oxford to LA would be that of a gradient gently rising to a higher and even more pleasant vantage point. I would pass seamlessly from a good life into a great life, like spring expanding into summer. The reality was inconveniently different. It more resembled a treacherous leap, over a chasm, from one S to another S. In the old world one might have reached the top, but in the new world one has to start at the bottom. Even if you manage to vault straight onto the summit of the second S, its snaking curve will surely cause you to backslide.

The 'Double S' model is designed to ruin the illusion that major change can pass off with no hitches. And yet that illusion has its advantages. Without it, we might never essay a jump at all. Because it provides the imaginative energy needed to get from A to B, such 'illusion' might better be understood as *adaptive fantasy*. By adaptive fantasy, I mean the acquired capacity to ignore unfavourable realities lest they get in the way of what could be a positive outcome. It is the mindset of the entrepreneur. After all, we only sign up for change in the belief that things will go better. If we thought that things would get worse, we wouldn't budge.

A tale of two tales

It was such an adaptive fantasy that, like a comet, had powered me towards LA in the first place. It gave me the confidence that all would be well. But something odd was going on. For I had indeed found myself in a position bizarrely similar to that which I had experienced in Perpignan a decade earlier. Then I had crossed the sea out of love for a woman, having broken off my career trajectory, to a foreign land where I had no rights and no money – but where she did – to share an apartment that she had rented. Now again, I had crossed the sea out of love for a woman, having broken off my career trajectory, to a foreign land where I had no rights and no money – but where she did – to share an apartment that she had rented. If it was the comet of an adaptive fantasy that had borne me to LA, that comet had a tail whose glitter lit up the past.

The similarities between the two cases are, I think, too striking to dismiss. At an unconscious level I was repeating myself. I say 'unconscious' because I never noticed the parallels at the time. But then, repetition of this psychological ilk usually is unconscious. It has to hide from us in order to do its work. Were we to catch it red-handed, we would be bound to call a halt to its blind strivings. In this sense, the unconscious is a repetition factory. The factory runs automated processes precisely to relieve its human owners from having consciously to intervene. As the factory churns, we can slumber, exonerated from such banausic activity.

But what exactly was being repeated in my case? Yes, there is the story that happens twice, first in France, then in America. It is the story of a woman, a journey, a lack of money and a dearth of work. But while the French and American versions of the story are spookily identical, they are themselves reiterations, up to a point, of the story of my parents' elopement. Going to America, just like going to France, represented an acting out of the template identified in Chapter 2: *Out of love, one follows the other across the sea.* First, I crossed the Channel to be with Simone. Now, I had traversed the Atlantic to be with Maddy. I wasn't just repeating myself: I was, at least to a degree, repeating my parents.

As if that weren't repetition enough, I was theoretically repeating my father's downfall again. Going to California meant throwing away my career, thus recapitulating the throwing away of my career when I went to France, which itself was a way of repeating my father's experience when his career came crashing down. Just like the move to France, my move to LA showed symptoms of self-sabotage. As when I dropped out as an undergraduate, I should probably have stayed on as an academic instead of jumping ship. Yes, the clock was ticking on my time at All Souls, but with enough determination and a bit of luck I dare say I could have found a passable replacement. Instead I threw it all in and simulated once more my father's ruination.

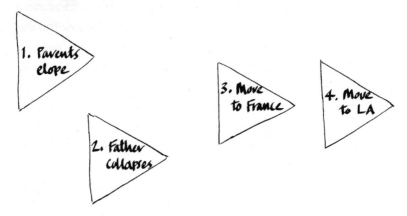

The diagram sets out these repetitions. Story 4 (LA) seems to be a clear repeat of Story 3 (France). In addition, Stories 3 and 4 (France and LA) could have been repetitions of either Story 1 (elopement) or Story 2 (father), or both. One might object that these 'repetitions' are resonances rather than perfect matches. But given that we are walking the mirrored halls of the unconscious mind, with its associative mode of operation, resonances were more than material enough for it to work with. Preferring association over causation, the unconscious gets us to repeat in whatever way it can. It improvises.

Boomerang *Schadenfreude*

So long as we are talking about the unconscious, we should take account of Sigmund Freud's dictum regarding repetition. Not only are we compelled to repeat, says Freud, but we repeat *what we don't understand*. Undoubtedly, those four stories feature lots of repetition, direct and indirect. But none of it is terribly hard to understand. So what was the not-understood core that was being repeated?⬇

To answer that question, I would go back to the notion of capital. When I set off for LA, just as when I absconded to France, I was risking all the capital that I had. I mean 'capital' in the broadest sense: not just money (of which there was very little) but my accumulated wherewithal. That was made up of my network, my experience, my expertise, family connections and cultural belonging. A solid foundation and a promising future. To jettison that capital wasn't far short of disposing of a whole life.

And why? To lose it all, even to destroy it, gave me a thrill. It

⬆ That question leads into a logical maze. If I understood what I don't understand, then I might understand it. But if I understand it, then maybe I'm understanding the wrong thing, because the thing itself is by definition not understood. And yet the definition of being 'not understood' differs from the definition of being 'not understandable'. Unless, that is, the 'not understood' is also 'not understandable', in which case I will never understand. Inevitably, therefore, any answer about the harder-to-understand thing will be speculative.

was a spectacle. I put the cost of damaging myself at less than the gratification to be had from the drama of so doing. It was a form of *Schadenfreude*, the cruel delight in seeing others in trouble. But it was a boomerang form of *Schadenfreude*, in that it rebounded on me. It came close to sadomasochism, though of a non-physical variety. The unpalatable premise, in every case, was that my own suffering would bring me pleasure.

In order to become that actor in my own drama, however, I needed to see myself as object rather than subject. There had to be some dissociation. Unless I split myself in two, with one half on stage and the other half in the audience, there would be no show at all. And although that might sound like the reasoning of a madman, it is only what every autobiographer does as a matter of routine. You, the writer, create a character who is the hero of the autobiography. Up to a point, writer and character are one and the same. And yet, as a written entity, the character will always be a construct, an artifice. He or she is an edited version of the writer, created by the writer. So writer and character are also different.

Besides, nobody really wants to suffer, not directly. The underlying purpose of that splitting, I think, was to deflect any harm that might come my way. If I got an actor to play me, then it would be he who suffered, thus sparing me in the audience. What would be attacked would be a projection of myself that I had fashioned and dispatched into the world like a tin soldier. While he ran to meet the arrows aimed at him, I would look on from a safe distance. If it was sadomasochism, it was a fake version: less sado-masochism than pseudo-masochism.

And yet I wasn't completely protected. How could I be? I didn't – I couldn't – literally crack myself into two halves like an egg. If things were going badly wrong for me in LA, which they were, there was nobody suffering my fate but me. Whatever ruses of dissociation I might have been employing in order to shield myself, the letters of rejection were still addressed to me. It was my bank account that was draining. I was the one going spare on the phone to the INS. There was no actor Robert taking the slings of outrageous fortune on my behalf. I had no body double. Everything that was happening to me was happening to *me*. The fantasy that I could absent myself from the present was precisely that – a fantasy.

Such would be my answer to the question about repeating what we don't understand. At a profound level, I hadn't understood that what was real was really real. The reason why I kept repeating scenes that were injurious to me was that I was clinging to the magical belief that I would come to no harm. According to that belief, the world inside my head would shelter me from any tornado in the world outside. It was the psychological equivalent of an invisibility cloak.

Learning that lesson took a while. Only much later would I come to accept that reality was not a drama I could observe from the port but the sea in which I was swimming. The fantasy lasted through my time in LA. It would last through the day of my blighted wedding to Maddy.

2–14 January 1998

I have to leave the US again as the second three-month visa period has expired. I fly back to England to see my family. I am missing my daughters. The arrangement isn't working. Also, the cost of these flights is eating up the rest of my money, and I have no income coming in. At their invitation, I give a lecture at the University of Oslo in Norway. The theme is autobiography.

15 January 1998

At Heathrow, on my way back to LA, I am questioned by border police and even by the Virgin Atlantic ground staff. They are rightly suspicious of the regular three-monthly stamps in my passport. 'What country do you live in?' they ask. 'England,' I lie. When I get back home to our apartment in West Hollywood, more rejection letters are waiting. I'm now living on credit. I still can't drive.

Fireflies

I can't drive legally, that is. But this is LA. If you don't drive, you can't play the game. And so I ask to borrow the white C class Mercedes that Maddy's grandmother hasn't driven for years. It sits like a stone dog in one of the parking bays on the long driveway leading up to her house, gathering sap from the pine tree over-hanging it.

Now, to drive a car with neither licence nor insurance, in the litigation-happy culture of California, is to take a foolish risk. To race your girlfriend along Sunset Boulevard at night without such documentation is especially unwise. Nevertheless, Maddy and I would sweep through Bel Air and Westwood as fast as we dared.

On paper it was an even match. Maddy also drove a C class Mercedes, a gift from her father (who owned an E class). The only difference was that Maddy's car was gold. Unlike me, however, Maddy knew the rises, dips and curves of the road as intimately as an infant knows the contours of its mother's body. Where she would swoop through the traffic light at Bellagio Drive just as it was changing, I, a split second behind, would have to slam on the brakes. I watched Maddy's tail lights disappear like fireflies round the bend.

As well as wounding my male pride, Maddy's small victories in our *grands prix* underscored the sense that this town was not mine but hers. Together with a stinging awareness of the failure of my Californian Gold Rush, that feeling sharpened into a point: a point of resentment that I angled at Maddy. I started finding fault with her. We quarrelled. In the midst of one such contretemps, Maddy's friend Briony, who was paying a visit, slipped a note under our bedroom door, imploring us to stop. We paused to read the handwritten missive, then carried on.

But Maddy and I were together now. I had risked all that 'capital' for this new life. We were clamped onto a track that led inexorably towards – well, towards marriage. What other conclusion to our story could there be? Besides, we both knew that marriage to a US citizen would smooth my way to a Green Card; that a Green Card would expedite my job search; and that my having a job would put us as a couple on a firmer footing. If we were marrying for love, that golden motive had become unavoidably alloyed with two less precious metals – an acceptance of the inevitable, plus the practical need for me to find work. But alloys or not, they added weight to the whole. The case for marriage had become compelling.

Her identification with the city having never waned, Maddy wanted the proposal to take place in San Francisco. Such, as the bride-to-be, was her prerogative. There was a particular patch of green, atop one of the many hills, where she envisaged the rite occurring. We took the short flight up the coast – descent following ascent, with no plateau in between – and made our way to this mini mecca. I brought out the silver ring topped with an amethyst, the gemstone chosen to vibrate with Maddy's 'steady state'. On that grassy knoll Maddy accepted both the physical object and my verbal offer.

The ring cycle

I say 'the' ring because it was new to neither Maddy nor me. I had bought it twice. The first time was when we were living in our eyrie in Park Town, Oxford. We had got engaged at the zenith of our love fever. There was a get-together in the flat to celebrate. Maddy wore a knee-length gold dress with a black lace overlay. But when some months later that fever had evolved into madness and Maddy bolted for California, she broke off the engagement. The ring came back into my hands.

Listening in self-pity to Radiohead's 'High and Dry', I would stare at this tiny, twinkling trinket. Its symbolism weighed so massively more than its substance. What does one do with a returned engagement ring? Does one save it for one's next fiancée? Obviously not! Does one keep it for sentimental reasons? Perhaps. But the sentiment associated with a ring that has been returned will at best be bittersweet. I conveyed it back to the jeweller's in Oxford as if carrying a dead pet in a box. I sold it for roughly half the price for which it had been bought.

That was just the first turn of the ring cycle. It was now more than a year later. Maddy and I had reunited and transplanted ourselves from Oxford to Los Angeles. We were to be engaged for a second time. So during that week in January 1998 when I was over in England, I returned to the jeweller's. Would the ring still be there? Amazingly – or not amazingly, I wasn't sure which – it was. Did its failure to sell imply that the ring wasn't very nice? Or had fate been keeping it aside for me?

Opening the shop door set off a bell that brought the saleswoman out of the back room, like a laboratory rat. Anxious not to be recognised, I conducted the transaction as briskly and as mutely as the purchase by a gentleman of an amethyst engagement ring can decently be made. I didn't mention that the price had been hiked up.

The word *redemption*, which is Latin in origin, literally means 'buying back'. In buying back the ring, my relationship with Maddy had been redeemed. But my awkwardness at the jeweller's speaks to an aspect of that redemption that was not so salutary. Yes, it was redeeming, but was this not another repetition? For all their psychic seriousness, repetitions run the risk of bathos. When Marx talks about history repeating, for example, he notes with grim pleasure that what the first time round is tragedy, the second time turns into farce. Although there was nothing so historic about my little redemption, the buying back of the ring, after the tragedy of the broken engagement, contained an irreducibly comic element. The pre-conditions for marrying were beginning to fall short of ideal.

11 April 1998

My three months is up again. I fly to England for a week. When I take the return flight back to LA, nobody from immigration, at either end, bats an eyelid. Maddy and I set a September date for our wedding. We agree that it must take place in Oxford, our origin.

I consider asking All Souls to host the ceremony. All Souls is my college. As its prestige will lend glitter to the occasion, Maddy expresses enthusiasm. But I am uneasy about enquiring. To conduct so intensely personal an affair as a wedding in the precincts of what is essentially my workplace is bound to produce tension. Who would choose to get married at the office?

There is an underlying reason for my hesitation. I have never shaken off that dim sense of being judged by my colleagues. Or – taking the monkey back onto my own shoulder – I feel less proud of my relationship with Maddy than I should. I'm all too aware of its flaws. Exposing it to the scrutiny of my peers makes me anxious.

On the tenuous grounds that Maddy and I held one of our early trysts in its cloisters, I approach another college altogether. The chaplain, a recent appointment who is no older than I am, and who wants to make his mark, acquiesces in the scheme. When we meet him for our prenuptial consultation, he makes a show of dispensing with his customary pep talk about fidelity and sacrifice. His intuition that Maddy and I will stay together for ever is so solid, he gushes, that it renders such counsel superfluous.

June 1998

Finally, two months later, in June, I am offered a job with a management consultancy. The firm is based in Century City, a twenty-minute commute from our apartment. That is the good news. The bad news is that I cannot start until October. October is the month when their other English hire, and my boss-to-be, is due to receive his own visa. There's no point in me joining without somebody to give me direction.

The additional good news is that they agree to sponsor a work visa – an H1B – for me too. The additional bad news is that the company fails to tell their immigration lawyers that I will be marrying a US citizen in September, before the job starts. I should be eligible not just for the H1B, but for a Green Card.

8 July 1998

Another three-month visa period comes to an end. This time I am informed by a lawyer that once I leave the US, I will not be allowed to return. The logic-defying reason given is that I have a job offer, but no work visa to go with it. In other words, I can no longer claim to be a tourist. Until that visa comes through, I face arrest if I try to re-enter the country, even if it's just to take snaps of the Statue of Liberty.

Apparently, the visa will be ready in October. I have not been told that the lawyers have not been told that I will be eligible for a Green Card once I'm married in September.

All I can do is go back to Oxford and wait. I find a single room for the summer. I am now liable for two rents, one in LA, one in Oxford, both paid on credit cards. Maddy remains in LA. I shan't see her until a few days before our wedding.

16 September 1998

With the ceremony less than a fortnight away, and with Maddy still in LA, I am advised that my H1B visa will be delayed by an unspecified number of months. I can't start the job in Century City. I will not be able to return to the US after the honeymoon as planned. We will be stranded.

The happiest day of my life

The morning of the wedding is the very morning on which I am obliged to move out of my rented room. After all, that will not be the threshold across which I will carry my new wife; nor is it where Maddy and I, as newlyweds, are going to reside. The rental period is up.

How do most grooms spend the final hours of singleness before their nuptials? Maybe they have a hearty breakfast, iron a shirt, joke with family or reflect on the vows that they are about to swear. Me, I was packing boxes, zipping up bags, hoovering, dusting, and hauling all my gear to a storage facility in the drizzle. I was fielding messages from the caterers with last-minute changes to the menu. I took a phone call from an old friend, cancelling his attendance because his sister had died from cancer the night before.

Faced with similar challenges, any of those other grooms might have asked their best man to assist. My best man was Cameron. As the person who had originally, if unintentionally, brought Maddy and me together, he was the man for the job. As somebody whose gifts were intellectual rather than organisational, he wasn't great shakes. Yet the problem was not the organising. It was that our friendship was broken. Throughout the big day, I had the unsettling feeling that Cameron was looking on from an ironic distance. I suspected that he saw his role as a last duty before signing off.

More unsettling still was the absence of joy in my heart. For this, I can blame neither Cameron nor anybody else. The night before the wedding, Maddy and I had laid on drinks for those making the trip from California. The occasion was jovial enough. The modern Americans were suitably awed by ancient Oxford. It was I who was looking on from the ironic distance. The bickering with Maddy had become habitual. My need for a Green Card, plus the sheer expectation that the two of us would marry, had to me become factors that loomed as large as any marrying for love.

My daughters, Anna and Ruby, aged eleven and seven respectively, were at that drinks party. Simone, their mother, had dropped them off for the evening. Maddy had never been anything less than loving and playful with the two girls. Her family had been more than welcoming. Yet the idea of becoming a stepmother was something with which Maddy had struggled.

It wasn't so much that in fairy tales the stepmother is wicked – although that didn't help. It was more that marrying me meant forfeiting the clean slate to which most brides can look forward. The wedding that you dream about as a girl, Maddy insisted, does not feature a husband with two kids by another woman. What could I say? Maddy was right.

Maddy asked me to make sure that when Simone dropped the two kids off, it was done out of sight of the other guests. I understood Maddy's reasons. Having the girls at the party was one thing. Having their mother in view would shine too bright a light on ghosts from my past. And so I agreed to Maddy's request. But in executing it I felt compromised. I was agreeing to an air-brushing of the truth.

Despite the consternation that I knew it would provoke, I snuck out of the party without saying goodbye. I walked ponderously up Parks Road and through Norham Gardens, back to my bachelor bolthole, tears on my cheeks. It was all wrong. I should have called the wedding off. But the momentum was unstoppable. *Unstoppable* is what I told myself.

The next words that I spoke to Maddy were at the altar.

October 1998

Maddy and I return from a honeymoon in Istanbul that began with a blazing row. It is not just the dynamic of the relationship that is causing strain. There is the exhaustion of having trans-atlantically project-managed the wedding by ourselves. More than anything, we are stressed about will happen next. Where we will go once we land back at Heathrow? What money will we be earning?

Bradley suggests asking the consultancy in LA if I can start my tenure in their London office. They are beholden to me, he argues, as their future employee. The fact that my visa has been delayed, and that I can't return to the US, is their fault, is it not, insofar as it is their lawyers who are on the case? The moment we get back to London, I make contact with the firm.

While awaiting a response, Maddy and I beat the pavements looking for a place to live. We find a tiny flat near that London office. Because it is a short-term let, the rent is charged at a higher tariff. My things are still in storage. Maddy's stuff is in LA, and she has only the honeymoon outfits in her suitcase. At further expense, we have clothes and some basics shipped over from LA.

After a fortnight of shuttle diplomacy between their Los Angeles and London offices, the consultancy firm agrees to my plan. I may work in London until the H1B visa comes through. The Green Card process is never triggered.

October 1998

I start at the office in Piccadilly Circus. Technically, it is a British subsidiary of the American parent, called Dyke Rollins. But because the acquisition is recent, Dyke Rollins has yet to become suffused with the American culture of its new owner. As it is staffed by not a few Oxbridge types like myself, and has the air of a barristers' chambers, I find the leap from academia to consultancy to be mercifully shorter than I had feared. My colleagues are charming, intelligent and warm.

At All Souls, I took my peers to be among the biggest brains on the planet. Such was their renown. Here, at this boutique consulting firm where I have washed up, I encounter men and women who are their equals. No, the consultants have nowhere near the depth of knowledge plumbed by the academics. But in most cases their minds are as sharp. They also work a lot harder.

When, like a shipwrecked sailor, I relate to these goodly people the saga of how I arrived here, they are by turns horrified, amused and sympathetic. Fortunately, my story helps to plant my identity among them. They could have seen me as an imposition. They could have treated me like the offspring of a poor relation and kept me at arm's length. Instead, they embrace me as the hapless victim of circumstance and an interesting, if temporary, colleague. I feel accepted.

So much for the Dyke Rollins culture. As for the work, I am out of my depth. The first meeting I attend is internal: no clients are in the room. The conversation is therefore informal, for which I am thankful. But it is also coded, as at a family dinner, with a lingo and in-jokes of its own. I find the abbreviations cryptic. What is a LOB? Why have a GTM strategy? How come the DOH are so important? Like a burglar trying combinations on a lock, I make a stab as to the meanings. The lock won't open.⬇

The leader sallies up to a flip chart. I have never been in a room with a flip chart. On it he writes a series of numbers. I have never been in a meeting where numbers, rather than ideas, are discussed. He circulates a printed PowerPoint pack. Each page spells out a dozen words in a childishly large font. Schooled in dense academic text and footnotes, I find the paucity of the content extraordinary, let alone the waste of paper.

There are monthly drinks. In the academic world, which was my benchmark, 'drinks' meant budget wine poured into white plastic cups, peanuts served in polystyrene bowls, and earnest exchanges about how 'depressed' we all were about the amount of 'admin' we had to do. The wine at Dyke Rollins is a full-bodied

---

⬆ LOB = Line of Business. Having been acquired, Dyke Rollins is expected to join up with other parts of the parent company – other 'lines of business' – in order to expand its offer to clients. GTM = Go to Market. A Go to Market strategy is a plan for what products and services you intend to offer, and how they will be more attractive than those offered by your competitors. DOH = the Department of Health, who are a key client. All this I find out only later, in miraculous moments when a colleague enunciates a whole phrase, rather than its acronym. I am too embarrassed to ask directly.

Hermitage, served in capacious glasses. There are canapés. I talk to a woman a couple of years my junior. She tells me that she has just bought a Saab 9-3 convertible. 'Surely not new?' I ask in all seriousness. 'Yes,' she affirms, surprised at my question. I smother the surprise of my own. I have entered a different world.

As for the interactions outside the office, with clients, I find myself scrambling up a similarly steep learning curve. I tag along with colleagues to meetings with officers and executives at the most senior levels of government and industry. Despite my gaping lack of experience, my opinion – by which I mean the few generalisations that I can cobble together on the spot – is treated with respect.

I realise that that is what learning is. It is the experience of non-mastery. As long as we feel competent, we are not learning, just doing. Learning is the transition from disability to ability. Mastery is skill become beauty.

January 1999

I am told that my visa will be delayed for a further unspecified amount of time.

9 February 1999

That amount of time tops out at five weeks. The H1B visa, with its watermark of an American eagle, has landed. It is good for three years. A week later, Maddy and I return to West Hollywood. The life that has been on hold for eighteen months – ever since that afternoon at the Randolph Hotel – can resume. We unwrap our gifts. We have the delayed sessions with friends to look through our wedding photos. For the first time in America, we are using the terms 'husband' and 'wife'.

I even get my driver's licence. Nervously, I make my way down to the DMV test centre in Hollywood. My apprehension is not justified. The theory exam is an easy multiple choice that takes ten minutes. The practical part lasts no longer. I get into the car with an examiner who resembles a middle-aged Diana Ross. As we exit the lot, she commands 'Turn right.' At the bottom of the street, she says 'Turn left.' We turn left along La Cienega and left again, completing a tour of the block, and cruise back into the test centre. 'You have passed,' she announces in a monotone. I understand just how fundamental the earthbound car is in this city of angels. The driving test is no test. It is the formality by which a birthright is endorsed. A legitimate driver at last, I pull out.

February 1999

Ten months after my interview, I begin working for the consultancy in LA. My manager is the other Brit, Giles, who was taken on at the same time. An experienced consultant, Giles has been charged with setting up the equivalent of a Dyke Rollins within the LA parent. The equivalent being a 'change management' function. Change management, as I have discovered in London, is the art of navigating businesses through times of transition, such as mergers, redundancies, restructurings and alterations to the strategy. It is less about the financial than the human side of such transitions, as if we were organisational therapists.

I had been led to believe that such a practice already existed within the LA office. But no. The inauguration of the change management function coincides with the arrival of Giles and me. But as I have barely three months' experience, and that experience was in the inapplicably different market of the UK, the onus falls squarely on Giles to get it up and running.

Until Captain Giles has reeled in our first clients, there is nothing for me to do. I'm like the cabin boy on a fishing boat that is plying a waterway without fish. There are only so many times that I can mop the boards. To keep me occupied – and squeeze some value out of me for the company – Giles loans me out to the 'benefits communications' team. I am to write leaflets about pensions for the employees of our clients. I have published books, haven't I? *Faute de mieux*, I accept the commission. It is even duller than it sounds. Had there been a competition for The World's Most Boring Job, I would have backed myself to win it.

June 1999

It is more than three months later. Despite his blandishments, Giles has failed to convert any leads into paid projects. The truth is, he has very few leads to speak of. The Californian marketplace doesn't get the idea of 'change management'. Although California might have a reputation for hippies, it couldn't be more hard-nosed when it comes to business. The concept of managing organisations through the human side of change sounds airy-fairy. Meanwhile, I am still drafting the damned pension leaflets. Poor Giles was already under pressure from his own boss above. Now he has me nagging him from below.

Even more demoralising than the tedium of the work is the office culture. Whereas Dyke Rollins, with its roll call of eccentrics and intellectuals, felt like an old-school English club, the Century City operation is as corporate as corporate can be. In the air-conditioned corridors, co-workers glide at a hygienic distance past one another. They exchange a rigid smile and say 'How are you' without supplying a question mark. All activity has to be entered onto a computer system, as if we resided in a capitalist sanatorium. The obedience to process is so devout that in order for me to move a pot plant from one side of the room to the other, I have to seek permission from HR. If I were to do my back in, I could sue the company.

After months of nugatory activity and soul-sapping rules, I have had enough. With a Green Card, I would have the freedom to look for another job. My H1B visa is tied to this specific employer. I don't have the energy to go through the palaver again.

In any case, the fairy lights of LA are popping one by one. Its caricature is real. The city is preoccupied with appearance. Apart from looks, money is the only thing that talks. It is near impossible to have an interesting conversation. Pleasantness serves as a barrier to authentic contact. The dependability of the sunshine becomes an unvarying torment. There are no seasons to speak of, so no opportunity to wear jumpers and scarves, and enjoy the snugness of coming in from the cold. There's no woodsmoke, no BBC and no black cabs.

Despite it requiring another upheaval, I can see no better option than begging Dyke Rollins to take me back. Meaningful work is the fulcrum on which everything pivots. London is where that fulcrum lies. The favourable impression that I made at Dyke Rollins during my unscheduled and protracted stopover in London pays off. They agree. Although Maddy is reluctant about schlepping back to the UK, she hasn't established a career foothold in LA, and has no binding professional ties. On the condition that one day we will end up in San Francisco, she agrees.

A scant few months after our stuff has been shipped from right to left over the Atlantic, we ship it from left to right. I will never live in America again.

Identity Jenga

In this book, I am trying to grapple with the question of what it means to be human. This chapter has focused so far on the human propensity for making mistakes, and on our vulnerability to things going wrong. Any plan we make will be weaker than the reality that it goes on to meet.

But our plans are not abstractions. They are bound to our

identity. We plan according to who we are and who we want to be. We make changes to our life that fit with our sense of self. The diagram below, which I call 'Identity Jenga', aims to express the connection between these two forces of identity and change.

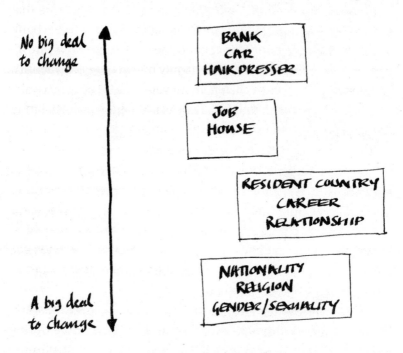

Broadly speaking, our identity is built of four blocks. The most fundamental of the four is comprised of three things: our nationality, our religious belief (or the lack of it) and our gender. Sexual orientation also belongs here. None of these markers of identity is unchangeable, but changing them is a big deal. Beneath the lowest block, as it happens, sits an invisible fifth that is even more fundamental to our identity. Namely, the point in history when we are born, coupled with the fact that we enter the world as a human being rather than as an animal. But that is a layer over which we have no influence. The bottom brick in the diagram, we have. We can convert from Christianity to Islam; we can make the switch from male to female; and we can adopt a different nationality. All three shifts are foundational, yet all three lie within our power.

At the top of the pile of bricks sits a set of affiliations that have a bearing on our identity in a far lighter way. Who we bank with, where we get our hair cut and the car that we drive are all aspects of our life that contribute, if only modestly, to our identity. Although we might not change them very often, we easily could, and doing so would be no big deal. As in a game of Jenga, lifting this top brick off the stack will have little impact on the bricks below. It won't set off a toppling of the whole structure.

The second brick down is where change becomes a bigger deal. Our identity starts to be materially, although not radically, affected. Moving to a new area or changing job will alter how we define ourselves. It will also shift how we are defined by others. When we meet somebody at a party, for example, it is often the two facts of what they do and where they live that we want to establish first.

This chapter has isolated the third brick down, that of resident country, career and relationship. All three were at stake during that period in the late 1990s. There was the to-ing and fro-ing between England and America; the faltering journey from academia to consultancy; plus the fragile nature of life with Maddy. It was as if, like a Jenga player, I had my index finger and thumb on the right edge of that third brick down. I was slowly drawing it out. In flirting with such a serious level of change, I was also playing with my identity.

On the one hand, the hazardous withdrawal of that third brick, along with the risk it created of causing other bricks to crash, merely adds emphasis to the self-destructive impetus in me that I have identified. If I was making what looks like a series of rash decisions, and gambling with the markers of my identity in the process, there was an ulterior motive. I was indulging a devilish desire for disruption.

But there is a more innocuous explanation. The shuffling of my country, career and relationship was a naïve attempt at getting my life onto the right track. If I found disruption seductive, I also yearned for the stability that would come with a secure base. When put together, the restless changes formed a zigzagging route towards peace. As a Zen master might put it, obliquity was the way. Perhaps the true function of an obstacle is to mark out the path.

Graham, the accountant from Purley

Not long after the return to London, at a conference, I would meet an accountant named Graham. He was from Purley, a characterless suburb a mile from where I grew up. Graham had stayed in the area all his life. Except that Graham now resided in Purley's hidden gem. This was the Webb estate – a grove of private roads with gravel drives, majestic pine trees, indoor pools, paddocks for horses belonging to spoiled daughters, and triple garages to house Dad's Porsche, Mum's Range Rover and the Bimmer for general use.

As in the first moves of chess, Graham and I rapidly established the connections between us. There was the geographical proximity. We were also the same age. Graham had gone to Whitgift, an independent school in Croydon that I had nearly attended. But that was where our worlds divided. After university, Graham trained in accountancy. He joined a blue-chip firm and rose to become partner. Financially literate, Graham had managed his money wisely. He had bought one of the stately piles on the Webb estate before turning thirty-five. Graham had had one wife, and remained happily married. I checked his gold ring. The couple were blessed with two children. The little angels were flourishing.

No longer do we give much credit to the idea of the grass being greener on the other side of the fence. We tell ourselves that nobody's life is perfect. But what if, in some cases, the grass next door really is more vibrant? Absorbing the gamma rays of Graham's contentment, a mountain in me melted. I longed to be him.

> Perhaps the history of the errors of mankind, all things considered, is more valuable and interesting than that of their discoveries.
>
> Benjamin Franklin

6

Office Politics

Even the striving for equality by means of a directed economy can result only in an officially enforced inequality – an authoritarian determination of the status of each individual in the new hierarchical order.

Friedrich Hayek

The phrase 'We are social beings' has become a routine assertion. It points to a natural inclination in us to form communities and support each other. Yet no less prevalent is the doctrine of the 'selfish gene'. That doctrine preaches how we are predisposed to favour our own interests above the common good.

Of these opposing visions of human nature, which is the truer? Are we *with* other people or *against* them?

Thomas Hobbes, writing in the seventeenth century, argued that, left to our own devices, we will always put ourselves first. Unless kept in check by an authority figure, we are likely to tear each other to pieces in an apocalyptic 'war of all against all'. A century later, Jean-Jacques Rousseau talked about the 'social contract' that we naturally want to make with one another. Rousseau's picture is irenic. Our instincts bend towards harmony. In the intervening period, between Hobbes and Rousseau, Adam Smith came up with a counterintuitive third option. The common good, Smith argued, is served best precisely when everybody pursues their own self-interest. We just need to let the 'invisible hand' of the market sort it out.

The very range of answers – and from such esteemed thinkers – indicates that none has proved conclusively true. Being human means having to make adjustments between individual and group; or competition and collaboration; or selfishness and altruism; or personal gain and the common weal. Whatever name we give to each side of the equation, they are equally indigenous features of the human landscape, like two mountains. We dwell in the valley of their overlapping shadows.

A cloud of gnats beneath a pine tree

We can also choose to go it alone: we can avoid groups altogether. But in doing so, we miss out on the fellow-feeling that a group can provide. In any case, it is almost impossible to live one's life without belonging to a group at some point. Whether the groups we join are formal, such as a degree course; or informal, such as a supper club; or even if they are transitory, such as the 'group' that we loosely form as passengers waiting on a crowded platform for a train; whichever it is, group-belonging represents a common feature of our lives.

But common isn't the same as comfortable. On that crowded train platform, an unspoken question forms as to who will get on first and whether there will be a seat. Even a group that assembles for social purposes will tax its members with questions that the members themselves may only half articulate. What is my place in this group? Am I important or unimportant? Do I come away feeling better or worse? Would anybody notice if I wasn't here? How can I feel more like I belong? Which people are on my side? Is anybody against me? Who is the leader? However light-hearted their purpose, groups will prompt us to consider our position within them.

Should it turn out that our position within the group is less comfortable than we would wish, we will want to change it. The same goes for the group's other members. Everybody has an interest in their own self-interest, as it were. The consequence is that we find ourselves competing. Sometimes the competition is subtle. At other times it's blatant. But whatever else they might be, groups are competitive environments in which the members seek to maintain, improve or prevent a falling-off in their position. The aggregate of tactics deployed during that jostling for position is what we know as politics. 'Politics' I define as *the practice of calculated self-interest within a group*.

In a work organisation, which is the focus of this chapter, the politics are no less active than in social groups. Indeed, work organisations tend to be more political altogether. Yet work organisations are ostensibly in business to compete with other work organisations, not with themselves. Everybody should be pulling together like the crew of a rowing boat. Instead the behaviour often resembles that of passengers on a cruise ship, sizing each other up.

The political manoeuvring that goes on within an organisation threatens to impair the organisation's performance against its competitors without. Intramural competition takes energy away from competing beyond the organisational walls. There are conflicting currents, as shown in the diagram overleaf. The big arrow of the organisation points one way. The small arrows, representing individuals, jockey with each other for advantage. They point in multiple directions.

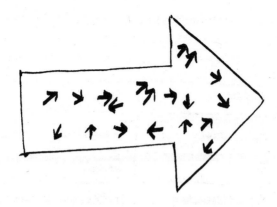

If enough of the small arrows swim against the direction of the big arrow, the organisation as a whole will capsize. But while most organisations have their mutineers, that scenario is exceptional. Internal disorder tends to hover beneath the level of the overall order maintained by the enterprise. All that fissiparous activity among the little arrows is contained by the big arrow. Homeostasis ensues. An image for it could be that of a cloud of gnats dancing beneath a pine tree. Despite the multidirectional energy, what prevails is equilibrium.

The question is how to manage self-interest within a group. That is a fundamental aspect of being human. Like it or not, we will find ourselves having to deal with the politics in the groups that we join. As Aristotle famously declared, 'man is a political animal'.

Them and us

By the time I got back to London in the autumn of 1999, the corporate culture of its American parent company was beginning to penetrate the quintessentially English Dyke Rollins. The table below sets out the contrasts between the two. It was as if an old-fashioned Bath Oliver cheese cracker had been dropped into a vat of Coca-Cola. Immersed in that acid bath, the cracker was dissolving.

THEM	US
American	English
Big	Small
Homogeneous	Heterogeneous
Numbers-driven	Ideas-driven
Transactional	Relational
Compliant	Questioning
Practical	Theoretical
Serious	Playful
Unsociable	Sociable

Among the change management fraternity, it is an article of faith that cultural differences are the single biggest factor in the failure of corporate mergers and acquisitions. Even when the financial case for a union between the two companies in question is sound, their personalities don't click. Instead of working together, and thereby realising the anticipated value from combining the businesses, people are reluctant to adapt. Sometimes an atmosphere of 'them and us' builds up. If you are the acquired rather than the acquiring party, that is especially uncomfortable.

Unless contractually bound otherwise, the acquired may think about leaving.⬇

The irony with Dyke Rollins was that it set out its stall as a change management house. At leading companies through mergers and acquisitions, it was an avowed expert. So when the firm was sold, it should have been attuned to such cultural risks. It should have been adroit at their mitigation. But when it found itself bearing the brunt of that cultural clash, Dyke Rollins could only echo the response that it heard routinely among its clients. The whispers in the London office insinuated that we were the last healthy cell in a body being devoured by a corporate cancer. It was just a matter of time before the predator advanced on us.

Not everybody at Dyke Rollins was so twitchy. For many, the acquisition meant they would be smaller fish but in a bigger pond. One might even grow into a bigger fish. From a mercenary perspective, you could earn more as a high-up in the larger American entity than in the British outfit on its own. The majority of Dyke Rollins staffers held on.

But the handful who did not was significant. First to go was the charismatic Harry Baker. Given that Baker was one of the founders of Dyke Rollins and had fronted the deal with the Americans, his departure was portentous. Dyke Rollins also felt the loss of his commercial acumen. Baker was a rainmaker. The silver-haired entrepreneur knew where to strike gold. His slip-

---

⬆ In the context of mergers and acquisitions, one often hears the word 'synergy' bandied about. The word's meaning has subtly changed over time. *Synergy* used to refer to the extra value that could be created by bringing two organisations together. The idea was that the whole would add up to more than the sum of its parts. Today, 'synergy' has become code for the job cuts that need to be made when two organisations merge, in order to remove duplication. In other words, value is now created through a trimming of the cost base, rather than through an uplift in the top line.

stream, when he left, threw a diaphanous membrane around the organisation, reminding everyone lightly but persistently of his absence.

A few months later, Harry Baker was joined by a second silver-back from Dyke Rollins. This was Martin Dawson. Much loved for his foibles, Dawson was no less honed a commercial weapon than Baker. He was also admired for his tradecraft with clients. I had a fondness for him. Martin Dawson was the kindly soul in London who had taken me under his wing when I alighted on the company windowsill, lost and confused, on the migratory flight back from Istanbul to Los Angeles. With Martin's going, my staying became moot.

The third musketeer to fall in with Baker and Dawson was Simon Cummings. Younger than the first two, Cummings hadn't racked up enough flying hours to have achieved the same status. But he was a rising star. That decided it. If those three had hijacked a space capsule and fired off from the mothership, I wanted a seat in it too.

When I told the powers-that-be at Dyke Rollins of my inten-tions, they were not amused. They felt that they had bent over backwards for me. First, in giving me a berth at the London office while I was waiting on the delayed visa. Second, in letting me back inside the tent when the Century City plan broke down. Now here I was, another defector to the Baker coalition. I was remiss not only in loyalty but in gratitude. Like that of the trio before me, my departure reflected back to Dyke Rollins their own misgivings about being taken over by the Americans. That was no less galling. Finally, there were business implications. That coalition of deserters was rapidly hardening into a direct com-petitor. The threat that they represented would only be increased, if marginally, by my swelling their ranks. The conversation was frosty.

Divided by the same language

As an English entity struggling to adjoin its culture to that of an American partner, Dyke Rollins wasn't alone. Its problems were a Xerox of my private life. The cultural gulf between Maddy and me was becoming ever more apparent and ever less easy to bridge.

Maddy too had landed a job in the London office of an American enterprise. Although she learned the ropes quickly and impressed her colleagues, it wasn't her *métier*. A few months in, she was petitioning for a sabbatical to pursue other avenues. In a handy example of the tussle between individual and group, Maddy's request was not authorised. The group (Maddy's company) needed the individual (Maddy) to demonstrate commitment to the group before the group permitted the individual to go off on a personal tack. The group appraised Maddy's self-interest and quashed it.

Maddy was no more at peace in her marriage than at work. Aggravated by the job pressures that we were now under in London – pressures that had been absent from life in Oxford and LA – the tension between us had risen. Our pattern was as follows:

get into a fight > analyse the fight > make a list of the things that we were going to change > fail to change them > get into another fight

We couldn't dig ourselves out of our own hole. It was as exhausting as it was wretched.

In the chapter before last, I wrote about love and hate. I suggested that, of the two, love is the primary. Hate arises either when love has gone wrong or when it hasn't been able to get off the ground. From this perspective, *extreme disappointment at the impossibility of love* would be a way of defining hate; or *recrimination for love interrupted*. Hate is a way of resisting the love that we secretly feel. Love and hate are not so much opposites as energies in fluid dialogue.

I would now argue that love and hate are intertwined completely. For if you fail to love what is *not* loveable in the person whom you love, there is a question as to how true your love can be. After all, it is easy to love what is loveable. It will sound a bit stiff, I am sure, to assert that you have to love what it is in the other person that you hate. Yet that is what love is. Love is the embodiment of the word 'yes'; and so, to be pure, love has to love the hateable as well as the loveable. It is the loving inclusion of what is hard to love that makes love love. As in the symbol for Yin and Yang, love and hate each contain a small, homeopathic dot of the other.⬇

Whether or not that theory stands up, it helps with diagnosing the malady affecting my marriage with Maddy. Although the sweet wine of love had once over-brimmed our relationship, it was mixed with bitters. Why was that? Such antagonism between two people can always be put down to a difference in personalities. As listed in the table below, Maddy and I certainly had many a trait that set us apart.

As will be immediately apparent, not every 'trait' is personality-related. There are the three differentiators at the

⬆ Technically, the Yin and Yang reference implies not only that we have to love what we hate, but also that we should hate what we love. I think it would be hard to mount an argument in support of that second claim. A possible angle would be to say that hate creates distance between two people; and that distance is necessary for those two people to relate to each other, rather than merge into one. I am not sure how convincing that is, though. It sounds like sophistry. Perhaps the true opposite of love is not hate but indifference.

MADDY	ME
American	English
Female	Male
Younger	Older
Unpredictable	Controlled
Emotional	Rational
People-oriented	Success-oriented
Funny	Witty
Impractical	Sensible
Outgoing	Introverted

top, which are structural rather than psychological. First among them is the fact that Maddy was American. Embarrassing though it is to confess, Maddy's Americanness was perhaps what I found hardest to love.

My prejudice wasn't entirely blind. I had undergone that dismal passage through California. The Golden State rejected me. When eventually I got a job, I found American corporate life stultifying. Having worked in offices on both sides of the Atlantic, I was in the unique position of following the carry-over of that corporate culture into Dyke Rollins. I saw a magic in the English firm and I saw the American proprietor constrain it.

Is it too pompous or self-serving to invoke the wider context in order to excuse my bigotry? No doubt it is. But that context existed. A wariness of American colonialism was in the air. America's foreign policy under George W. Bush was seen as overweening. The American aura of entitlement put many people off. Such churlish sentiment built on a post-war grudge against America for having purloined Britannia's crown as ruler of the waves. The 'special relationship' with America had always been ambivalent. We were allies yet we were rivals. If Britain as a nation had a chip on its shoulder, I as a British national had a chip of that chip.

Besides, Maddy wanted to be back in her homeland. London was nice for a spell, but not her ultimate destination. She had left her heart in San Francisco. She also missed her family and friends in Los Angeles. Not to mention another branch of the family tree, on her mother's side. They were dispersed in various domiciles on, or within a tight radius of, that cattle ranch amid the pine forests of the Midwest. Maddy associated the ranch with childhood, nature and freedom of spirit.

During our last summer together, in the year 2000, Maddy and I flew there to visit her relatives. Owing to the ranch's remoteness, the final leg involved a twin-engine eight-seater. Midway we hit a patch of turbulence that blew the plane about like litter. Maddy panicked. Her face turning white, she scribbled a note on a napkin. The note read:

Bury us <u>both</u> at the ranch.

It was not the moment to protest. Or maybe it was. The plane was taking a series of aerial uppercuts, plunging after each by a hundred feet. The turbulence matched that caused in my heart by Maddy's note. It was vexing enough that I hadn't been consulted on my after-death wishes. Admittedly, I had never got round to writing a will, but that didn't mean I was ready to have somebody else write it on my behalf. Did I want to be buried? Did I prefer cremation?

Those questions, about the manner of my last rites, were important. But they weren't as urgent as the following:

1. Did I want to be buried *with Maddy*?
2. Did I want to be buried *at the ranch*?

By that point in the summer of 2000, I wasn't sure that I wanted to stay with Maddy for the remaining four months of the year, let alone eternity. I had begun to despair about our marriage. So no, I did not wish to be buried with Maddy. It was with horror that I watched her double-underline the word *both*.

Still more visceral was my reaction to a burial at the ranch. My exeat in California had demonstrated not how cosmopolitan I was, but the reverse. I was English, dyed in the wool. England was where I belonged. Aside from any prejudices, my own identity had become clearer. Nothing American attached to it. With its cowboys, hunting rifles and evenings around the campfire, the ranch was the essence of America. A spiritual home it might have been to Maddy, but to me it was anything but. When she enthused about it, I murmured assent. Underneath, I felt as alienated at the ranch as I would have felt on Mars. Bury me, but please do not bury me there.

On the final morning of my visit to the ranch – Maddy planned to stay on – our tribulations came to the boil. Maddy announced that she wished to move back to the States by herself. She proposed that, first, I would continue renting the flat in London, but that, second, as her husband, I should rent another flat for her, in San Francisco. Once in Fog City, she would reconnect with friends and consider her next move.

No dice, said I. How could we possibly add a second rent, subtract her income and still balance the books? We could not. I perceived her suggestion as naked self-interest. But Maddy believed that what she was proposing was a mature collaboration between two partners. As grown-ups, we could live separately and support each other from a distance. Just because we were married, we didn't have to live under the same roof. She had followed me around on my haphazard career, hadn't she? Who was I to clip her wings? Our relationship, in any case, was on the rocks. Time apart would do us good.

That is the balance which every relationship must strike, between collaboration and competition. What is good for the couple vies with what is right for the individual. In a relationship context, the word 'competition' might carry unappealing connotations. Yet the couple must serve the interests of the individuals as individuals, as well as the interests of the relationship as a whole. That involves the individuals ensuring that they take what they need.

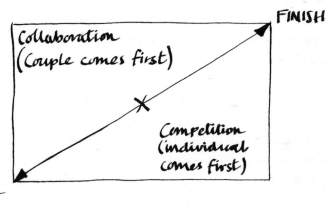

The diagram tries to express these dynamics. Most relationships set out from the bottom left-hand corner. The balance of collaboration and competition lies wholly in the former's favour. Both parties are keen to give their all to the couple. They can only say yes. Inebriated by romance, however, they risk sacrificing their own needs. So the relationship gravitates towards the top right-hand corner. Up to a point – marked by the X – that movement is healthy. The needs of individual and couple inch towards parity. Beyond that X, the couple loses out to the individuals who comprise it. That is a movement which leads to the end. Each individual denies the needs of the other, in the interests of its own. Yes gives way to no.

Even if it was better for us as a couple to live apart, as she claimed, I had said no to Maddy. After she had thundered out, I was left alone. We were lodging in one of the shacks dotted among the ranch's acreage. Having packed my bags for the journey back to Heathrow, I went to sit on the toilet. When I flushed, the water rose rather than sank. When I flushed again, the water rose further, to just beneath the brim. I left with my shit swirling in the bowl.

Those four months to the end of the year were indeed enough to bring our marriage to a close. The last time I ever saw Maddy was in London, in February 2001. It was Valentine's Day. She flew back to America that morning.

The cultural thermostat

Leaving Dyke Rollins was more ticklish than I had bargained for. From the hour when I handed in my resignation, I was treated as *persona non grata*. Being the youngest of the gang of four to quit, and the one with the least experience, I felt scapegoated for the treason of all. Or, to take a different animal, I was the infant buck trailing at the back of a herd of deer, the one who gets picked off by the lion. I found myself isolated. The collegiate warmth that I had enjoyed turned chilly. On me, the cultural thermostat had been dialled down.

My upset would have been less, I think, had I not hailed

from a university background. The higher education sector sees academics come and go between institutions, and rarely is there any bad blood. Universities happily host speakers from other universities. They frequently collaborate on research projects. In theory, universities must compete for students, and to that extent they participate in a market. Since there are entrance criteria for them to satisfy, however, those students are chosen as much as they choose. If higher education is a market, it cuts both ways.

The point is that an academic is unlikely to feel in head-to-head competition with the university down the road. A scholar's resignation is typically treated with nothing more barbed than curiosity. I expected a similar reaction when I handed in my notice at Dyke Rollins. But Dyke Rollins was not the public sector. In evolutionary terms, we were engaged in a competition for resources. The more that was appropriated by the Baker rump, the less there would be left for Dyke Rollins. My resignation meant transferring my labour to a competitor, that is, a rival for market share. Small wonder that within the London office, I was sent to Coventry.

I had a notice period to work out. It required me to occupy that murky overlap between collaboration and competition. On the one hand, I was still a colleague to all at Dyke Rollins, and part of the team. On the other hand, I was a competitor. More exactly, I was at once an ex-colleague-to-be and a competitor-in-waiting. In a manner reminiscent of the half-blood/half-water position of my father in his family business, my belonging became equivocal. Nothing about me had intrinsically changed. I was the same person. Yet that extrinsic change in my position changed everything. Further evidence perhaps that *where* we stand in a system counts for more than *who* we are. Place trumps personality.

An abortive attempt at cloning

If quitting Dyke Rollins was uncomfortable, joining the break-away group led by Harry Baker was no shoo-in either. According to my fantasy, the new company would be a clone of Dyke Rollins – cloned, to be sure, on a date when its corpus was still intact, before the American infection had set in. I would bind on, as in a rugby scrum, and we would continue as before, with the same bonhomie.

That fantasy was based on the best information I had at the time. From where I was still sitting, in Dyke Rollins, I saw only the three men whom I admired – Baker, Dawson and Cummings – ride off into the sunset. Obscured to my view was a fourth figure among them. This was Stephanie Rogers. Rogers was not a Dyke Rollins team-mate, which explains how she fell within my blind spot. Like a tributary flowing into a river, she had merged with the Baker group from another source.

In the furtive conversations that I had about my hiring, Baker, Dawson and Cummings separately warned me that without Stephanie's say-so, no such recruitment could transpire. From their tone, it was clear that the one woman among the men was a force to be reckoned with.

Whence did Stephanie Rogers derive her power? It was she who had been the first to combine with Harry Baker. Rather than having 'led a breakaway group', as my romantic fiction had styled it, Baker had set up on his own. He registered a company under the made-up name of Burton Harcourt. Soon after, though before the arrival of either Dawson or Cummings, he met Stephanie Rogers. Baker and Rogers decided to make a go of it. Contrary to the yarn that I had spun, Burton Harcourt had its origins not as a band of brothers, but as a mother and father. I would have to join as a son.

Stephanie Rogers had built her career in marketing and communications. Her expertise lay in straplines, messaging, branding, positioning and presentation. These were all the things that, at Dyke Rollins, had brought us out in a rash. Relative to our more psychological approach, we adjudged them to be vapid. But Harry Baker himself had done a stint with an advertising agency, which made him sympathetic. He was also attracted to Rogers' ambition of packaging the esoteric discipline of change management and, as she put it, 'tying it up with a bow'. It caused Baker's commercial glands to salivate.

The selling of change management as a suite of packaged products – rather than as wise counsel – had implications for how the business of Burton Harcourt was to be run. Because those products were off-the-shelf, you could have junior people delivering them. As if cooking from a recipe, it was a matter of following the instructions. Baker and Rogers pictured Burton Harcourt as a pyramid that operated on 'leverage'. The seniors would broker the project with a client and keep an eye on the relationship. The juniors would do the legwork. Simples. One of the laws in life is that it is the servants and not the masters who are busy. Today we might claim to be busy as a way of stating our importance. But such a claim points to our enslavement.

Whilst the leveraged model was the one on which Baker and Rogers concurred, it was not, oddly, the one on which they recruited. At the point when Martin Dawson – a Dyke Rollins partner – came on board, there was just one rookie on the payroll. This was a young Antipodean named Cassie. That made three seniors and one junior. A pyramid there was – just the wrong way up.

What's more, Martin Dawson had little truck with that productised approach to change management. It wasn't that he took against it. He was just his own man. Dawson's style was to build the closest links with the heaviest hitters in both Whitehall and the City. Like a tailor, he would provide them with a service that was entirely bespoke. I picture him as a consigliere. Rather than dis-crete projects, Dawson would cultivate long-term relationships, and follow his clients' fortunes with an intimate propinquity. It was as if he were an honorary member of the boards he advised. Clients valued him for his intellect, his integrity and his fiduciary attention to their cause.

Those professional qualities, coupled with his talent for win-ning business, meant that Rogers and Baker were loath to correct Dawson's deviation from Burton Harcourt dogma. Besides, they all got along famously. But the upshot was the opening of a fault line that forked through the company. In his mock-erudite way, Dawson dubbed it a 'doctrinal schism'. On one side, you had the New School, with Stephanie Rogers as its head girl. The New School swore allegiance to products, leverage, hierarchy, teams and projects. On the other side, Dawson represented the Old School, whose beliefs were the diametric opposite. In that he talked like the New School, but walked like the Old, Harry Baker made for an ambiguous mixture of the two. Simon Cummings vacillated.

Having apprenticed myself to Martin Dawson at Dyke Rollins, it was his Old School approach that I espoused. Moving to Burton Harcourt would be a way of carrying on in the same vein. What I failed to appreciate was that, in the Burton Harcourt context, that vein was not neutral. It positioned me on a particular wing. Which suggests a lesson for anybody thinking about moving to a new organisation: *Don't wait until you join to figure out the politics.* Use the precious time before official induction to have as many unofficial conversations as you can.

It was for all the above reasons that, when it came to my applying to Burton Harcourt, Stephanie Rogers put up her guard.

I embodied the Old School. I was another white, Oxbridge-educated male. Rogers had already tolerated the inclusion of three men from Dyke Rollins, and was minded to pull up the drawbridge. Why should she let in a fourth? The cloning of Dyke Rollins was precisely what she sought to resist. Moreover, at thirty-five, and with my academic back catalogue, I wasn't sufficiently junior. True, I had barely eighteen months' experience in consulting. But it would be hard for Rogers to bat me as far down the organisational pyramid as she hoped.

In the end, what swayed Stephanie Rogers was a simile. For my interview, she and I met over coffee at Starbucks by Charing Cross station. She likened the work that Burton Harcourt did to 'sprinkling the fairy dust'. We take a brief from a client, she explained, instructing us to recast the way that they communicate to their staff. In the process, we add a certain sparkle. Inwardly, I cringed. I had no interest in 'internal comms' as it was known. I wanted to do the big, strategic stuff with Martin Dawson. I also recoiled from the 'fairy dust' image, which I found saccharine.

But this was an interview. If I could just get over this hurdle, I would be able to reconnect with Dawson and we could do our thing. It was a question of meeting Rogers on her own terms. 'I see,' said I. 'It's like you put the angel on the top of the Christmas tree?' 'Exactly!' she beamed. I was in.

The miracle of multiples

So who founded Burton Harcourt? The 'About Us' page on its website at the time began with the words, 'Founded by three partners . . .' The phrase has the ring of a legend. But was it true?

As I had gone on to discover, Harry Baker had set up on his own. The name 'Burton Harcourt' was his creation. Only subsequently did Stephanie Rogers come along. If it was the two of them who founded the company, then Rogers' part in that founding was retroactive. The same goes for Martin Dawson, who came along a little later still. It was through legerdemain, in other words, that you arrived at your 'three founding partners'. As if by magic, two of the three partners who had founded Burton Harcourt – namely, Rogers and Dawson – founded it after it had been founded. Chapeau!

As for Simon Cummings: by the time he tapped on the door, the magic had been burned up by the others, like oil from a lamp. Cummings was a mite tardy to be anointed as a founder along with them. That can't have been easy on his pride. More than once I would overhear Simon introduce himself to clients as 'one of the four founding partners'. Would those clients think to cross-check his claim against the website?

The reason why the question of foundation is crucial is that it determines the distribution of power. The earlier you pitch up, the bigger the say you will have. As in physics, power concentrates near the origin. Hence Simon Cummings' forgiveable untruth. Above all, getting in early means that you are there when the rules are set. Since you can therefore influence those rules, you are going to influence them in accordance with your self-interest. And because those who come after you are admitted on condition that the rules are obeyed, they will *de facto* work in service of what is best for you. That is the essence of power: getting other people to put your self-interest above their own.

It comes down to multiplication. In the beginning, all the resource that you have to deploy in your self-interest is yourself. You are a unit of one. That forces you to compete with all the other units of one – all the other individuals – who are doggedly pursuing self-interest of their own. If you want to get your nose in front, you have to labour harder. Labouring really hard, you might double, or conceivably treble, your output. But that is about the limit; and there could be a cost to your health. How much smarter it is, therefore, to convert the self-interest of others into the self-interest of your own. That way, the others become multiples of you, working on your behalf. As soon as you have enough people to produce more than you could produce, you're golden.

Setting up a business is one of the surest ways of achieving that end. For a business is a sovereign entity. Somewhat like a family, a business provides a fenced-off space for the making up of one's own rules. Although there will be legalities to observe, you as its founder can dictate how the business will operate, and how the people in it are to behave. With that sovereign sceptre in hand, you are at liberty to command the masses to multiply your individual self-interest many times over.

And not just in terms of increased production capacity. Capacity is but a means to an end. The glory of a leveraged business is that the juniors multiply the money. In a professional services firm such as Burton Harcourt, the rule of thumb is that the juniors keep a third of the fees that they earn from clients, as salary. Another third goes to cover overheads, made up mainly of the lease on the premises and the wages paid to administrative staff. The final third goes to the seniors. As if by a miracle, the seniors are therefore paid for work that they personally have not done. Their self-interest is served by others.

In sum, being a senior brings juridical and financial benefits alike. A senior both stipulates the laws and becomes disproportionately enriched. Power translates into money.

The mystical foundation of authority

Perhaps I am guilty of conflating the terms 'founder' and 'senior'. There are similarities between them, it is true. But there are also differences. The following diagram tries to express both. While there is no founder who is not a senior, there are many seniors who are not founders. Having been there at the origin, a founder can claim a priority in time that a mere senior cannot. Admittedly, there may be no detectable difference in the executive power held by founder and senior. Big decisions can be taken by either. Because that broad equivalence in power drives a broad equivalence in pay, founder and senior might also earn a similar amount. On those two tests, of power and pay, there's barely the width of a cigarette paper between founder and senior. But on the test of time, they separate. The founder always comes first.

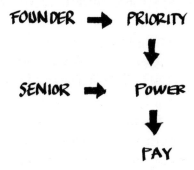

That priority in time adds a dimension to the founder's power that the senior is denied. So close is the founder to the origin that the founder *becomes* the origin – identical, even consubstantial, with it. Again, the effect is one of magic. Magic radiates like a nimbus from the origin of an enterprise. The founder or founders bask in its golden light. There are five interrelated reasons why that should happen:

1. Nobody can get closer to the origin than the founder. That makes the origin an exclusive enclave. Those who don't have access can only wonder at what lies within. The origin is a sacred space.
2. Nobody can belong more to the enterprise than the founder.

Being there at the origin, the founder has the privilege of absolute belonging. Again, that is unavailable to those arriving later. They kneel before an intensity of belonging which they will never attain.

3. Because the acts of foundation take place before others arrive, they involve no independent witnesses. Founding is a private rite, so what happens isn't easy to verify. That leaves it open to being distorted or mystified. Hence the foundation myth at Burton Harcourt, whereby the one founder was theologically transformed into a trinity.

4. The founders are sovereign, so there is no greater authority holding them to account. Or rather, nobody owns the account more than they do. If the founders wish to mythologise that account, they can. Just as history is written by the victors, so the founders own the story of the foundation, and can embellish it to suit.

5. Origins attract stories, because stories need beginnings. When narrating the story of a business, one will likely start with its foundation. That keeps the founders in the picture, and so confers upon them a kind of fame. With fame comes an aura of the untouchable.

Origins, founding, power and storytelling: all swim together, forming a submerged collective enigma like a shoal of nuclear submarines. Jacques Derrida calls it the 'mystical foundation of authority'.

A cure for deafness

As well as of Derrida, I am reminded of Prospero, the protagonist in Shakespeare's *The Tempest*. Prospero is the bookish Duke of Milan who neglects his civic duties in favour of studying magic.

It is a choice that leaves Prospero vulnerable to plots for his removal. Sure enough, cooperation with the Duke morphs into competition for his seat. Prospero's own brother, Antonio, tiptoes up on Prospero's blind side and usurps him. Along with Miranda, his baby girl, Prospero is hounded out.

Father and daughter tip up on an unnamed, unpeopled island. But what from Milan looked like exile, on the island feels like conquest. As the first one in, Prospero becomes the island's constructive founder. The power lost in Milan is thus balanced out by the power gained on the 'desolate isle'. For virgin territory is precious. No matter how inauspicious it might appear, the fact that the land has not been claimed means that it is open to being so. Mutely, the island extends an invitation to sovereignty. Prospero snaps it up.

Founder's power is enhanced by Prospero's newly acquired skills in wizardry. By placing them under a spell, he enslaves two of the island's native creatures – a sprite called Ariel and the earthy hominid, Caliban. The pair are pressed into serving Prospero's self-interest as if he were a colonial master. Prospero already wields power over Miranda. To put it baldly, he is the boss. The island might be small; it might be remote; but Prospero enjoys dominion. He becomes the potentate that in Milan he never quite was. Exile evolves into executive authority.

Exile also affords Prospero the leisure to fashion a plot of his own. He devises a three-pronged scheme: first for revenge against his dastardly brother; second for the marrying-off of his rapidly maturing daughter; and third for a restoration of his status. Never again will he be politically outmanoeuvred. Life in Milan will be organised according to his design, just as it has been on the island. Prospero will prosper once more.

In short, that rich mix of founding, power and magic is embodied in the island's canny maestro. As is the final element, that of storytelling. In the famous second scene of Act One, Prospero answers the now pubescent Miranda's questions. She is curious as to how they came to be on the island in the first place, when she was still an infant. Miranda – whose very name alludes to 'wonder' – is rapt. Her father's tale 'would cure deafness'. To somebody who was not conscious of them at the time, a narrative of origins can only be a marvel.

The butterfly effect

In a macro version of the micro schism at Burton Harcourt, a battle between Old and New schools was simultaneously raging in government. The administration of the day – the early to mid 2000s – was Labour. Or rather it was 'New Labour'. Tony Blair had dug the party up by its gnarly Old Labour roots on the Left, replanting it as a red rose on centre ground, in the sun. There it would attract more votes like bees. Blair was effectively re-founding the party. He was the re-founder.

The old guard, especially the unions and the grassroots, was suspicious. Blair's efforts at refreshing the party's appeal, though sorely needed, threatened to compromise traditional values. Modernisation, moreover, meant embracing the newfangled yet mysterious religion of communications (and yes, I am drawing a parallel with the stated expertise of Stephanie Rogers). New Labour was associated with 'spin'. That involved employing a figure who sounded like a virtuoso from the Magic Circle: the 'spin doctor'. One could imagine the Spin Doctor rising up through the trap door of a stage, revolving his head through 360 degrees, and doing tricks with phosphorus and sulphur. Was there any substance to his prestidigitation? Or was it all smoke and mirrors?

Commentators claimed that the ideological friction between Old and New Labour began with that between Chancellor and Prime Minister. Though a co-architect of New Labour, Gordon Brown was the more old-school of the pair. Where Brown looked backwards and down, Blair looked forward and up. Yet the antipathy between Numbers Ten and Eleven went beyond ideology. It was personal. The bad feeling between the supposed brothers-in-arms wouldn't stop floating to the surface, as irrepressibly as a rotten egg in water. What's more, the two had agreed at the outset of the New Labour project that Brown would one day replace Blair as top dog. As that day kept receding, Brown – a sort of Antonio to Blair's Prospero – became increasingly impatient to yank 'TB' from the throne. He wished to perch on it, raven-like, himself.

The greatest divisions of all opened up in 2003, over the Iraq War. As expected, a prospective deployment of British troops in Iraq offended the sensibilities of those in the heartland of the Left and associated activists. Less predictably, it enraged swaths of the middle class, New Labour and Tory voters alike. That made for opposition that was as genteel as it was principled. At the February march against the war – in which I took part – the spelling on the placards was impeccable.

Not a small part of the opprobrium was directed at Tony Blair himself. By insisting on war, he was seen as acting in a unilateral, even autocratic fashion. Worse, he had got into bed with the Americans. 'I am with you whatever,' swore the Prime Minister in a note to the President that later came to light. Blair created the impression of being keener to ingratiate himself with friends across the pond than to champion the people of Britain.

So whose self-interest was Tony Blair actually serving? Britain's? America's? Tony Blair's? And what was a *Labour* Prime Minister doing dancing so intimately with a *Republican* President? George W. Bush was a key figure in the right-wing 'Neocon' movement that had emerged in the American 1990s. Didn't Blair's choice of Bush as political partner confirm those doubts about spin? Maybe 'New Labour' was so new that it was Labour in nothing more than name. Maybe it was just a vehicle for Tony Blair to gain power, first in the UK and now on the global stage.

Certainly, it was hard to pin down a less ambiguous motive for getting mixed up in Iraq. Rumours that the country's leader, Saddam Hussein, was stockpiling weapons of mass destruction proved impossible to verify. The suggestion that Saddam could launch these elusive weapons 'within forty-five minutes' turned out to be scaremongering. The threat had been 'sexed up'. Finding a solid justification for war turned into a game of grabbing the bar of soap in the bath. Every time you got hold of it, it slipped out of your hand. Was the point to engineer regime change in Iraq? No doubt, Saddam was a loathsome dictator. But in that, he was far from unique. Okay, remove him – but what good would it do Britain?

Where in the UK the motive for deposing Saddam Hussein never shook off the uncertainty that clung to it, in the US it was clear. Chasing the despot out of town was part of a long-held Neocon ambition to replace Saddam with a pro-American leader. When 9/11 happened, the White House wasn't going to waste a good crisis. The response was to declare a 'War on Terror'. That war would sweep up not only the conspirators but a motley of vestigial enemies to America, including Saddam. It didn't matter whether such enemies had perpetrated the attacks on the World Trade Center and the Pentagon. Henceforth all could be tarred as 'terrorists'. Saddam's innocence in regard to the 9/11 attacks was a fact that the Neocon establishment deftly omitted to clarify for the American people. That establishment profited from the confusion.

Such was the scepticism of the time. Formidable. Yet there was one thing that the scepticism was powerless to doubt. Namely, that after 9/11 we had landed in a globalised world with no ticket home. From now on, events from Washington to Baghdad and beyond would have repercussions that we in Blighty would not be able to duck. The 'butterfly effect' made famous by chaos theory had become geopolitical reality.⬇ We were an island no more.

Globalisation was the defining phenomenon of the day. Its arrival was hymned by voices across the political and business spectrum. Yet the clarity with which globalisation entered upon the stage did not exempt it from ambiguity. Was it a hero or a villain? Under globalisation, we were all members of a 'global village', interconnected and levelled out. By the same token, we could see just how different we all were. As much as we found ourselves in one big family, we suddenly took in how many more people we had to compete with. So whether globalisation was good or bad, nobody could conclusively decide. If it was a fact, it was no less a conundrum.

COMPARTMENTS

Opportunity or threat, globalisation didn't just affect foreign *policy*. In the UK, it directly impacted the Foreign *Office*. The gentlefolk of the diplomatic fast-stream would have to rethink their assumptions about how the world worked.

I pick out the Foreign Office not only because it stood in the eye of the globalisation storm. It had also become a major client for us at Burton Harcourt. Against competition from the alpha management consultancies, we, a minnow, had landed a major

---

⬆ The oft-cited example from chaos theory says that a butterfly flapping its wings on one continent can be enough to set off a chain reaction that leads, ultimately, to an earthquake on another.

contract. That was quite a coup. But it wasn't solely our brilliance that swung it. Burton Harcourt was benefiting from an initiative by New Labour ministers. True to their neoliberal colours, those ministers were instructing officials to procure services in a newly market-oriented fashion. That meant not always falling back on the usual suppliers. Amidst the oligopoly of Goliaths, there was room for a smattering of Davids.⬇

And so the Foreign Office retained us – us being, to my delight, just Martin Dawson and me – to modernise the way that they were structured. It was time for this historic organisation, founded in 1782, and a bastion of Empire for well over a century afterwards, to catch up. 'The Office', as it was called, needed to start reflecting that new globalised reality, and pretty darned quick.

But before Dawson and I could roll up our sleeves, there was the vetting. We had to be cleared in order to read the papers classified as SECRET that would form part of our briefing. Beyond SECRET lay TOP SECRET, though that was where our clearance ran out. Not that TOP SECRET was the highest level. There was COMPARTMENTS, an alluringly opaque word that to me suggested a series of tall black panels behind the curtain of a theatre. Perhaps there was still another classification beyond COMPARTMENTS. If so, it vanished into the blackness.

As for the vetting process, one was required to give unidentified officials consent to rummage in one's cupboard for skeletons.

⬆ In adherence to the dogma that competition would drive up quality, the public sector as a whole was now being asked to behave like a market. As well as fishing in a bigger pond for services, public organisations should be competing with one another, for the ultimate benefit of the 'end user', i.e. the customer. Apart from the ideological issues thrown up thereby, the problem with competition was that the same public sector bodies were simultaneously being asked to 'work in partnership' with other public sector bodies. The contradiction between competition and collaboration was resolved by branding it as 'Collabetition'. Needless to say, that didn't resolve it at all.

That was unsettling enough. But more so was the rapidity with which a profile of the subject under scrutiny could be established. All I was asked to supply was my name and date of birth. From those two minimal data points, the team behind the vetting, itself shadowy, could generate all the information they required.

Once given the 'all clear', Dawson and I were admitted to the Foreign Office headquarters on King Charles Street – or KCS, as it was familiarly known. With our lanyards and papers, we were shepherded through a turnstile, under CCTV cameras, past security guards, by a reception desk, and under more cameras. We debouched into a quadrangle just like that of an Oxford or Cambridge college. Given that such a high proportion of diplomats were Oxbridge graduates, the continuity in architectural styles made it seem that their move into employment was less transition than trans*position*. Upon graduating, they had been picked up by a white-gloved mechanical claw in the sky, and set down fifty miles away in Whitehall.

The continuity applied to their activities too. Having dusted themselves off, they carried on as before, writing papers, debating issues and attending drinks. Though who were we to judge? Dawson and I came from the same stable. Perhaps the fact that we had been taken on had nothing to do with competition at all. Perhaps the Foreign Office had merely hired us in its own image.

In that quadrangle, there was even a falconer with a falcon. Not a recondite security measure, as it turned out. Once a month, the falcon was flown around the building's alcoves, ledges, pilasters and statuary. The purpose was to spread a cortisol-inducing scent for pigeons who would otherwise daub the Grade I-listed façade with their gobs of grey-white excrement. The quad's elegance didn't prevent it from being used by the diplomats as a car park; though among the workaday hatchbacks there sat an imperial 1965 Citroën DS that could have chauffeured President de Gaulle himself.

Inside the Map Room

Dawson and I discovered that The Office was organised, as expected, along geographical lines. A London HQ formed the hub, with a network of embassies flung far and wide. It was a set-up in keeping with Britain's colonial past. Indeed, the mosaic corridors at KCS boasted the original murals.

They showed Britannia, a notably masculine woman, subduing natives and restoring peace. It seemed as if she might engirdle the whole globe. Through a mixture of Victorian education, Christian evangelism, resolute administration and, where necessary, brute force, the world would hearken to Britannia's vision. If the UK had an embassy presence in all the main countries, it was partly a legacy of that colonial hauteur.

How it worked now was that the ambassador in post would represent British interests to politicians, bureaucrats and businesses in the host nation. He (sometimes she) would report back to the relevant London desk in turn. From time to time, London would intervene. Having lighted on a theme such as human rights, London would task the ambassador with challenging the local leaders on their record. The ambassador was generally happy to comply.

As in many a geographically structured operation, however, tension between 'the centre' (London) and a particular region (the post) would sometimes flare up. The post would accuse London of meddling in matters that it was too remote to understand. In return, London would decry the post for having lost sight of the big picture. But for the most part the 'ambo' was left to his own devices, sovereign in his realm.

Dawson and I divvied up a small sample of embassies so that we could see for ourselves. The first I visited was in north Africa. Arriving in a forty-degree heat haze, I opted for a short-sleeved, open-neck shirt. When I shook the ambassador's hand, his face fell. Feigning a need to take a phone call, he disappeared, only to return with his own jacket and tie removed. Upon sitting down to lunch, he instructed the staff to leave the wine on the table so that we could pour it ourselves rather than having it poured, 'since we are being informal'. Thus I was simultaneously indulged and humiliated. Diplomacy in action.

Modernising the Foreign Office was about more, of course, than updating the dress code or the protocol on serving wine. It was about tracking the political jet-stream and rising above the local perspective of the ambassador in his country. What globalisation implied was that the nation-based conception of the world was fast becoming obsolete. Thanks to technology, tourism and trade, national boundaries were already porous. That process was now accelerating. Looking at the list drawn up in London of strategic issues that were coming to the fore, one couldn't help but notice that none was country-specific:

- climate change
- drugs, the trade in illegal
- migration
- pandemics
- people trafficking
- terrorism

They all criss-crossed the globe in complex patterns that bore little relation to the artificial lines drawn on the map. Trying to address such issues through a single-nation lens was pointless.

As if those arguments for a transnational perspective weren't persuasive enough, there was the fact that nations themselves weren't the natural, incontestable units for which they were popularly mistaken. The point came home to me in the Map Room at KCS. The historic maps were preserved in the wide, shallow drawers of mahogany plan chests. One of them showed graphically the Sykes–Picot agreement of 1916. That agreement had contrived to parcel up the Middle East on lines favourable to the colonial ambitions of both France and the UK. But what was favourable to France and the UK was distinctly unfavourable to those with a stake in a unified Arab homeland. That homeland spread across the very Syrian and Iraqi borders imposed by Sykes–Picot.

It was, in part, the demolition of such artificial walls that was now motivating al-Qa'ida and their affiliates.⬇ In other words, what was denounced by the West as 'terrorism' could be seen as a cave-aged Arab response to the West's own deeds of violent appropriation: deeds whereby national blocs were superimposed on pre-existing patterns, like tiles glued over a fresco. More fool us in the West if our memories were short. Maybe the vintage maps needed to be dusted off more often.

For the Foreign Office to reflect globalisation in the present, it would have to take account of such forces from the past that didn't coincide with national boundaries. Not to mention all the other border-defying phenomena on that list – climate change, drugs, migration, pandemics and people trafficking. As regards cracking the problem given to Dawson and me as consultants, all roads led to the same conclusion. The Office should restructure according to transnational issues rather than nation states. Geography must bow down to theme.

⬆ That spelling of al-Qa'ida is the one that I picked up at the Foreign Office. It was the version that diplomats were expected to use. I saw a notice to such effect pinned above the desk of one of my clients.

Not that you would pull ambassadors out of their countries. For now, those countries still existed. They were functional political entities. Britain needed representation in them. Nor would you eject the ambassadors' opposite numbers in London, the directors who were responsible at HQ for such countries. They would still have to communicate. But what you would do is put in, also in London, an elite cadre of 'Directors General', known as 'DGs'. Each DG would take responsibility for one or two of those cross-cutting themes. For example, there would be a DG who would hold the UK counter-terrorism portfolio for the globe *in toto*. Given the portfolios' breadth, the DGs would need to sit higher up the tree than ambassadors overseas and geographical directors in London alike. Operating from those lofty branches, the DGs were to become the organisation's 'strategic brain'. They would look out across the savannah for any massing on the horizon or rapid accumulation of black cloud.

How else, practically speaking, could globalisation be brought alive in the structure of The Office? Every alternative that we brainstormed led to the same solution. *Of course* you had to move to a theme-based model. Our client nodded his assent. Indeed, it felt as if Dawson and I were merely putting an external stamp on what had been internally agreed. We had been hired, it seemed, to ratify the obvious.

A single ball of wax

Obvious was one thing: popular was another. Although the maps in those plan chests were out of date, they stood, as statements of nationhood, for a geographic view of the world that many in The Office were disinclined to surrender. Those who resisted were no Luddites, however, blankly refusing to recognise how much the world had changed. There wasn't a soul alive who could plead blindness to such seismic geopolitical shifts. The reason for their resistance was more human: an implied diminution in power. Several London directors with country briefs, in particular, were being lined up to report to the theme-owning DGs. Quite a comedown. Many ambassadors felt similarly. Accustomed to sovereignty in their missions far and wide, they already jibbed at the idea of being at London's beck and call. Having an additional set of London supremos above them took the biscuit.

In short, Dawson and I had underestimated how dearly held that geographical world picture was. Or rather, we hadn't bargained on the degree of self-interest vested in it. At the prospect of being thwarted, that self-interest expressed itself rather less than diplomatically. There was a gang of Office malcontents who lampooned Dawson and me as managerialist vandals. Our business-school solutions were inadequate to the texture of the situation; our touch too coarse for leafing through the delicate palimpsest of reasons as to why geographically was the only way that The Office should be run. In any case, it wasn't broken, *so why the hell fix it.*

Under attack, Dawson and I dug in. We got sucked into Office politics despite our purported objectivity as advisers. But negotiating with diplomats – and especially with disgruntled diplomats – was a battle with a foregone result. Negotiation, to them, was mother's milk. Along with dexterity in rebutting an argument, they possessed the reserves of diplomatic oil necessary for running the issues out of time.

In other words, if those recalcitrant directors threw themselves into wrestling with our proposals, it was as much to defer a final decision as it was to refute the substance. And while such delaying tactics were invaluable in situations of military threat, for the managing of an organisation they were maddening. Churchill had said that jaw-jaw was better than war-war. He was recommending talking over fighting. Well, yes. Indisputably, jaw-jaw was better than war-war *when* a war-war was in the offing. When it wasn't, jaw-jaw was hot air.

The problem was that in the eyes of those directors this *was* a war. There was a doctrinal schism between two world pictures. The one was based on geography, the other on theme. As to the side on which Dawson and I had come down, it was blindingly obvious. More to the point, it was obvious *that we had landed on a side*. Far from being brought in to independently endorse a view that had received universal backing, we found that we were *parti pris*. We had become the ventriloquist's dummies of those in the centre. Those being the very clients who had hired us.

Had we been played? Yes and no. By proposing the solution that we proposed, Dawson and I were manifestly shoring up the power of our paymasters. And yet restructuring by theme was the logical response to globalisation. Too bad that we couldn't isolate the logic from the politics. It was a single ball of wax.

The ultimate decision lay with the Foreign Office Board. The Board was itself an organ of the centre, a fact from which conclusions both could and couldn't be drawn. Whatever the motive – objective logic, subjective self-interest, both or neither – its members ultimately accepted our recommendations. Our job had been done. To quote a phrase of the day, The Office was set to become 'fit for purpose'.

Shade-loving plants

Long after those recommendations had been accepted and Martin Dawson had moved on to another client, I was putting in four days a week at KCS. My motives for doing so were plural. Professionally, I wanted to see those recommendations through, and to be there as the changes were implemented. Emotionally, I connected with the organisation. I had made friends, and I found the culture sympathetic.

Why was I so at home? Perhaps my tarrying at the Foreign Office was a way of being overseas without having to leave England. Yes, I had sworn never again to live in America. But I clung to a fantasy of myself as an Englishman abroad. Working at the Foreign Office was a proxy for foreign experience. Like a diorama, it extended a theatrical recess into exotic lands without transporting me anywhere physically. I was passing my days in an exclusive, ornate departure lounge. A liminal space between nations.

If I am honest, my final motive for prolonging the engagement at KCS was the avoidance of Stephanie Rogers. Although the chemistry between Rogers and me was toxic enough, it was what Rogers represented that I found problematic. Namely, 'communications'. Like those chary of New Labour spin, I saw it as faintly mendacious. To me it seemed that in the communications playbook a glossy enough surface could paper over a multitude of sins.

So I had an aversion to what I perceived as fakery. But what needled me even more about Stephanie Rogers was that I was answerable to her. The business was her baby. Of the 'three founding partners', Stephanie Rogers was first among equals. She was unassailable. That made everybody answerable to her, not just me. Yet I felt a particular heat. Stephanie hadn't fully trusted me at my hiring, and she hadn't fully trusted me since. True, she did hold down the drawbridge long enough to admit me to the castle of Burton Harcourt. But once I had passed through, I felt under her surveillance as if by a drone. Was it only because I was bringing home the bacon, in other words enriching her as a senior, that she didn't dispatch a missile my way?

Maybe I was demonising her. Maybe Stephanie trusted me no less than she did the others. Even so, I struggled with being accountable. I found it demeaning, regardless of who was doing the holding-to-account. It didn't matter that it was Stephanie Rogers: she just happened to fill the role. What irked me was giving public testimony regarding actions that I felt I should have been allowed to keep private. That bacon was being delivered, wasn't it, so why all the attention?

In Oxford, I had been trusted to get on with my research, like the independent scholar that I was. My motivation and self-discipline were taken as read. But where the academy provided nooks for private study, the business environment was all open-plan seating, published billing targets and strip lights. Hardly the conditions for a shade-loving plant like me. Businesses are designed for cacti that can flourish under an unblinking sun. With nowhere to hide, I wilted. I also wondered how businesses could ever hope to foster the innovation they so bruited, when everybody had to sit in each other's company all day long with the lights full on. It was like a penal colony. With no escape from the brightness, what chance did the unconscious have of pursuing its subterranean works of transformation?

Yet my problem with accountability pre-dated Oxford. What being called to account made me feel like was a naughty boy. It activated memories of my father summoning me into the kitchen to report on my day at school. This was when he was still working and the MS remained in abeyance. He would sometimes be tired, often irascible, and always ready to judge. The very fact of standing in court made me feel like a felon. Fearing 'the slipper', I would quake. The best outcome that I could hope for was to be dismissed without further comment. Praise was out of the question.

In the worst case, I would be sent to my room. There I was

obliged to await 'six of the best' from that slipper. I lay upstairs in dread, listening for the scrape of the kitchen chair as it was pushed back, the clearing of the throat in the hallway, the heavy step on the stairs, and the sweep of my bedroom door over the green carpet, as it was opened wider. Daddy filled the room. He kicked the slipper off his right foot. Accountability went hand in hand with fear.

In other words, Stephanie Rogers unwittingly acted on me as a psychic trigger. Being held to account by her brought up fearful memories. Having to be present played havoc with my need to withdraw. Despite the difficulty that I had with Stephanie's doctrine of presenteeism, however, it did help me understand why trust is spoken of as 'blind'. When you trust somebody, you don't need to follow them. You believe that wherever they are, they are doing what they say they are doing. It is like the childhood game in which you close your eyes and fall backwards into the arms of the person behind you. Trust and blindness are bedfellows. Conversely, it is mistrust that drives the need to monitor. Which is why the modern enthusiasm for *transparency* is perhaps misguided. It is thought that transparency fosters trust. In reality, transparency is that which *removes* the possibility of trust, by calling for continuous monitoring. Under a transparency-based system, blindness is swapped for vision, faith exchanged for certainty. That arguably amounts to a net loss.

The infinite tuning-fork

In 2004, Burton Harcourt threw itself a Christmas party in Brighton. The plan was to do a 'Secret Santa'. A few days prior to the event, we had all drawn the name of a colleague from a hat. The person you picked was the person for whom you had to buy a token Christmas present. My Santa was Stephanie.

After the bibulous dinner, Stephanie passed me my little package along with a Christmas card. The gift was a pencil with a tiny eraser plugged into its non-writing end. The card read:

To the self-effacing Robert!

Stephanie explained that the rubber symbolised my personality. I nodded and smiled. But in my mind I was turning a steel wheel to release a stream of invective that gushed like a foul liquid through a sewer. Case in point: I effaced my reaction. I rubbed out the feelings that would have otherwise been sketched on my face. Perhaps Stephanie was right.

After the event, my thoughts refracted in two, as if that pencil had been stood in a tumbler of water. I had both won and lost. The skilfulness of my attempts at hiding from Stephanie, both physically and emotionally, had been proven. If she had caricatured me as self-effacing, it was because I had surgically excised my true feelings from every interaction I had with her. I presented her instead with a work face, like a mask.

There was no such complacency in the other half of my refracted thoughts. How could Stephanie be so poor at reading me? And how could she be so gauche as to convey that misreading with such brio, on a Christmas card? Not to mention the diminution of me that came with it. *Self-effacing!* Effacement is the process of deletion. I remembered the Etch-a-Sketch kit I had as a boy. Having drawn a picture in carbons, you could wipe the slate clean with the twist of a knob.

The inevitable byproduct of my presenting Stephanie with a mask was that she misunderstood who I was. I had hidden myself so well that what she saw was a diffident person to whom she could condescend. What a dangerous thing a weak opponent is, I railed. All of a sudden, I wanted her to know me. I wanted to be seen. Or did I? No, not really. I wanted to carry on hiding. Help! I was tied in a double-bind of my own making.

It came back to transparency, or the lack of it. I had made myself so non-transparent, so opaque, as to be almost a different person from the one that I put forward. If Stephanie – or others – misread me, it was because I had deliberately fed them the wrong script. As a decoy, that was pretty nifty. But it came at a price. It ruled me out of receiving any true empathy from others. Space, yes: that it bought me. Yet the cost of space was isolation. Worse, my masking tactics implied that I was no less fake than I had judged Stephanie for being. Maybe what I was reacting against in her was a capacity for deception in myself. In that sense, Stephanie was entirely right about me. In calling it self-effacement, she was actually being kind, considering that its truer name was *duplicity*.

The point is that the dynamic prevailing when I signed with Burton Harcourt never faltered. Like the note struck on a tuning-fork, it went on for ever and without variation. I was under the illusion that I could join the fraternity I wanted to join rather than the matriarchy that it was. I believed I could put Stephanie Rogers in brackets. I was wrong on both counts. Stephanie Rogers was indeed the queen of the castle. There was no bracketing her off. Indeed, she was the main text: Chapter One and all the chapters that ensued.

The spectral beauty of the West Pier

As well as the sustained after-effects of Burton Harcourt's foundation and the politics that they fuelled, there were the occupational stresses of life as a consultant. These included long hours; a dreary commute; back-to-back meetings; a rushed sandwich lunch; relentless pressure to meet targets; and an obligation to be civil at all times to clients, including the few with no manners of their own. I was constantly fatigued. In hindsight I would say that I was in a depression that was shallow but long. When I awoke most mornings it was with a feeling of dejection.

I also missed writing. By 2005, five years into my tenure at Burton Harcourt, it was a decade since the publication of *Derrida and Autobiography*. In desultory fashion, I had been chipping away in the evenings at a book on Freud's theory of the death-drive that I had begun at All Souls. But having left the academy, I had lost sight of why publishing another academic tome was a good idea. It was similar to preparing a meal to which I wasn't invited.

My frustration peaked one summer's evening. I was cycling home over Westminster Bridge. Tourists thronged the pavement to my left, taking photos of Big Ben, peering down into the Thames, listening to the buskers or buying caramelised peanuts from a cart. So crowded was it that a few people had spilled over onto the road.

I picked out my man fifty yards ahead. With his back to me, he was strolling nonchalantly along the cycle lane. *My* cycle lane. I wasn't going to ram him full on, just glance him with my elbow to show my displeasure. Which is exactly what I did. What I didn't do was reckon on it being me, not him, who would come off worse. The contact threw me off balance. I crashed into the path of a bus coming up behind. The bus swerved. The injuries to my body were minor. But my soul was clearly in a bad way.

If I was going to staunch the leaking of my spirits, I had to act. Taking a day off work to think through what form that action might take, I went back by train to Brighton. I took up my thinking-post on the pebbly beach by the West Pier.

Already derelict, the pier had been set on fire in 2003. But rather than destroying the building's beauty, such a violation had turned that beauty spectral. Where, in its heyday, the con-

Brighton's West Pier

struct with its puffy white domes had looked like a joyful bride, now it gave off the sorrow of one jilted at the altar. The West Pier was forever fixed in a defining moment of loss, her dress torn away.

Gazing out at the abject structure, I reviewed my options. What kept coming to mind was a Philip Larkin poem called 'Toads'. Its first stanza runs as follows:

> *Why should I let the toad work*
> *Squat on my life?*
> *Can't I use my wit as a pitchfork*
> *And drive the brute off?*

I took the poem's message literally. I should use my wit as a pitchfork to drive off the toad of work. What did that mean in practice? It meant using my brains to pen a different kind of book, popular rather than academic. A book that might be read by more than a coterie of specialists. A book that might even sell! If I were to be paid an advance, I could bundle it up with the money that I had saved. I had been steadily inflating a small

237

cash cushion to buoy me along after leaving Burton Harcourt. I couldn't bear to be in a collective any longer. Since all my behaviour was oriented towards maximising my autonomy within it, why not go the whole hog and strike out on my own? I would work as an independent consultant. I had to have room to breathe. On the train home from Brighton, I began roughing out ideas for the new project.

Il faut cultiver son jardin

In this chapter, I have been looking at how we preserve our self-interest within a group. It boils down to three scenarios, set out in the table below. The three are ranked 'low', 'medium' and 'high', according to the amount of self-interest that each scenario is likely to secure.

	In a group, with limited power	Alone	In a group, with significant power
High self-interest			X
Medium self-interest		X	
Low self-interest	X		

In the bottom row of the table, you are part of a group, but with limited power of your own. Your potential for maximising self-interest is therefore low. In the next row up, you operate as an individual. Your self-interest score necessarily rises, but only as far as medium. It is capped because your power extends only over yourself, like a roof with no eaves. There is nobody multiplying your self-interest for you. In the top row, you are the leader of a group, or at least senior enough to exercise power over it. With others working on your behalf, your self-interest score rises to high.

By leaving Burton Harcourt to go solo, I was taking just the one step up the staircase in the table. I was hopping from the X in the bottom left to the one in the middle. But it was a start. The journey from the 'effacing' of my self-interest to the nurturing of it had begun. I was following Voltaire's admonition to 'cultivate one's garden'. *Il faut cultiver son jardin*. What's more, I would rid myself, once and for all, of office politics.

Before all else, be armed.
Niccolò Machiavelli

7

Near Death

This is where the serpent lives, the bodiless.
His head is air. Beneath his tip at night
Eyes open and fix on us in every sky.

Wallace Stevens

The catechism of logic informing this new chapter runs as follows:

QUESTION: What does it mean to be human?
RESPONSE: *Among other things, it means having a body.*
QUESTION: What does it mean to have a body?
RESPONSE: *Among other things, it means being in time.*
QUESTION: What does it mean to be in time?
RESPONSE: *Among other things, it means moving towards death.*

Like lovers in a Gothic painting, death and the body are intimately entwined. It is their intertwining that is the theme of this chapter. But in order to work up to that theme, I need first to go back to the early 2000s. I will start the narrative at that same point of transition from Dyke Rollins to Burton Harcourt, though with a different focus. That focus will fall on events outside work, events occurring in parallel.

The one-way dolphin

The question of what it means to be human sounds, initially, abstract. It invites us to ruminate on fate or loss or change or hope or truth or love or courage. All important. But all intangible. Whereas one of the most fundamental aspects of being human is that of having a body. The being of a human is made of flesh and blood. Little can be more tangible than that.

And how wonderful that tangibility is. Having a body delivers benefits that would never be available if, say, we were pure spirit. How, without a body, would we dance, shower, have sex or eat chocolate? How would we travel? What would laughing be like with no diaphragm or lungs or mouth? Were we not physically incarnate, we'd never feel the sand between our toes, hear the crashing of the waves or taste the salt on our lips after dips in the ocean. There'd be no way of sniffing the aroma of fresh bread; cuddling a baby; licking ice cream from a cone; hearing the rain drip from a pine tree; or observing the sky redden at sunset. What chance would there be of enjoying a massage without a body to lay down on the bed?

If only all bodily experience was like that. As much as they are a conduit for pleasure, our bodies, alas, are convenors of pain. Bodies are where hurt hurts: hurt doesn't hurt outside bodies. The surrounding air doesn't flinch. It's only because we have a body to experience such afflictions that we get sunburn or cramp or diarrhoea. So, being bodiless, like that spirit, would have its upside. It would release us from a panoply of ailments ranging from the trivial to the grave. In a state of bodilessness, there'd be no stubbing one's toe, no pulling of muscles, no flu, no broken bones, no diabetes, no arthritis and no cancer.

On whether it prefers to bring us pleasure or pain, the body is agnostic. It is simply our vehicle in the world. As such, the body courses indifferently through the sublunary elements in all their variety. It experiences delights and dolours, from orgasm to injury, in random order. One minute we are giving our partner a quick kiss as we prepare dinner. The next we cut our finger slicing peppers. We are hiking a fell in the Lake District, taking in the stupendous view, when all of a sudden we sprain our ankle. We're watching our favourite band at a festival and some leery fool stumbles into us, spilling his pint of lager down our arm. The good and the bad alike are what the body brings, without prejudice towards either.

That worldliness is the point – the fact that the body is precisely a body and not a spirit. It is, as Hamlet says, all too solid. As such, the body fixes us in space. We can't be anywhere except where our body is. It remains glued to the spot, even as the spot changes. Our minds, by contrast, may wander, free birds that they are. With no concrete weighting them to a geographical location, our minds are at liberty to wing the universe. But our bodies remain bound, heavily. When we walk in the sunshine, the shadow that we cast is a reminder that we cannot be anywhere else. That moving impression which we make upon the ground is the stain of presence. It is a shadow that we cast even in the darkness as we sleep. Invisibly, it shows that our body is there, now, and nowhere else.

One consequence of the body's embodied condition, of its unremitting occupancy of the place where it is, is that it can never hide. I mean, it *can* hide. From toddlers playing peekaboo to outlaws on the run, people do hide. But the physical substance that is a body makes that body inherently findable. Even if we go off grid, avoiding detection for years, we can still, in principle, be found. That is why we need to go into hiding in the first place – because we have a body. Say you had committed a heinous felony: would you not consider trading your body for that spirit? That would be ultimate hiding. We, the embodied, can always be found. To that extent, we carry an existential concern about who might be coming for us. Thankfully, the source of that concern is an equal source of comfort. For if having a body means that we can always be found, we can also be rescued.

The body is no less fixed in time. Just as a body has a continuous *where*, it has a continuous *when*. Space and time are the body's abiding dual coordinates, the two inalienable axes that plot our lives. As Merleau-Ponty says, 'We must avoid saying that our body is *in* space, or *in* time. It *inhabits* space and time.' The being-in-time of the body again sets it apart from the mind. In our heads we can time-travel. We can remember episodes from the past or look ahead to the future. The body has no such licence. From birth forwards, we cling to time as to the dorsal fin of a dolphin, forever streaming one way. Not only can we never go back: we cannot outpace time and get ahead of ourselves. It is impossible to be older or younger than we are. We are always exactly the right age, the precise distance from our birth that we ought to be. The tireless dolphin never fails, even for a second, in its task of maintaining its rider in the Now.

While the time since our birth is so invariably precise, such precision escapes us when measuring the time until death. For most of us are completely unsighted as to when we will die. Our date of death remains as obscure as the road beyond a bend. We know that the road is there but have only a vague idea of its length. Not that we're eager to find out: it's too morbid. We would rather not be reminded that when we die, it will be on a specific day – perhaps a Wednesday – in a specific month

– say February – and in a specific year. For, like birth, death cannot happen outside the scheme of the diary. We are creatures in time.

If I say that 'most' rather than 'all' of us don't know our exact date of death, it is because I have in mind three exceptions to the rule:

1. Prisoners on death row who have a day of execution assigned to them. They will know their death-date with an intimate clarity, as if it were stamped on their inner wrist.
2. Those suffering from a terminal illness. Their doctor will have communicated if not an exact date, then a window of time within which the end will come.
3. Suicides. The suicide's death is just as bound to time as that of anybody else. Ergo the suicide is obliged to pick a time at which to do the deed. They can't operate outside the calendar either. Indeed because they consciously choose a time, suicides are all the more embedded in that calendar. Thus they educe a certainty about when they will die that is not readily available to the masses. They might pay for that certainty with their life, but by that point their life, on their own assessment, has shed its value.

But those three cases – death row inmates, the terminally ill and the suicidal – represent the outliers. As for the bulk of humanity, we are in the dark. Our death date remains unknown.

For all its significance, however, the question of when we die ranks a whole division below the fact that we are going to die regardless. The necessity of death overshadows the timing of death like a colossus rearing above a crowd. The breathing animal that we are and that allows us to experience life with its manifold pleasures and pains is the very animal whose breaths are numbered, not infinite. For having a body – to name it – makes us mortal. A body is temporary. That is the more imponderable truth.

Improbable origins of the double divorce

It was in February 2001 that Maddy said goodbye to both her English husband (me) and the English nation. About a year before that, as in a relay race, Maddy had connected me with the woman who would connect me with the woman who would come to replace her in my life. Could it be that a bit of Maddy wanted to do just that? Given the rotten state of our marriage, Maddy's unconscious might well have wished to release the uxorial baton, passing it on to a delegate with a delegate. Maddy would have thus made sure that any connection to me was doubly abjured.

The flat that we were renting was in Kensington. From there, Maddy would go for her constitutional jog around Hyde Park. One winter's day, another jogger ran past on the other side of the rimy grass, going in the opposite direction. Like Maddy, the mysterious woman had the hood of her sweatshirt tugged over her head, to insulate against the cold. All that Maddy could see of her was a nose peeping out from the swaddling. But the gait gave the stranger away. Just as she was passing out of Maddy's peripheral vision, like an actor making an exit, Maddy gave an instinctive shout.

'Emily!'

The figure stopped and turned. She trotted over. 'Maddy?!'

If ever there was a moment of fate in my life, this was it. Does it matter that I wasn't there? Not a jot. My absence means that the two women's encounter and what flowed from it were all the more out of my hands, and all the more fateful as a result. It was as if, in a glassy supernatural realm, two of the three Fates, represented by Maddy and Emily, were toying with my life. There was Clotho, who spins the fabric of life. And there was Lachesis, who deals that fabric out. The two Fates have a third sister in Atropos, who cuts the thread. Atropos is the figure of death: for now she was waiting to make her debut.

I don't even recall my whereabouts on that pregnant morning when I was being acted on from such extraterrestrial distance by the other two. All I can say is that, at the time, I had zero idea that the encounter was taking place. What was it that made that encounter so portentous? The fact that for me it would lead to both a second marriage and a second divorce. A second divorce, moreover, that would necessitate an uncoupling not from one woman but from two. The two of them in this case being first Emily, the runner in the park, to whom Maddy would soon introduce me; and second the woman to whom Emily would introduce me in turn, named Helen. Cutting my ties with the one meant cutting my ties with the other. They were inextricably linked. In effect it would be a double divorce.

For now, however, I had not clapped eyes on Helen, let alone married and divorced her. I had yet to meet even Emily, the intermediate baton-holder. The point to emphasise about that wintry linking-up of Maddy and Emily is that it so nearly didn't happen. Which is another reason, along with its occurring out of my sight, why the Fates might have had a hand in it.

The default was for the two women to keep on running. The fact that they didn't raises the question of whether everything that happens has to happen. Aristotle's answer was yes. But he wasn't referring to fate. He was saying that every effect is the necessary result of its cause. More precisely, he was saying that for every cause there exists a delimited field of possible effects. Probability, in short. Although an event will narrow the possibilities for what may proceed from it, it won't shrink those possibilities down to one. When, for example, I cast my fishing line over the water, it is more probable that I will either catch a fish or not catch a fish, than that I will spark a third world war.

Looking back we are justified in saying that everything that happened had to happen. I caught a fish because I was fishing. Looking forward, we can anticipate a limited number of outcomes arising from the prevailing circumstances. In that qualified sense, Maddy and Emily were destined to re-meet each other. Given that they were both living in west London, both female, both in their late twenties, both middle class, both keen on jogging, et cetera, the chances of their bumping into each other were not astronomically remote. Their meeting was, one might say, an amazing coincidence that took place within a range of not unlikely scenarios.

There is a Chinese proverb that says, 'No coincidence, no story'. The proverb helps to disclose an underlying point. However we may rationalise or reduce it, every coincidence glints a little with a golden seam of the miraculous. Only a portion of a coincidence can be captured by logic; the remainder continues to glow in that part of our soul where we register wonder. And the only way that we can deal with wonder is to repeat it – by telling and retelling the story. In other words, if we are pleased to share the coincidences that happen in our lives, it is partly because the miraculous quality of a coincidence means that relating the story of it will always feel more natural than trying to account for that coincidence rationally. So not only, as the proverb proclaims, would there be no stories without coincidences; but the very nature of coincidence is such that it will generate story. To present it as a maxim:

A coincidence cannot be thought, therefore it has to be told.

	3 Maddy, 1995-2001	4 Helen, 2001-2015 Greta b. 2006
Marriage		
No Marriage	1 Astrid, 1983-1986	2 Simone, 1986-1995 Anna b. 1987 Ruby b. 1991
	No Children	**Children**

*Given the potential for confusion,
I offer the table to the right as a
way of making sense of the various
relationships under discussion*

The semi-stranger

At the moment when Maddy shouted across the park to Emily, their relationship was a long way from being established. To call them friends would be a stretch. When they got talking in the morning mist, the two women rehearsed their meagre history. Emily, who was English, had studied for a year abroad in America while Maddy was still living there, before leaving for Oxford. A mutual friend, Grant, had put the two women in touch, though they never physically met at the time. When they did, it was a while later, back in England, and then only once, and only as part of a group. So at the moment when Maddy hailed Emily across the park, you couldn't have called them bosom pals. Had Maddy not shouted out, it is perfectly possible – nay probable – that the two women, semi-strangers in effect, would never have seen each other again.

The phenomenon of the semi-stranger represents a not insignificant part of our lives. Every few months, I will catch a glimpse of such a person as I go about my day. I mean an ex-colleague, a fellow participant on a course, somebody with whom I went to school, a couple from a holiday, another student in my year at university, the mother of an old friend, or a party guest to whom I once chatted. None belongs in my inner circle but nor are they completely anonymous. Together such people make up a demographic of appreciable size. I would suggest that we all know more semi-strangers than we have genuine friends. Certainly, when we think about all the semi-strangers that we *could* see out and about, their numbers quickly mushroom.

Given that the defining characteristic of semi-strangers is their capacity to return at random from the past, they share some DNA with ghosts. They are revenants in the literal sense of *those who come back*. If nothing else, they remind us of a certain period in our lives. Perhaps that is their function: to signal such a period in the past on the grounds that it contains a lesson for the present.

I am speculating. The practical question regarding such persons of undead status is whether to say hello. No such question arises with a true stranger. With a true stranger, we are at liberty to keep walking. Such is the relief of anonymity. It is why, despite their populousness, cities provide such a sense of freedom from the burden of other people. Strangers make no call on our con-

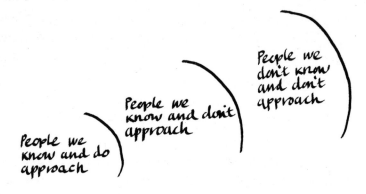

People we
know and do
approach

People we
know and don't
approach

People we
don't know
and don't
approach

science. Semi-strangers, by contrast, present us with that dilemma: to approach or not to approach?

My comfort zone lies in the middle of the three in the diagram. On seeing a semi-stranger, I tend not to approach. No sooner has the moment passed, however, than I rebuke myself. *I must do better at reaching out. Think of the rewards of human contact. Perhaps this could lead to something good. What is there to lose?* I curse my dependence upon my independence.

All of which assumes that semi-stranger relationships are a one-way street. Yet to others I am a semi-stranger too. It stands to reason that I will be ignored about as often as I ignore. Should I be offended? The truth is that I myself don't particularly care for some of the people whom I avoid. So if it works both ways, then yes, I should be offended somewhat. Although I cannot know when I have been ignored, I can draw the general conclusion that, given the option of approaching me, some people prefer to keep their distance. As a truth in life, that is to be welcomed. As a reflection on who I am, it makes me feel bad. Sometimes we are even avoided by a person whom we would unhesitatingly greet, a member of our inner circle. Is that also a welcome truth? Maybe it is just a fearful hypothesis. Still, it must happen.

Maddy's temperament was such as to never let a semi-stranger go by unintercepted. She was always for approaching. Where I would have jogged on, Maddy pulled up and hollered at the half-known other in the morning whiteness. Her action thereby demonstrated another law of life:

If you want things to happen, you have to leave the house.

Or leave one of your three bases, anyway. We spend the majority of our lives being in, or going between, the place where we live, the place where we work, and the places where we socialise. In the diagram, the three are labelled 'home', 'work' and 'play'.

An ordinary day for a working person might involve starting at home; then commuting to work up the left-hand line of the triangle; taking the horizontal line to see friends in the evening; and returning home down the right-hand line. Home sits at the bottom because it is our anchor, though the other two points also provide security. The closer we stay to the points of the triangle, the safer we feel. All three work like tent pegs driven into the earth.

Where that certainty begins to lose its tautness, like a sail crinkling, is in the large area in the middle. It represents the space that we occupy when we are out and about. We might be shopping, walking the dog, getting the car washed, attending a dentist's appointment, or indeed travelling between home, work and play. We might, like Maddy, be out for a run. Whatever the activity, the people around us in this open space are random. As in a mournful ballet, it is where strangers and semi-strangers move among each other without interacting. Having left the familiarity of home or work or friends, we find ourselves in open country. There, events are less predictable. It is the place to go to experience the unexpected, and yet this destination is all around us, like a theme park without signposts.

Three visits to a country house and one excursus on death

I first met Emily on a train to the English countryside in early 2000, the last year that Maddy and I were together. After that chance encounter in Hyde Park as semi-strangers, Emily and Maddy had become friendly. That naturally led to Maddy wanting to introduce Emily to her husband, me; and to Emily wanting to be introduced. So Emily invited the two of us, along with some other friends, for a weekend at her father's substantial retreat.

Contained in that last sentence are two clues about what Emily valued. First, friendship. If there was one thing that mattered to Emily, it was her friends. Second, having something the friends could enjoy: in this case, her father's commodious home and its extensive grounds. She could thus be the warmth-giving hostess, a sun around which those friends could gratefully orbit. Like the other guests, Maddy and I slid happily into our planetary positions. Winding up her orrery and letting it run, Emily ensured that the weekend was lauded by all.

The next time I visited the house was in the summer of the same year. I had just returned from the ranch where Maddy and I had held our shouting match in the shack. What with Maddy proposing to move back to California and my increasing vexation at her changeability, our marriage was hanging by a thread. So while Maddy stayed on at the ranch, I came back to London. Hearing that I was at a loose end, Emily invited me for a second weekend of friendship and feasting at her father's.

It was on that second visit that I met the famous Helen, the baton's final recipient. I say 'famous' because in the short time I had known Emily, I had more than once heard her brag about her friend. *Top totty with brains* was Emily's impious-yet-venerating phrase to describe Helen. And so it turned out. Helen was both beautiful and clever, without being big-headed. One couldn't help but be impressed.

Yet I was still married, albeit unhappily. Helen had pitched up to the house with a boyfriend, Dylan. The road to romance was blocked. I also sensed that at that roadblock stood Emily herself. Was she watching like a border guard for signs of amatory contraband passing between Helen and me? I assumed that Emily was trying to protect a relationship, be it the one that I had with Maddy or the one that Helen had with Dylan. Up to a point, my assumption was correct. Emily was indeed protecting a relationship, only it was neither of the aforementioned two. If Emily was on guard, it was for her own bond with Helen.

Ever the conscientious guest, I had brought my hostess offerings. These included two boxes of cream cakes to have with afternoon tea, as befitted weekending at an English country house. Like a blindfolded archer, I had little idea whether my gifts would hit the mark. Preferring salt to sugar, I rarely ate cake. But as luck would have it, the strawberry tarts and coffee eclairs recommended to me at the patisserie were a bullseye. Especially with Helen. Svelte as a model who makes other women envious, Helen tucked in sans regard to calories.

Sugar was not the only need of Helen's that I met. After tea, she and I found ourselves sitting together on the bed in my allotted guest room. Where was Helen's boyfriend Dylan at this time? A hundred and twenty yards away, south-south-east of my guest room, sunning himself in a deckchair on the lawn. Where was Maddy? Approximately five thousand miles further away, in the American Midwest, in an altogether different latitude and a time zone that put her under the bedcovers, asleep. As for Emily, she had been forced to abandon her checkpoint in order to prepare a well-thought-out dinner downstairs, great chef that she was. Thus neutralised, none of the three watchmen was watching.

The satisfaction to which I am alluding was not sexual, however. As she was grappling with a doctoral thesis related to my own interests, Helen chose to use our unchaperoned hour for quizzing me on Freud. I was notionally finishing my book on the Freudian death-drive. I would fiddle with it in the evenings after a day at Burton Harcourt, like a hobbyist with a classic car in his garage. All I was doing was taking the engine apart and putting it back together again, not making the vehicle roadworthy. It certainly had no wheels. This being the year 2000, many moons would have to pass before my epiphany on Brighton beach in 2005 to the effect that I should give up on academic books and turn to writing for a general audience.

So Freud was still my thing, nominally. My account of his theory of death – the account that I gave to Helen – went as follows:

> Running against the grain of thinkers before him, Freud does not believe that human beings are fundamentally rational, social or political. No such grown-up adjective accurately describes our true nature. The reason being that our true nature is shaped in childhood. And what defines us as children is wanting to have our wishes satisfied. That is our earliest and most fundamental instinct. Even when we do become adults, that infantile desire to have desire satisfied remains with us. We are universally driven by the need to fulfil wishes. Thus wish-fulfilment is the engine of the psyche.

Helen listened attentively to my impromptu lecture. I say that the encounter between the two of us was cerebral, and superficially it was. But I don't deny the non-cerebral plane on which we were simultaneously communing. There we were, alone on a bed, on a sunny afternoon, away from normal life, our partners out of the picture, exploring mutual interests, and I was talking about fulfilling wishes. There was at least one lead plugged into the erotic circuit.

I continued:

> We are out to find pleasure. That is the famous 'pleasure principle'. But pleasure is not the end of the story. The purpose of fulfilling a wish is to remove it. For to wish is to lack what you want. As long as we lack, we are restless. And we don't like being restless. What we like is being at peace.

Up to this point, Freud's thinking makes reasonable sense. Helen, for one, was not moved to object. *In seeking to fulfil our wishes, we are searching for peace.* Yes, why not? As a hypothesis, that is not particularly contentious. It is his next step that makes Freud's argument harder to swallow. For if, he speculates, what we are pursuing via pleasure is peace, then our ulterior motive is suicide. For what is there to tell peace from death? Absolute peace equates to total inertia.

As if it were not bold enough, Freud adorns his theory with an ostentatious biological justification. It is not just that in trying to satisfy our wishes, we are surreptitiously aiming for a deathly quietus. We are also zooming backwards in evolutionary history, like a time machine travelling through a narrowing field of stars to the dawn of dawns. Freud points out that the human species began, all those millennia ago, as a single-cell organism. Our evolution from that matutinal point has been a story of increasing complexity. We have gained cells, skilful bodies, agile brains and consciousness of a depth that is unfathomable even to ourselves. Unfortunately, the complexity hasn't suited us. It causes too much inner disturbance, the opposite of peace.

What it means to be human, in other words, is to be over-evolved. And so we are plagued by nostalgia for our phylogenetic origins. Our profoundest instinct is to go back to a simpler state of things. Whenever we seek to fulfil our wishes – in even so lowly a manner as consuming cream cakes – we are acting as agents of that unresting mission on the part of the species to satisfy our wishes, destroy our craving, settle our desires, calm our seeking and return to zero.

Like many others, Helen might not have bought Freud's theory in all its pomp. It is a lot to take on board. Nevertheless she seemed appreciative of my efforts at explaining it. After departing the house that weekend – she to Brighton where she lived and I to London – we continued the conversation by email. And while the text of those emails was heady, the subtext vented from a different source. The pleasure principle had stirred.

It was on my third visit to the father's house that our moment came. Emily had gathered another group of friends, this time to see in the New Year. Again the group included Helen, though by now the boyfriend had been discarded. And I was alone again too. Tellingly, Maddy had gone to visit her American relatives for the holidays by herself. Even more telling was the fact that not once did either of us pick up the phone to call the other, as had been our custom when apart. Not even to say Happy Christmas. The mutual frustration had turned into antagonism. Antagonism had worn itself down to a talc of indifference. The talc of indifference was now being blown away on the wind. So no telephone calls were made. A funereal silence reigned.

If on the morning of the last day of that year my relationship with Maddy wasn't technically dead, its final death was assisted by what happened that night. Under the camouflage of the New Year celebrations at the house, Helen and I kissed. For Maddy, it was the kiss of death.

Half in love with easeful death

My preoccupation with death went beyond the academic. For many years, I had suffered from night terrors. I would wake up in the darkness in a state of horror at the thought of dying. Though my voice made no sound, my mind clanged like a spade that is plunged into soil only to strike granite. The impact of metal upon stone sent shockwaves back up along the shaft of the spade, through my wrists and into my core. The heart, the liver, the lungs, the kidneys, the stomach, the spleen, the brain: every organ was sheathed in its vibration as by a demonic fascia.

One hears about the fear of uncertainty. In me it was the opposite – the fear of certainty – that set off such existential alarm. The certainty that I would, that I will, die. My own death. The implacable unavoidability of it. The no-getting-round-it. The utter immoveability of the wall ahead. The sheer impossibility of prising my body off the railway track of time that was transporting me inexorably towards that wall. The wall's infinite breadth. Its infinite height. Its infinite depth as the bricks stretched down and down beneath the ground. No skill that I could ever learn to scale it. No feint by which to outflank it. No conceivable cunning that would allow me to burrow underneath. That's what it means to be human, I thought. It is to be an animal for whom the cost of living is death.

It was partly with the aim of stamping out such fires of terror that I had embarked on the Freud book. Insofar as the process of writing situated my mortality within an intellectual frame, that aim was met. It enabled me to look upon death with one degree more detachment. That helped a little, but why no more than one degree? Because a frame is but a frame. Even if it does help us comprehend the intractable matter under discussion, a frame holds that matter in place. That is, situating my fear of death within an intellectual frame helped me to understand it better, but like a museum cabinet the frame also gave that fear a permanence. Behind the glass the death animal still quickened, an undying mess of blood and fur. Thanks to the book, I might have been able to see death more clearly, to observe its body pulsing, but still I lacked the tools to dispatch it.

Was it my love of life that made me so scared of losing it? I did indeed love life. It follows that the answer is yes. Indisputably my love of life was the cause of my fear of death. Not that that is unusual. For is anything more worthy of love than life itself? Where death makes nothing possible, life makes possibility itself possible. And how can we not love possibility? Life is the genius of opening, and love is nothing if not expansive. There is a natural affinity between the two. Perhaps speaking about the mere love *of* life doesn't go far enough. Perhaps the very point of love is to allow life to flow more fluently. Love is life's principal canal, and our job as humans is to keep it unclogged. Being life's agents, we should be scraping away the build-up of ego and resentment that so insidiously causes the tunnel of love to narrow, restricting the flow of life.

All well and good. Yet if I was scared of losing this life that I allegedly loved, I must answer for the opposing fact that I had long entertained fantasies of suicide. My love of life was matched by a love of death. Starting in my twenties, I would routinely survey the options for self-murder: pills, razor blades, guns, hanging, drowning and jumping. The contradiction ran deep, like a crevasse. On the one side, I was petrified of dying. The abhorrence of nothingness gripped me. On the other side, I was taken up with the technologies of surcease.

The closest that I came would be during my marriage to Helen, though I didn't feel I could tell her. I approached Dignitas, the Swiss organisation that specialises, as its name suggests, in 'dying with dignity'. Its core business is assisted suicide. Meta-phorically speaking, Dignitas polishes the ramp that leads to the underworld, then nudges its clients gently over the rim so that they slide down in a beatific glissando. Theirs is the art of what Keats called 'easeful death'.

It sounded so effortless. Effortlessness was important because the research I had done showed that, for the most part, suicide is no easy business. Though an ever-present possibility, a good suicide takes planning. It is a murder, after all. Guaranteeing a smooth operation is harder than one might imagine. For you can't kill yourself without killing your body. That is, you can't kill your *self* without killing your body. It was my self that I wanted to do away with; I had little against my body. But the body had to be killed in order to kill the self. And that was a challenge. Hang-ing can leave you only half dead; an overdose can cause terrible pangs before the end comes, if come it does; and obtaining a gun, at least in the UK, is no piece of cake. Jumping from a great height enjoyed the best success rate, but to me it wasn't instant enough. One had to endure the fall. Not to mention any pain upon impact. Painlessness was key.

That is why I approached Dignitas. Their USP was lethal injec-tion. The needles pump the body with rocket fuel that propels it to Lethe in the twinkling of an eye. I emailed saying, *Please tell me if you provide your services to individuals suffering from depression.* They emailed back the next day. The subject line contained the single word, *Information.* That word both reassured me with its discretion and frightened me with its detachment. No surprises there: mixing human warmth with clinical coldness, itself a lethal combination, was their forte. The Information informed me that no, I could not be considered. The reason? Depression didn't count as a terminal illness. Here is their reply in full:

Dear Mr. Smith

Thank you for your e-mail.

We sadly confirm the receipt of your inquiry, which we truly understand as well as we understand why you are struggling with your difficult situation.

Unfortunately Dignitas is unable to help healthy people or people with a mental illness or psychological problems. Whilst it is legal for Dignitas (and for the other right-to-die associations in Switzerland) to help people suffering from such ailments, we are unable to help because there is no Swiss physician cooperating with our association who would be ready to assess such requests and possibly grant the 'green light'. Furthermore, the Swiss association of psychiatrists advised their members not to support their patients or right-to-die associations in any way if they see that the aim is to prepare an accompanied suicide. Also, there are some uncertainties in the Swiss law which lead to several court cases which are up for decision.

We are working on the issue as our association is fighting for the freedom of choice – no matter what the illness may be. However, this takes some time as our resources are very limited and support for our association is small.

Yours sincerely

Dignitas

Just as with a common-or-garden rejection letter, my reaction to this ultra-rare variety was wanting to mount a challenge. How, philosophically speaking, can one, as an adult, be debarred from the prosecution of one's own death? Since I could at any point have jumped off a building, by what authority had this suzerain veto asserted itself?

I had described my condition as 'depression' because that term had the medical credibility for which I believed Dignitas would be looking. It missed the mark, as depression was categorised as 'psychological' and therefore invalid. But nor was depression the right word for what I felt. What drove me into such bleak corners was less depression than inconsolable disappointment. Disappointment that my love of life was so infrequently requited. That the moments of adrenalin in which life loved me as much as I loved it were so rare. That so much of life was humdrum. When you have experienced exhilaration, how can you settle for existence? Life was insufficiently lively.

I look up, I look down

The refrain 'I look up, I look down' refers to Jimmy Stewart's character, Scottie, in Alfred Hitchcock's *Vertigo*. Scottie is a San Francisco policeman. He is forced to go on sick leave after a rooftop chase with a fellow cop whom Scottie witnesses slipping to his death. The event leaves Scottie with an intense fear of heights. Scottie's female companion encourages him to overcome his phobia by walking up and down a stepladder in her apartment. He is supposed to 'face his fear'. Unfortunately, facing his fear leads Scottie to experience it all over again.

It was in vertigo that the contradiction between my terror of death and my attraction to it took its most demonstrable form. As for many a sufferer from vertigo, mine was not exactly the fear of heights. Whenever I found myself looking out from a tall building, or standing on a high bridge, or driving along a road with a sheer drop, the overwhelming feeling was rather that of *temptation*. I was tempted to fling myself off. Any fear that I had was of my impulse to do just that. Vertigo meant that I ran towards and away from death simultaneously, like a half-broken wind-up toy bound in a juddering dance.

Contrary to Freud's hypothesis, my death-drive was not directed at finding peace. Quite the reverse. What more dramatic gesture could there be than to step out into thin air with no parachute? It was the absoluteness of the thrill, the dare, the risk that enraptured me. Not inertia but adrenalin. To the extent that I was afraid, I was afraid that I lacked the strength to curb my desire for such an unsurpassable rush. What terrified me was that the diabolical frisson of abandon would win out over the angelic instinct to protect myself. For the achingly slow seconds during which the outcome of that struggle remained in the balance, and I was watching from the sidelines, I would feel nauseous and giddy.

Needless to say, the angel always saved me. She swooped and held me back each time I was about to jump. She would arrive at less dramatic moments too, not just when I was at the edge of a precipice. I mean times when I was sitting alone, stewing over my problems and unable to see a way out. She would land on the roof tiles with a soft thud, brush through the window and settle behind me. Once installed, she would make of her wings a canopy to stop the shower of self-destructive thoughts from clattering on my mind.

Two white lines

It was that yearning for exhilaration which made me so ready to leap into the arms of cocaine. The New Year's party at Emily's father's house was when I was first invited to sample the drug. In an adult version of wink murder, nods and whispers were exchanged among a select few of the guests to the effect that someone had in their possession a wrap or two of the 'naughty salt'. One by one, the designated partakers would slip out from the living room only to reappear a few minutes later as if having gone for an innocent pee. Their reappearance served as a signal for the next insider to go up.

When it came to my turn, I excused myself politely from the conversation in which I was engaged. I made my way up the spiral staircase to the appointed bathroom. I knocked gingerly on the door like a member of the French Resistance gaining admission to a clandestine meeting.

There were two officiates presiding over the ceremony. Knowing that this was my initiation, they answered my questions with a mixture of encouragement and condescension. Those questions came from the nerves that so tingled at this new threshold. Apart from one or two tokes on a spliff that I had taken as an undergraduate – tokes that had made me feel sick – I had never consumed an illegal drug up to that point. It wasn't just the illicit nature of the activity that made me pause. It was the warnings about cardiac arrest. Would ingesting cocaine induce a heart attack? I had no reason for believing that I suffered from a weak heart, but nor did I feel like playing Russian roulette in order to find out.

Given that I was now tapping on the bathroom door, I must have made my decision. Curiosity killed the doubt. The officiates bowed over the preparations as over a debased Eucharist. One tipped the white powder onto the surface of a handheld mirror, making a hillock, then chopped it up with a credit card. When the hillock had been flattened and elongated into a narrow ridge, the other placed to one side of it a ten-pound note rolled into a tube. This would serve as the drug's pipeline into my nostrils. I knelt and bowed my head.

What struck me first was the acridity. Whether owing to its active ingredient or the cement and battery acid used to bulk it up, the powder caused a smarting of the soft palate. Cocaine was indeed a chemical – as though it could have been anything else. This was not sugar and spice, and it wasn't very nice. It was nasty, even if it had been manufactured for earthly delight. We the human race had tumbled a long way from the Garden of Eden.

But after a few minutes the grains of white powder spread out like a thousand Storm Troopers from *Star Wars*. They swarmed into the vein tunnels, firing their weapons and hitting the pleasure sensors over and over. Or, to speak non-galactically, the difference between before and after snorting the line was like plodding up a mountainside only for a mighty gust of wind to spring up behind and carry me bodily to the summit in one unbroken sweep. At the top I felt like a superhero from the novels of Ayn Rand. Into my being there flooded a delicious mixture of exertion and ease, of actual and potential energy. In explaining the notion of confidence, Friedrich Nietzsche, Rand's chief creditor, speaks of 'a continual feeling that one is climbing stairs and at the same time resting on clouds'. For what I was now feeling, Nietzsche's description was spot on. Cocaine is chemical confidence. It told me that I was brilliant in every way. My heart pounded in delight.

It would be false to say that I became addicted. Yet it would be true to say that I found it impossible to stop at one line. At the minimum, I would vacuum up half a dozen of the frail white trails. But that's not unusual. And I restricted my usage to weekends. In this, I was merely following the habits of the metropolitan liberal elite whose dinner parties would conclude after the cheese course with a convivial round or so of charlie.

More concerning, perhaps, was the space that the drug colonised in my mind. Where I might not have been overly using cocaine, I was overly thinking about it. That is part of its power. It's not the body alone that cocaine keeps on a tether, yanking that body back to the bathroom every thirty minutes or so for another zap. It is also the mind. Cocaine converts the mind into a snow-dome, its softly floating flakes creating a scene so much more bewitching than everyday life.

The concomitant anxiety was that the snow would stop falling. For the first few months, I was reliant on the person at the party to supply me from his supplier – who was supplied in turn from his supplier, and so on, in a canon of percentage deductions that mounted back to Colombia as to the top of a spreadsheet. 'If only there were Fairtrade coke!' was the standard quip at those dinner parties. But as my preoccupation with cocaine increased, I would blench at seeing my need reflected in my seller's eyes. Some disintermediation was called for. I got my supplier's supplier's number.

To limit my traceability, I dialled from a phone box. But that was the beginning and end of my savvy. How was the request to be phrased? It wasn't going to be like ordering my organic vegetable box.

'Hi, I was given your number by X.'

'Oh, right, cool,' said a soft Irish accent.

Pause.

'I'd like to come to the same arrangement with you, please.' It appeared that at times of nervousness, what surfaced in me was public schoolboy formality. Perfect for the first interaction with a drug dealer.

Another pause.

'Yeh, sorry, sure. I'm in a faraway place, if you know what I mean.' I didn't know what he meant.

'Cool,' I said, changing my persona to suit.

'Okay, so two white lines, right?'

Well no, I thought. Two lines aren't going to be enough. Oh, he means grams. But if you're going to use a euphemism or a metaphor (which was it?) to limit traceability, then why not use a euphemism or metaphor that is discernibly different from the word or words that it replaces? I decided that this must be a use of synecdoche on the pusher's part. Synecdoche is the trope by which the part stands for the whole: *pars pro totis* in classical rhetoric. The schoolbook example is that of a shark's fin. From the visible fin (part), we infer the invisible body (whole). Thus from the citing of 'two white lines' I was to deduce two whole grams. Such is the gratuitous mentation involved in the purchase of illicit drugs by an Oxford English don.

'Right,' I confirmed.

I was to meet him upstairs at a coffee shop in the West End. Upstairs because there was no CCTV. His Irish accent on the phone had led me to expect a man of Celtic appearance, but he was black as ebony. As he sat down, he produced from his back-pack an A4 manila envelope. Quite loudly, as if wanting to be overheard, he announced, 'Here's your mail!' So that was the ruse: we were flatmates and he was bringing me my post. I thanked him, matching his loudness and method-acting my way into the role. I assumed he would leave as soon as I'd settled my debt, but no. To make the flatmate conceit properly plausible, we had to soldier on and have coffee. And so we performed our wooden playlet for about twenty minutes. Twenty minutes during which I itched to get away from the incriminating company of a drug dealer.

Whenever I ran out, I had to go back. And so, like ageing actors on an interminable West End run, we were obliged to keep churning through our performance. It was not least because of the tedium of these encounters that I restricted their frequency. Apart from once, I kept my consumption to a level that would be described as 'recreational'. I'd never use cocaine on a school night. The insomnia would have been ruinous. The exception was my stag do, in the lead-up to the wedding with Helen, a couple of years later. Of course, there's nothing original about doing coke on a stag. What was unusual was the quantity I consumed. It was double my usual dose. This time, it took nearer three days than the usual one day to recover. There were longueurs of sleepless-ness, teeth-grinding and tears. But once the comedown was over, I felt normal. That was that, I thought.

In the mountains, there you feel free

A week later, I found myself in the mountain ranges of the Picos de Europa in northern Spain. Helen and I were on honeymoon. In the opening stanza of T. S. Eliot's *The Waste Land*, there is a line that goes, 'In the mountains, there you feel free'. For me with my vertigo, mine was the freedom to jettison myself from the mountainsides into nothingness. As I drove the rented Opel Corsa around bends that looped, rope-like, over the granite heads, my foot would quiver malignantly on the gas pedal. I knew I had to surrender the driving to Helen. Once in the passenger seat, I'd close my eyes and lean inwards, away from the abyss that pulled me so magnetically towards it.

After one such outing, I arrived back at the chalet feeling dis-combobulated. When it came to bedtime, I looked upon the horizontal of the mattress as a relief from all the mountain ver-ticals, somewhat as a sailor might embrace dry land. But in the darkest reaches of the night, I sprang upright in bed, gasped and blacked out. When I came to, I knew that my heart had stopped. I stayed awake the whole night, terrified of falling back to sleep, with Helen reading Dickens of all things to distract me.

On our return from the mountains, I went for tests. The first doctor instructed me to strap an ECG around my chest for twenty-four hours. It showed an irregular heartbeat and persuaded him to recommend a pacemaker forthwith. I had not confessed to him the marching powder binge. As the drug can create effects for several weeks after ingestion, like aftershocks following an earthquake, I had wondered whether it was the cause of my vital blip. What if the readout from the ECG was simply a delayed reaction to the cocaine? I used my secret knowledge to resist the pacemaker suggestion. I asked for a second opinion.

The tests this time were fancier. I had a fine wire inserted through my groin and up into the heart. The wire was connected to a motor capable of speeding my heart up and slowing it down, like a throttle. The procedure itself made my heart quicken out of anxiety, so I had to be sedated. That is, my mind had to be shut down so that my heart could be put through its paces. So I lay there asleep at the wheel, so to speak, as my heart was driven by a passenger in a white coat.

The conclusion was twofold. Yes, I had a somewhat irregular heartbeat. The more worrying finding was that my resting heart rate was so low. At night, when I was asleep, that heartbeat slowed to a periodic boom, like a far-off drum in a jungle. At altitudes where the oxygen thinned out, it could drop to inertia. The condition was known as 'athletic heart', words that disguised the curse as a blessing. The heart has a series of electrical triggers that kick in if it fails, like a back-up generator. As if agents of the Freudian death-drive, athletic hearts are too languid even to activate the back-up. That inertia is what they court. The condition particularly afflicts cyclists because of their exceptional fitness. Indeed, cases of night-time death among the hardcore cycling community are disproportionately high. I was no athlete, but I shared the same condition. A rarity in general practice, the doctor's advice was to exercise *less*.

The question of whether the after-effects of cocaine had been a factor in my mountain blackout was to remain unanswered. I tend to think that they were. Either way, I was rattled. I scaled back my consumption of the narcotic accordingly. The final nail in the coffin of my dalliance with cocaine was the law. Some months later I was hurrying through St Pancras station with two white lines in my pocket. Up ahead, beyond the passengers at the Eurostar terminal, I glimpsed a pack of sniffer dogs patrolling the concourse. I swivelled on my heels and walked briskly towards the exit. In my snow-dome reverie with cocaine, I had lost touch with the brute fact that being caught in possession of Class A drugs could lead to prosecution. Those dogs served as a reminder. I would never contact my 'flatmate' again.

The animus cake

I say that I was no athlete, and so much is true. And yet during the period in question, the early to mid 2000s, my routine involved cycling to Burton Harcourt's offices every morning for thirty minutes; dropping off my bike; walking to the gym for an hour's workout; putting in a long stint at work; and cycling back home again. A good two hours of physical exertion daily. I was also at the gym on weekends. This being before the doctor's tests, I had no idea that I was making my athletic heart the more athletic, thereby jeopardising rather than improving my health.

The point is not that the regime was *excessive*: it was *obsessive*. Each element had to be ticked off without deviation: each rep on the pec deck; each kilometre on the treadmill; each stretch on the mat. Omitting any one of them put me out of sorts. And why? There was, to begin with, the doughy feeling of under-extension that bothers any regular gym-goer. I would also miss the endorphin release that only a full workout could deliver. It provided a semi-orgasmic reward that represented an addictive hit of its own.

But the greatest cause of my perturbation was the incompleteness itself. In other words, what distressed me about failing to complete the full routine was the sheer failing to complete it. It meant that I had left an imperfection in a perfect design. That had nothing to do with physical exercise. My vexation was abstract, formal, aesthetic, totalising; and perhaps therefore a little fascistic. It didn't matter that the exercise routine I had prescribed for myself was arbitrary – thirty minutes' cardio, twenty minutes' resistance training, ten minutes of stretching. Once the blueprint was dyed into my mind, that routine needed to be adhered to. Even a minor falling-short invalidated the whole. Ninety per cent was as good as nought.

As for many obsessive exercisers, my regimen was more akin to self-harm than to self-care. It was as punitive as if I had become a sergeant major to myself, sadistically insisting on autotelic and debasing activities for the troops. Certain people will speak of 'getting out their frustration at the gym', and no doubt that is the outcome they achieve. Exercise, for them, functions as a purge of negative feelings. But for a different, smaller group, it works the other way round. Repetitive exercise hammers the negativity further inside, compacting it into a dense, resinous and flammable cake of animus. It was to this second group that I belonged.

The obsession extended to my bodyweight. After showering at the gym but before breakfast, such being the moment in the day when I calculated that I would be at my lightest, I would step onto the scales. I would peer down at the gauge between my feet. If the dial flickered by a hair's breadth to the right of twelve stone, my day was spoiled. Needless to say, the figure of 'twelve stone' was no less arbitrary than the structure of my workout. But once I had set twelve as a target, it stood as my absolute. The arbitrary became the arbitrator, the judge not just of my weight but of my worth. Exceeding twelve stone meant that I had failed.

The absolute did have permission to move to the left, however. Less than twelve stone was allowed. Indeed there had been a few periods previous to the 2000s when my weight had dropped to nearer ten. For somebody like me, six feet two inches in height, ten stone in weight nets out into a particularly narrow silhouette. There is a photo of me taken by Simone, on a hotel balcony in Paris in 1986, that shocks me to this day. I look like a spider, so narrow is the waist, so ethereally long the limbs, so blow-away the frame.

That was the period when I had dropped out of Oxford and was living in the box room at my parents'. It was soon after my father had been sacked and was shuffling around at home in the no man's land between un- and under-employment. I have speculated in earlier chapters about whether, out of misguided loyalty, I was mirroring his demise. Adding to that speculation now seems apposite, for not only did I bail out of my degree, I almost stopped eating. I'd take a brown bag with fruit in it for lunch to the summer job where I met Simone; and that was my sustenance for the day. Had I not moved to be with her in France with its abundance of cheese, bread and wine, I might have withered away. Besides, Simone and I were about to become parents. The focus would shift from starving myself to nourishing our baby.

Adamantine™ and the chronic emergency

By the mid 2000s, which is the timeframe of this chapter, that baby, Anna, born in 1987, was a teenager. She was engaged with the world, had good friends, looked attractive, enjoyed her hobbies and was achieving excellent grades. At parents' evenings her teachers cooed over her abilities. As her father, I was proud as Punch.

On the August bank holiday of 2002, I took Anna to the

Notting Hill Carnival. We slipped blithely enough into the maelstrom: the throng of people, the throb of reggae from sound systems, the passing floats, the smoke from barbecues, the Technicolor costumes and the grassy smell of skunk. And as we strolled we ate: salmon and dill sandwiches that I'd picked up en route. But long after I had finished my sandwich, Anna was still holding hers. Amid the hubbub it was hard for me to see, but she seemed to be picking tiny pieces of bread from one of the slices as if delousing it. She rolled each piece between her forefinger and thumb, then let it drop to the ground. I saw her do the same with the salmon. Had it not been so crowded, one would have seen a trail of crumbs stretching for yards behind.

I decided to challenge her. 'I'm eating it!' protested Anna the first time. 'I'm not that hungry,' she parried the second. Did those two responses not contradict each other? After another ten minutes, the depleted sandwich still in her hand, I let my irritation show. 'Eat the bloody sandwich!'

'Dad!' she retorted angrily. My irritation had merely justified her obstinacy. I was silenced.

The showing of my irritation was equally the hiding of an emotion with a far darker hue. For down in the lightless bottom of an inner well of knowing, there lay a problem. Anna's growing aversion to eating was abnormal. There were contextual factors. She was a teenager undergoing her hormonal metamorphosis. She was at a single-sex school where the competition was as much about looks as books. And yet. So were all the other teenage girls teenage girls; and so were all the other girls at the girls' school girls at the girls' school. None of them was affected. The 'contextual factors' were simply that: they provided no explanation. What my irritation hid was dread.

A few weeks later, on my way to meet Anna before a concert, I saw her double heading straight towards me. This other Anna wasn't an exact lookalike. She was at least a decade older, in her mid to late twenties. Her hair was more finely spun, her eyes set in silver-grey saucers of fatigue. The stylish jeans that she wore stood loose from the waist. The skin over her cheekbones shone taut and limpid as if to illuminate the skull beneath. The strap of her shoulder bag was kept in place by a scapula jutting upwards like a flint.

The doppelgänger did not, however, swerve to one side of the pavement as she approached. It seemed that her business was with me. *A messenger of sorts?* I wondered nervously when she came within spitting distance. All at once I realised that this was no double but Anna herself. That feeling of dread soughed in its well like steaming bitumen. This was Anna as creature of the grave. She had sent her vaporous body up through a drain on the road in order to pay a visit from the underworld.

Thus began what might be termed a chronic emergency. It was an emergency insofar as the trajectory of anorexia is sufficiently life-threatening to induce panic. On the other hand, anorexia is not a condition for which one can dial an ambulance. It is more chronic than acute. With no option to use first aid, all we had to work with was words. Unfortunately, pleading with Anna to eat was futile. Reasoning with her was futile too. As was threatening her, comforting her, cajoling her, admonishing her and reassuring her; not to mention the scores of other rhetorical strategies that from time to time we deployed. The words failed.

They failed because words are weaker than the will. Medical definitions notwithstanding, a modality of the will is what anorexia fundamentally is. The specific will of the anorexic manifests as the refusing of food, but arguably the food-refusing comes second to the will *per se*. In literature, the word 'will' is often qualified as 'adamantine'. That adjective refers to an artificial substance developed by The Celluloid Manufacturing Company of New

York City, and patented in 1880. 'Adamantine' alludes, however, to the natural stone of diamond. That was precisely the character of the anorexic Anna's will: the universe contained no material harder than it.

The doctor's orders were to take Anna out of school and install her at a specialist clinic. There, though steeped in the arcana of *anorexia nervosa*, the staff had learned that such sophistication was of limited value. They too had experienced the feebleness of words in the fight against the will. Yes, there were talking cures in the form of counselling groups and individual therapy sessions, but such activities were very much complementary. The core methodology was blunt: forcing the patient to eat. Confronted with a human being who is literally starving themselves to death, nothing else held as much weight (pun intended). And so a nurse would sit in front of Anna during her meals, to make sure that the food went into Anna's mouth and nowhere else. After the meal, Anna was accompanied to the bathroom to inhibit any self-induced vomiting. When it came to the daily weigh-in, Anna was kept under watch for the hour beforehand so that she didn't artificially add a kilo by gulping down water.

It took many months to pull Anna back from the brink, but back from the brink she was pulled. She returned to school and resumed her studies. And yet 'coming back from the brink' and 'getting back to normal' are two different things. It would take several years before the anorexia fully released its grip.

Two important phrases: 'Release its grip' and 'I will live'

The phrase 'release its grip' is barely less hackneyed than 'adamantine will'. The reason for using it is that it relates to one of two ways in which I made sense of Anna's eating disorder. According to the first, you distinguish between the patient and the illness. Anna didn't need to be identified with the anorexia besetting her. But that was easier said than done. For when observing what is effectively a walking skeleton, one cannot help but think:

I am looking at an anorexic.

Yet an alternative interpretation does exist. One can choose instead to think the following:

I am looking at somebody who for now happens to be suffering from anorexia.

I recognise that that could seem like a distinction without a difference. Yet at the time the distinction helped. The therapist at the clinic encouraged us to construe the anorexia as a separate creature squatting on Anna's shoulder that had temporarily taken control of her. I pictured that creature as a psychotic crow with its beak tilted towards her head. A frenzied despot trembling with power and rage, the crow would croak ear-splitting instructions at Anna not to eat. If there was a softening – even by an iota – of Anna's resistance to food, the crow would dig its talons into her flesh. That is why for me the otherwise washed-out image of 'releasing its grip' maintained some colour. If we could just get Anna to see that it wasn't her but some maleficent djinn who was directing her behaviour, then maybe she would reject it. If she could be disabused of the idea that it was her will which was regulating the intake of food, maybe she would desist. Anna's true will, the force which that djinn was attempting to strangle, was the will to live.

The phrase 'will to live' provides the segue into the second way of making sense of Anna's anorexia. To state the blindingly obvious, Anna was my daughter and I was her father. As such, the biological link between us could not be gainsaid. Yet 'biological' might be too narrow a way of putting it. Derived as it is from the Greek for life, *bios*, the word marginalises the importance of death in the study of animate creatures. For there is no life without death. Life begins on the condition that it ends. Instead of 'biology' we ought to say 'bio-thanato-logy', the study of life and death combined.

What I'm driving at is that I was connected to Anna as much by death as by life. For a start, the death of the parent is implicit in the birth of any child. The baby's arrival signals that the species has put in place its continuance, and in that teleological sense the parent has served their purpose. What's more, parents and their children are by definition of different generations, which positions the parents nearer to death in time. Patently some parents survive their offspring, but in generational terms that represents an aberration. The natural law stipulates that the older generation should die first.

One side effect of that generational turnover is that it lays down in the child's mind a constitutive anxiety. For children know, as a rule, that they will live to see their parents die. And whilst that knowledge is unlikely to cause them to feel anxious in any conscious or quotidian way, it remains fundamental to a child's relationship to their parents. Hence calling it 'constitutive'.

Anna was no less a carrier of such a constitutive anxiety than any other child. What made her case special was that her own father had leanings towards suicide. That is, her constitutive anxiety about her father's death would have been augmented by the fact that the father was preoccupied with bringing his own death forward. (I phrase it as 'bringing his own death forward' because, given that we are all going to die anyway, suicide can be seen as a variety of impatience.) Anna's father's interest in accelerating his inevitable death could only have ratcheted her anxiety up.

But was Anna *actually* anxious about my death? If so, did it *actually* have a bearing on her anorexia?

During the phase of the anorexia when Anna's life was most at risk, and none of those complementary techniques was producing any noticeable effect, I turned to an alternative source of help. Desperate times called for desperate measures. I enrolled for a workshop in 'Systemic Family Constellations', or 'Constellations' for short. The workshop beamed a bright light on Anna's anorexia.

The light revealed that Anna's illness and my suicidal tendencies were indeed connected. Both, after all, were attempts at self-erasure. However, that last sentence makes the connection sound like happenstance, which it was not. Anna didn't just *happen* to be embarked upon a drawn-out suicide attempt at the same time that her father was considering taking his own life. Nor was she simply mimicking him. Rather, the Constellations process suggested that Anna was offering up her own life so that her father wouldn't have to forfeit his.

So yes, the constitutive anxiety borne by children concerning the death of their parents was heightened in Anna's case by the fact that I, her father, was ruminating on bringing my own death forward. But what really counted was the sacrificial nature of Anna's response to that elevated anxiety. Out of love and loyalty, Anna was trying to step into my place. That was the ultimate aim of her starvation. Anna was silently saying:

Rather me than you.

Such was the diagnosis of Anna's anorexia offered by the Constellations process. Indeed, in Constellations theory, the limitless but misplaced loyalty of children to their parents is a pivotal theme. But if that was the diagnosis, what was the cure? How to confiscate from Anna the fantasy that her death could save me?

The answer was disarmingly logical. If the root cause of Anna's attempt to hasten her death was her father's desire to hasten his own, then conquering the father's suicidal desires was the key. The person who would have to make the change was not Anna but me. I had to turn away from death and look back towards life. The facilitator of the Constellations workshop gave me the following mantra to repeat:

I will live.

It might have been sheer coincidence, but it was from roughly the point at which I started reciting that phrase to myself that the crow on Anna's shoulder began to release its grip.

Kindertotenlieder

Whilst still an undergraduate at Oxford, before becoming a father, I had a friend who introduced me to the music of Gustav Mahler. Other than *Das Lied von der Erde,* I didn't especially take to it. Then I heard Mahler's *Kindertotenlieder,* and my mild dislike curdled into superstitious avoidance. The German title translates as *Songs on the Death of Children.* It was to the title rather than the music that I reacted. I couldn't bear the image of children dying. I pictured a charnel house of tender, pellucid limbs. It was appalling. That the intent of Mahler's score was elegiac made no odds. To compose a suite of songs about something so terrible was too much. He had shoved into focus a monstrosity that ought to have been left untouched.

Soon after, I did become a father. In 1987 Anna's life began.

Many years later, in 2002, when Anna became anorexic, that life was saved. And yet I hadn't been entirely free from the death of children. I had also, at one point in my life, been the co-author of a conception that was aborted.

There are two ways in which I do *not* plan to talk about the termination, as they both fall outside the philosophical scope of this book. First, the whys and wherefores of the decision to end the pregnancy. Suffice it to say that making such a decision was as heart-wrenching for the two parties involved as it would be for anybody. Second, the politics of abortion. The various opinions on the subject are routinely rehearsed and can do without another airing here.

To say that barely a day goes by when I don't think about my unborn child would be a gross exaggeration. And yet I do think about him or her every few months. I'm obliged to use the laborious construction 'him or her' because I never knew the gender of the foetus. Yet he or she would have been a he or a she, rather than the neutral entity that the word 'foetus' suggests.

In fact, I wonder whether not knowing the gender is itself a reason why he or she continues to fidget on a ledge in my mind. Whenever I think about him or her, I think about whether he or she was male or female. The question remains unclosed and indeed unclose-able, not unlike a coroner's report that records an open verdict. I have to be content with not knowing, even as the not knowing is what stops me from being content.

What I am implying is that to have the question of gender settled would help to settle my memory more generally. But is that truly what I want? After all, the 'settling of my memory' is a circumlocution for forgetting. I'm arguing that if I knew the gender of the foetus, my memory would be less disturbed, making it easier to forget. Candidly, I'm not sure my conscience could live with that. Indeed I have made an unconscious choice in kind. To spell it out: the unsettled feeling that comes of not knowing the gender remains preferable to the guilt of being the father who forgets the foetus whose prospect of life he had a part in shutting down. It is the lesser of two evils.

Not that forgetting is such a crime. It is possible that the dead *want* to be forgotten. I say 'the dead' in relation to the foetus fully aware that the epithet 'dead' can apply only to an entity that has enjoyed life. In the case of a foetus that claim is questionable. And yet if the foetus hadn't been alive, he or she would not need to have been aborted. Ergo I can speak of my unborn child as having died despite never having lived. Paradoxical but true. The larger point being that the dead creature might feel no need for me to keep him or her alive in my memory. What help is it? Perhaps my unwillingness to forget my unborn child is as much about my need to posit myself as a good person as any disinterested act of mourning. By keeping him or her alive in my mind I am distracting myself from my role in bringing that 'life' to an end. Perhaps forgetting, unriddled with my ego, would be the saintlier course.

The invention of zero

The further ambiguity concerns the number of children that I have had. The title of an earlier chapter in this book is 'The Dream of Three Daughters'. That phrase is based on the fact that I had two daughters with Simone and one, later, with Helen, after we were married. Two plus one makes three. About that chapter heading there is nothing deceitful. And yet in doing the arithmetic I'm aware of a missing element in the form of the unborn child. There is a zero that is weightless and yet has a presence. Instead of 'two plus one makes three', the more faithful formula would be expressed as:

$$2 + 1 + 0 = 3$$

Different data, same result. The unborn child is a zero but not nothing. That doesn't change the fact that I am the father of three children, but to that fact the zero adds resonance. Metaphorically speaking, it is the same three-note chord played on a piano, but now with the foot pressing on the sustain pedal.

It was medieval Arab scholars who invented the concept of zero as a device for facilitating number theory. Little could they foresee the uses to which their concept would later be put. For the zero counts; and moreover Constellations theory agrees. That theory calls on us to remember not only the children born to us but the total number of conceptions. The zeroes have their place in the working out. Partly, that is to honour the past. We also spare ourselves thereby from the hidden costs of exclusion. When we fail to give a place in our heart to all members of our relationship system, somebody somewhere will suffer.

Constellations theory also asserts that couples who have a termination will struggle to stay together. The premise being that the love between a couple peaks with the birth of their first child. From that premise it follows that interceding against a first birth puts a cap on the love between the parents. Even in a hypothetical situation where a first birth that has been fore-stalled is 'redeemed' by a later birth that is allowed, both partners will carry the memory of the first. Because it produces a dreadful intimacy, at once close and sickening, the sharing of the decision to abort is analogous to co-committing a crime. The knowledge of the other person's act, combined with the knowledge of the other person's knowledge of one's own act, is terrible to bear. That reciprocal knowledge generates a high-temperature bonding that anneals the souls of the two 'perpetrators'. At the same time, the shared knowledge of their act sends both parties bounding away into different landscapes to hide among the hills.

> . . . the total emptiness for ever,
> The sure extinction that we travel to
> And shall be lost in always. Not to be here,
> Not to be anywhere,
> And soon; nothing more terrible, nothing more true.
>
> Philip Larkin

8

The Forms of Things Unknown

The true sign of intelligence is not knowledge
but imagination.

Albert Einstein

Somewhat like a riddle, the question 'What does it mean to be a human being?' contains a clue to its own answer. According to my dictionary, the adjective 'human' yields the following cognates: 'fallible', 'weak', 'frail', 'imperfect', 'vulnerable', 'susceptible', 'erring', 'error-prone'. The phrase 'all too human' also crops up. Whatever it means to be human, it seems, it is to have limits.

Planets of knowledge

One of those limits provided the theme for the last chapter. Namely, the limit imposed on us by the allied conditions of having a body and being in time. Those two conditions braid together to form our mortal coil. But while death marks the ultimate limit, it is not unique to humans. All creatures great and small find themselves curbed by it. So what limit might be more exclusively human?

A possible candidate is our capacity for knowledge. But perhaps that's an odd one to pick. After all, we as a species seem markedly eager to extend the demesne of what we know. We have explored, traded, experimented and studied; and in the process have discovered ever more about how the world works. With the emergence first of anatomy and later of psychology and neuroscience, we have also probed within ourselves. The sum of that knowledge, both outer and inner, is prodigious. All the signs point to its increasing.

Where, then, does the limit come in? If what we know is ever-expanding, how, in respect of our knowledge, are we limited? The answer lies in changing that 'we' to an 'I'. Whilst as a species we have colonised extensive land masses of the unknown, as individuals our conquests remain modest. So modest that it might be fairer to say that our ignorance, at an individual level, is vast. Each one of us would struggle to absorb a fraction of the knowledge that we have accumulated collectively. The world's leading experts will humbly attest that they don't know everything to be known even within their own discipline. They will be humbler still regarding subject areas in which they have no expertise. That being the case for experts, what chance is there for the rest of us? Nobody is omniscient, and the majority of us know very little indeed. Moreover, the fabric of our knowledge is continuously eaten by the forgetting-moths in our mind. That said, if we remembered everything we'd be paralysed. A certain amount of forgetting is a precondition for acting.

For us as individuals, the scale of the unknown is to the known as the Pacific Ocean is to our bathtub. The difference is huge. The ratio of the one to the other can also be pictured as planets. I offer the following non-scientific diagram to illustrate. In the diagram, the planet marked 'What I know' is smaller than 'What we know',

WHAT I KNOW   WHAT WE KNOW   THE UNKNOWN   THE UNKNOWABLE

which is smaller than 'The unknown', which is smaller still than 'The unknowable', the latter being the most sizeable planet of all. Needless to say, the planets are not to scale (as if they could be). Nor are they static. On current trends, the circumference of 'What we know' should expand as 'The unknown' contracts. For as we learn more about the world around and within us, what there remains to know will shrink. That assumes that the unknown is finite, however, which might not be the case. The unknown could continue to widen. Take the fact that as time passes, history piles up. There will be ever more for us not to know, and ever more to forget.

Then there is the unknowable. By definition, it is that which we cannot know. We can't even know that it's there: the planet may not exist. Indeed to those of an empiricist cast of mind, it absolutely does not. For them, all knowledge can in principle be harvested – though it might take many an autumn to do so. As such, the concept 'unknowable' simply doesn't pass muster. To believe that there are things that can't be known speaks at best to scientific laziness. At worst, it smacks of witchcraft.

Real Imaginaries

Back in the 1990s, when still at All Souls, I had a colleague named Andrew Harvey. Technically. By the time I joined he had moved on, but one continues to be a member of the Fellowship even after leaving. So Harvey and I were 'colleagues' even though we never met.

I first came across Andrew Harvey when I was lent a book of his called *A Journey in Ladakh*. Through a friend of a friend I learned that he lived in Paris, near St-Sulpice. Harvey was part Indian, wrote poetry, wore flamboyant clothes and was said to be handsome. Those markers made for a glamorous portrait. Unbeknownst to him, I placed Andrew Harvey on my inner alcove.

By 'inner alcove' I mean that part of our mind where we stow the image, like a figurine, of people who have made an impression on us. It's a practice that often starts at school. There is a person, perhaps a year or so above, who occupies a position similar to, but not quite the same as, that of role model or hero. We don't necessarily want to be like them or to worship them. Nevertheless, they stand out to us, and we follow them from a quiet distance. When their name comes up, we hear it with a sharpened sense of interest – an interest that we are likely to disguise. We ourselves might try dropping their name into conversation – though ever so casually – to see what reaction it elicits or what further information it draws out. As to our reaction to the reaction, again we're inclined to keep mum. The secrecy is part of the pleasure. To let the secret out would be to oxidise it. Oxygen is poison to secrets.

The label I give to such precious statuettes in our inner alcove is 'Real Imaginaries'. The word 'Imaginaries' alludes to imaginary friends: Real Imaginaries are the adult equivalent. Along with their largely secret status, both Real Imaginaries and imaginary friends serve as screens upon which to beam our projections. That is, we bestow idealised attributes upon them. Sadly, the projective nature of the relationship suggests that the intimacy we feel is one-sided. No matter: we create enough intimacy for two. Thus we are soothed. And whilst imaginary friends will be fictional and disembodied, where Real Imaginaries are living people with a physical presence, the act of installing a Real Imaginary on our inner alcove alters their ontology. They become a little less mortal and a little more mythic.

For me, Andrew Harvey was a Real Imaginary. He took on that mythic quality in my head. But Harvey had a Real Imaginary of his own. Or so it seemed from his book.

Why the spirit is no spade

Andrew Harvey's *A Journey in Ladakh* is a story of spiritual awakening. So we are to take the word 'journey' in the title as both literal and metaphorical. As Harvey penetrates the remote terrain of Ladakh, hoping to study at the feet of a Buddhist master or 'Rinpoche', so his understanding deepens.

I would suggest that the Rinpoche represents for Harvey a Real Imaginary, or something close to it. The Rinpoche stands as an object of Harvey's idealisation. He has been granted some turf on the inner alcove. Furthermore, as spiritual teacher the Rinpoche already cuts a somewhat mythic figure. What is different perhaps is that rather than maintaining an admirer's stealthy distance, like a birdwatcher in a hide, Harvey steps out and makes a frontal approach to the Rinpoche's personage.

The contact between them, however, in no way dims the Rinpoche's aura. If anything it brightens it. After all, the subject matter is non-trivial: it concerns spiritual enlightenment. To an awestruck Harvey the Rinpoche dispenses the following guidance:

A man is starving in one dark room, while in another room just across the corridor from him there is enough food for many lives, for eternity. But he has to walk to that room, and before he can walk to it, he has to believe that it is there. No one else can believe for him. No one can even bring the food from that room to him. Even if they could, he would not believe in the food or be able to eat it.

With his parable of the uneaten food, the Rinpoche is effectively challenging that dictionary definition of 'human' as creature-of-limits. Or, more accurately, the Rinpoche is indicating that to be human is very much to have limits, but that those limits are self-imposed. We humans are the authors of our own constriction. And whilst that could be taken for a counsel of despair, the Rinpoche's message is rather one of hope. Since we are the ones who threw those chains upon ourselves, we are also the ones who can shimmy them off. It's down to us. The food is waiting in the other room. We just need to have faith that it's there and go help ourselves.

So much for what the Rinpoche says. No less important is the way that he says it. For the Rinpoche tends to speak in parables. In that he is not unusual: it is common guru practice. Consider the following text from the Eastern Rinpoche's Western contemporary, Eckhart Tolle:

A beggar had been sitting by the side of a road for over thirty years. One day a stranger walked by. 'Spare some change?' mumbled the beggar, mechanically holding out his baseball cap. 'I have nothing to give you,' said the stranger. Then he asked: 'What's that you are sitting on?' 'Nothing,' replied the beggar. 'Just an old box. I have been sitting on it for as long as I can remember.' 'Ever looked inside?' asked the stranger. 'No,' said the beggar. 'What's the point? There's nothing in there.' 'Have a look inside,' insisted the stranger. The beggar managed to pry open the lid. With astonishment, disbelief, and elation, he saw that the box was filled with gold.

Where the Rinpoche invites us to picture a starving man who is blind to the fact that there is a banquet laid on for him, Tolle portrays a beggar unknowingly sitting on a stash of gold. In their message, the two parables are virtually identical. If we could just let go of our limiting beliefs, spiritual abundance lies within easy reach. So easily reached is such abundance that the puzzle of enlightenment lies as much in our human predilection to shrink from it as in any numinous quality that enlightenment itself might possess.

Instead of calling a spade a spade, the Rinpoche opts, through the image of a starving man, for the parabolic style. But why communicate in this riddling manner? Assuming the Rinpoche's intention is not to obfuscate but to illuminate, should he not speak more plainly?

One reason for adopting the periphrastic approach might be that the Rinpoche is addressing a novice. There is Andrew Harvey, all agog in the master's presence, and wanting perhaps in the maturity to comprehend that which radiates before him. By describing spiritual enlightenment – which is highly abstract – with a metaphor of uneaten food – which is very concrete – the Rinpoche hopes for Harvey's sake to make the strange familiar. That way, Harvey might be able to get a firm foothold on a chalk face given to sudden rock falls. In the terms of this chapter, the Rinpoche is bridging the gap between the unknown and the known. His motive, in any case, is didactic.

A weightier reason for the Rinpoche's indirect method might be that he has no choice. Although I am insinuating that the Rinpoche could have instructed Harvey more directly, the under-lying question is whether spiritual enlightenment can *ever* be conveyed in a non-roundabout fashion. For matters of the spirit are nebulous. It's woven into the very word 'spiritual' that it is unearthly, as different from worldly matters as gas is from ground. It may be that the spiritual Thing the Rinpoche is describing is unknowable in any form other than the metaphorical or parabolic anyway.

When it comes to the spirit, it seems, calling a spade a spade isn't an option. The spirit lacks the requisite substance for empirical description. Being gaseous, it can't drum up the density. And because the spiritual Thing declines to hove into our sightline, we will at best glimpse it obliquely, using the peripheral vision afforded by metaphors. No sooner does one turn to look at the Thing full square than it vanishes like a clown.

The Thing

My reason for crowning the word 'Thing' with a capital letter is to allude to Immanuel Kant. Famously, the German philosopher argues that we can never know the 'Thing in Itself', or the *Ding an Sich* in the original. By 'Thing in Itself' Kant means the essence of reality, though using poetic licence I would stretch that to encompass reality of the spiritual kind. Enlightenment, in other words. The spiritual Thing lies beyond human knowledge and so is unknowable. As regards knowing what the spiritual Thing is, we may as well give up and go home.

Yet nor is Kant's a counsel of despair. We are not doomed to endless night. For even if we can't know it directly, an understanding of the Thing is within our grasp. That is one of Kant's subtler points. Between knowing and understanding, a difference obtains. I have attempted to express that difference visually.

In the diagram, knowledge surrounds the star-shaped Thing. The Thing has identifiable contours, yet it and knowledge are

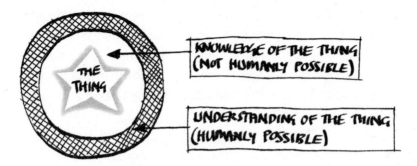

hewn from the same substance. The two are more similar than they are different. The spaceship of knowledge hovers over the Thing and sucks it up into itself until the whole glows like a lamp. Knowledge and the Thing each irradiate the other. In this apogee of knowingness, any line between perceiver and perceived lique- fies. The contours smudge.

For us humans, meanwhile, such unmediated knowledge remains out of bounds. We are confined to the periphery. The reason is that we are defined by having minds; and minds are mediators. Their very *raison d'être* is mediating the unmediated. Between us and the Thing, our minds intercede.

Not that it is all downside. Sliding in between us and the world like a lens dropped into its slot at an eye test, our minds bring that world into focus. And thank goodness that they do. Our minds translate the Thing, which is not human, into terms that are. For the Thing is like an alien species with which we cannot breed. The mind reconstitutes the Thing into an entity with valence in our world. A little gets lost in translation, but at least we gain the benefit of understanding. Most importantly, understanding is the *only* mode in which we can apprehend the Thing. For us mor- tals it's a straight choice between understanding and ignorance. Knowledge is the preserve of the gods.

So what exactly is understanding? It is precisely seeing the world through metaphors rather than knowing it directly. Understanding just is that peripheral vision. In fact, Kant explicitly says of metaphors that they provide no knowledge though they do help us to understand. They are the best that we have. They are all that we have. The Thing is not ours to know.

Meditation ≠ mediation

I was inspired by Andrew Harvey's book to take up meditation. I would sit in the lotos position for two bouts of thirty minutes a day. It wasn't just a surreptitious way of copying my Real Imaginary, of imitation-at-a-distance. There was a brace of supplementary motives.

First, my daily regime was a variant of the zealous self-discipline outlined in the last chapter. Meditation can be catalogued together with those manifestations of masochism such as lowering my calories and upping my exercise. In sticking so religiously to my cross-legged practice I was imposing upon myself another arbitrary edict, not to mention inflicting pain on the knee joints. By way of alibi I would point out that even some Buddhist monasteries operate more like military academies than nurseries for spiritual flowering. They embrace discipline for discipline's sake. The avowed goal of enlightenment is largely symbolic, like a flag that flies unnoticed above a building.

Masochism notwithstanding, I had (second) the sincere intention of making spiritual progress. I had fixed on inching towards enlightenment and was fascinated by the prospect of attaining it. I believed that through sitting meditation I might shuffle on my bottom at least a few feet along the path.

But what on earth does 'spiritual progress' mean? That is, what does it mean *on earth*? Spiritual progress can never be an entirely earthly endeavour. Given its vaporous quality, any 'spiritual' process must involve lifting up and away from the earth like an aircraft. That path, if it exists, is a runway.

Yet the upwards vector of the spiritual aircraft presents us humans with a conundrum. We observe it from the landing strip with the same multilayered longing with which Humphrey Bogart watches the planes take off from Casablanca. We dream of winning a passage on it. But cling as we might to the under-carriage, we feel gravity tugging on our belts. The etymology of 'human' leads down, as if into the soil itself, to a root word mean-ing 'earth'. It reminds us that we are earthly beings. On earth it is that we dwell, not in heaven. We never were engineered for flight into the divine stratosphere. Say you had invented water, music or light: then you might have a claim to divinity. But it's hardly likely. Nor is it just the dictionary that defines the human, with all our limitations, in contrast to the godly. *Gods versus mortals*: that primordial division is made universally in myth, religion and literature. So for a human to pursue spiritual enlightenment, well-intentioned though it may be, is either unnatural or hubristic or both.

That conundrum – the tension between upwards and down-wards – is one that meditation manages to find a way around. It does so by disabling the very thing that is most distinctive about us human beings. Namely, our minds. They need to be emptied. Indeed Andrew Harvey will often substitute the phrase 'empty-ing the mind' for meditation itself. It is a question of mental auto-evacuation. But why would the mind require emptying? Surely if our ignorance is so ginormous, we should be doing the opposite?

The problem is that the mind, whose instructions were to mediate the world around us, has a habit of wandering off the job. Rather than looking outwards and helping us to under-stand reality, the mind turns inwards. It becomes absorbed with worries, preoccupations, doubts, theories, fantasies and other flotsam and jetsam. *Mental chatter*, it could be called. That chatter drowns out the world beyond. What results is an extra layer, as in the diagram below, separating us even further from the Thing.

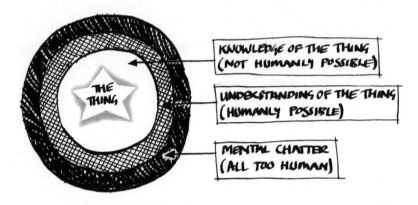

The aim of meditation is to strip away that outer layer. It is to shush our mental chatter. We reach for the knob on the radio that's been gabbling away in the kitchen, and switch it off.

Gap.

Only when the silence returns do we notice how much of a drone there has been, and how much mental capacity it has been tacitly consuming.

Handing over your sunglasses

Yet meditation is more than mediation restored. There is a next step – what Buddhists expressly call 'No Mind'. We actually cross the threshold of the inner circle. Once within, we become a part of everything around us. The result would look like the next diagram. No layering, no mediation, just unfettered knowledge of the Thing.

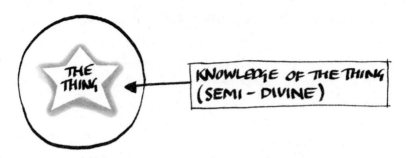

In this state of No Mind, we access the real Thing. The previously impermeable membrane between us and knowledge dissolves. As does that separating knowledge from the Thing in itself. What such a lifting of the veil feels like, nobody who has not experienced it can say. Buddhists call it Nirvana.

But let us be careful what we wish for. Nirvana comes with the following health warnings:

1. In gaining knowledge, we lose understanding. Practically speaking, we no longer have any need for metaphors or parables or indeed any form of indirect expression. Stories, poetry and even imagination become redundant. Now that we have unrestricted access to the spiritual Thing, we can dispense with those oblique strategies for processing our experience. They might have entertained us but in doing so they diverted our attention from the higher reality. It is as if we were having a nice time watching the matinee while outside the sun was shining and we were missing out. What's more, we can now look at the sun without squinting. Only problem is, we are required to hand over our beloved sunglasses.

2. It's not only understanding that we sacrifice in accessing knowledge. It is our humanity. For the realm of knowledge is the realm of the spirit, i.e. not the human. Our presence there is indeed unnatural. It follows that to be admitted to this

non-human environment, we must change our nature. We must agree to being transfigured.

The stakes, in other words, are high.

A feather tied to an anvil

Thanks to my meditation discipline, I did indeed make spiritual progress. So much progress that I had to put a stop to it.

The meditating itself was hit and miss. Sometimes I'd sit there, counting my breaths in and out, and I just couldn't get my mental chatter to switch off. Thoughts would keep coming as if from a bubble machine, winking to get my attention. When it wasn't my mind that distracted me, it was my body. My back would ache, my stomach would rumble or I'd get an insufferable itch on the calf. Mind and body conspired to wrench me away from my spirit, like twin toddlers demanding to be played with when all the parent wants to do is read their book.

But every now and then I'd manage to dissociate from the thoughts. It was like walking past a football stadium during a match and hearing the roar of the crowd. You know what's going on but you are not invested. In other words, I'd allow my thoughts to come and go without getting led away by any one of them. Bodily sensations I simply logged. Such moments never lasted long, though when they came they brought welcome relief.

Once in a blue moon I'd find myself without thoughts altogether. There was being but no thinking, the longstanding couple decoupled. So much for the cardinal apothegm of René Descartes, *I think therefore I am.* In those rare-as-hen's-teeth instances, I could have confidently claimed:

I don't think, yet I am.

Of course, the *cogito ergo sum* of Descartes declares that we can't think without being, not that we can't be without thinking. Nevertheless, the French philosopher forged the link between thinking and being so powerfully that it became a girder of modernity. Ever since Descartes, to be human has been to be a thinking being. Absence of thought has little place in the definition of the human in the modern West. That is why today any notion of being-without-thinking can come across as subhuman. It evokes less enlightenment than lobotomy.

My own experience of being-without-thinking certainly felt like it had a non-human aspect. I hesitate to call it 'spiritual' precisely because that term is so wispy. Besides, at such times I would feel *more* earthed, not less so. My centre of gravity dropped from brain to gut. Which is precisely where it needed to be. For the mind makes you floaty; the head is a balloon. Neither is much use to the spirit, which, being so filmily light, seeks the weight of a body to ground it. One could say that the spirit is like a feather asking to be tied to an anvil. Tying it to the mind would be attaching it to another feather. Together they would get blown away.

I would go so far as to classify being-without-thinking as an *animal* state. Not bestial, but animal. Since we humans are defined by our minds, the animal must be what remains when the swamp of the mind is drained. Yet 'animal' comes from a Latin word, *anima*, that is also used for 'spirit'. That suggests that although animals are typically ranked lower in the chain of being than humans, they deserve to be equal. Their relative absence of mind affords them easier access to the spiritual. Which is to say that when we over-thinking humans embody our animal self, it might be that we get closer to the spirit. Put baldly, our animal being is our spiritual being. It is that mode of existence which precedes the accretions of the mind. With a little effort we can always return to it.

Blood of gold

Animal or spiritual, whatever it was in my case, it was too much. Matters came to a head after a meditation class in Oxford. Meditating in a group can be more intense than meditating alone. For every unit of meditative energy that the individual expends, the group reimburses two. The atmosphere thickens.

Owing to that extra intensity, my session had been a powerful one. It was with a feeling of serenity that I came out onto the dark street. Students were chaining up their bicycles; tourists were quaffing ale in the Eagle and Child; and college windows revealed solitary academics at their lucubrations. As if still meditating, I observed it all with pacific detachment.

Small wonder: I *was* still meditating. Although no longer sitting in the group, I had carried the momentum beyond the end of the hour. It was just what we students of the spiritual were encouraged to do: embed meditation in everyday life. But I had never managed it before. Moreover, I was doing so without really trying. The meditative mode had started infusing through me, turning my blood from earthly red to spiritual gold.

There I go too – trying to portray the spiritual and reaching for metaphors. Golden blood? When attempting to describe their experience of transcendence, mystics will often use images such as 'being at one with the universe' or 'feeling part of a larger whole'. It is paradoxical, no doubt, that practising detachment makes you more connected. But for a whole minute now, walking north beneath the plane trees that lined the avenue of St Giles, I had found myself in that state. All the mystical, hippy or New Age terms that I might have ordinarily scorned were suddenly apt. It was as if I was resonating with the cosmic vibration.

Who's to say whether mine was a version of the transcendence reported by the mystics? It might have been a psychotic episode or a freak of brain chemistry. In any case, the experience quickly spoiled. What came over me next was a feeling of intolerable loss. The loss of my sense of self. A self that was full of anxieties and sorrows and egotistical fantasies, I admit. Yet it was through such imperfections that I recognised who I was. Who would I become in this brave new world of enlightenment? It was disorientating. My impulse was to reject it.

That impulse is one that the Rinpoche tackles just a few pages after his parable of the uneaten food. He says that refusing the spiritual gifts on offer is like saying, 'I do not want to endure my own perfection, I do not want to bear my own reality.' Now, I make no claim that during those few minutes after the Oxford meditation class I had sidled up on perfection. But I did perhaps get the briefest whiff of what, were I to devote myself, such perfection might potentially be. It was like coming into a clearing after a tiger has passed through and picking up its scent.

And yes, the reality of even that tiny intimation was unbearable. I lacked the plasticity needed for the transfiguring of my self. I had an identity, and for that identity to be identified it was important that it have a fixed form. Which it did. My identity was a panel with edges, made like all identities to remain identifiable and resist alteration. Under spiritual heat it might discandy, distend and remake itself into a shape that I would no longer recognise. And so, having unexpectedly accelerated along the spiritual path and passed through a first gate, I beat a hasty retreat.

A free lottery ticket

As far as my spiritual advancement was concerned, that might have been it. I had ventured so far, freaked out and turned back. Then a few years later I espied in Blackwell's bookshop a new work by Andrew Harvey. Its title was *Hidden Journey.* By now, the word 'journey' in the title had lost all literality. It was purely meta-phorical. Any journeying was so internal as to be 'hidden'.

It appeared that the Rinpoche had been supplanted in the role of Real Imaginary. The name of his replacement was Mother Meera. And if the Mother Meera website is anything to go by, one can easily see why Harvey should have shifted his attention her way:

Mother Meera is an embodiment of the Divine Feminine, the Divine Mother on earth. Mother was born in 1960, in the state of Andhra Pradesh, southern India. Today, she lives in Schaumburg, Balduinstein, a small village in the German countryside. Here, and during her travels around the globe, she gives her unique blessing of Darshan. The free transmission of Light, Love and Grace is Mother's gift to the world.

That is a fair bit to take in. Again, those of an empiricist bent – along with other rationalists, sceptics and atheists – will most likely pooh-pooh it. If I personally didn't fall into that camp of little faith, choosing rather to keep an open mind, it was for three reasons:

1. Andrew Harvey being my Real Imaginary, I was the more amenable to being seduced by what had seduced him.
2. Even if I had performed a U-turn on the spiritual path, I bore the memory of that epiphany after the Oxford meditation class. Not to mention the numerous occasions during meditation when, maybe for the duration of a heartbeat only, I had felt a

minor echo of it. What I had experienced softened me to what I had not.

3. The basal yearning that I dragged around with me like a ball on a chain. Namely, a yearning that my disappointment with life would be compensated for by the miraculous. I thought that Mother Meera might just deliver that miracle.

There was a final reason why I didn't simply scoff at the phrase 'Mother Meera is an embodiment of the Divine Feminine' and the words that followed. This reason was less emotional than the three above, and more properly ratiocinative.

I took my cue from Pascal's wager. Blaise Pascal mixed theology with mathematics to concoct a simple but compelling argument for why believing rather than not believing in God is the safer bet. In Pascal's words, 'If you gain, you gain all; if you lose, you lose nothing.' Believing brings either (best case) heaven or (worst case) nothing. Not believing in God will end in hell.

I repurposed Pascal's wager for my analysis of Mother Meera. What resulted was the ready reckoner in the diagram below. It plots Mother Meera's divinity against my belief in it.

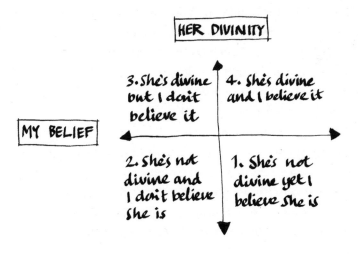

My lo-fi calculator generated four options. Starting in the bottom right-hand corner and proceeding clockwise:

1. Mother Meera is not divine yet I believe that she is. I'm a gullible fool. I might even have psychological issues. Perhaps the 'Divine Mother' makes up for deficiencies in my own childhood experience of being – or not being – mothered.
2. Mother Meera is not divine, nor do I believe that she is. Me, I'm with the empiricists. Let others slip and slide on the mudflats of their ignorance. The white coat that I wear – vestment of the scientific observer – stays clean.
3. Mother Meera is divine but I don't believe it. More fool me. Could I but scrape together enough belief, it could be cashed in for spiritual bounty. I would receive a banquet of food, a chest of gold or a similar metaphor for sublime satisfaction. But no, I turn my back on the treasure and stride off.
4. Mother Meera is genuinely divine and I believe it. I do not turn away. I surrender to the divinity's divinity. Heliotropic, I lift my face to the sun.

We know how Pascal would respond to those options. Crediting Mother Meera with her divinity is simply the most rational thing to do. Like being given a free lottery ticket, doing so costs nothing and could result in a spiritual jackpot. Not believing, by contrast, means that you don't even have a ticket. As the strapline says, you've got to be in it to win it.

Rational as it is, the Pascalian approach still doesn't answer the question of whether Mother Meera is divine. It merely gives us a strategy for responding to the likelihood thereof. That is not a verdict on the shortcomings of Pascal's gambling methodology. Regarding the divinity or otherwise of Mother Meera, there just is no conclusive evidence. Even if she were to perform a miracle, the naysayers would continue to cavil. That is why we humans have no choice when it comes to the divine but to exit the system of knowledge and enter the realm of belief. Once there, we can believe or not believe. Knowledge, regrettably, we are forced to relinquish.

My own position was not so much believing in Mother Meera as suspending my disbelief. *What if she actually was divine?* How exhilarating that would be. If only on the grounds of the amazingness of that possibility, I chose to keep the dogs of my cynicism locked up.

The sheep dip

In January 2008, the beginning of my last year at Burton Harcourt, I learned that Mother Meera would be coming to London. That she might physically descend into my world was astonishing. Mother Meera was my Real Imaginary's Real Imaginary. Twice removed, she was two parts Imaginary to one part Real. The prospect of those proportions being inverted left me blinking.

Mother Meera would be giving Darshan ('the free transmission of Light, Love and Grace') in a hall off the King's Road. I took a bus from Soho after work. Arriving early, I killed time over a beer at the pub opposite. At seven I went in.

With a dais at the far end, notices reading SILENCE PLEASE, and thirty-odd rows of plastic chairs, the scene resembled nothing so much as a school assembly for grown-ups. How it differed was that for the first hour, before 'Mother' appeared, we were expected to sit in private contemplation. Then, without fanfare or introduction, a diminutive middle-aged Indian woman, swathed in a crimson sari, entered stage left. Dispensing with all theatrics – no wave, no twirl, no catchphrase – she walked directly to the chair in the middle of the platform and sat.

Those in Row One were gestured at by Mother Meera's elves to file up to the stage on their knees. Each person knelt before her. Mother Meera put her hands on their head for about twenty seconds. Then she removed her hands and the supplicant looked up. Mother Meera gazed into their eyes. After another twenty seconds, Mother Meera closed her eyes and looked down. The blessing was done. Standing briskly, the individual returned to their seat and resumed their private contemplation. The next person shuffled forwards. The procedure was repeated – and repeated, again and again, as in a sheep dip. The size of the audience numbering over two hundred, it took a good couple of hours to process them all. Once finished, Mother Meera sat briefly with the whole congregation, her head bowed. At last she rose from her seat and quit the stage. In the ongoing silence, we gathered our belongings and went our separate ways.

That might make it sound like I was a spectator. I was not. I too had a turn. I knelt in front of Mother Meera and bowed my head. I felt her hands on my hair. After a few moments, she lifted them off. I raised my chin and met her gaze. At the closing of her eyes, I got to my feet and went back to my seat.

As for miracles, I can report a plentiful absence thereof. There were none.

The gift of grace and how not to avenge it

Was Mother Meera a fraud? Possibly. Then how to explain the fact that she charged nothing, said nothing and appeared to want nothing? What would have been her motive? It wasn't about the performance. The performance was as toned-down as toned-down could be. I didn't see anything suspect. Besides, what she did was harmless. Actually it was beneficial. For even if Mother Meera wasn't divine, convening a group of people to sit in silence for an evening was restorative in and of itself, especially in the big city.

Perhaps the problem lay with me. I went looking for a miracle. I was expecting too much. And where my expectations were high, my capacity to receive was low. I had rocked up to the venue with a pint of beer in me, aiming to collect my free miracle and bugger off. I was also bored by having to wait so long for my turn, and wait again afterwards for those who hadn't to have theirs. Not so gracious on my part. I felt ashamed.

From that shame I was able to extract a lesson, however. To increase our chances of winning a spiritual prize, we must ensure that we are well prepared. Humility is vital. Gifts are wasted on people who won't value them. Perhaps the question is not 'what would I like to receive?' but 'how can I be a worthy recipient?' It is rather about attracting the gift than expecting it. We should pay less attention to the object of our desire and more, as it were, to the desire of the object.

That led on to a further thought – about grace. For the capacity to receive humbly must be what grace is. Related to the English 'gratitude' and Spanish *gracias*, grace increases with our ability to take what is offered and in turn to offer thanks. In its simplicity, that is a disarmingly childlike position to assume. We adults get so easily enmeshed in the power dynamics of exchange. As Nietzsche reminds us, to receive a gift is to become indebted. That weakens us in relation to the giver, and a part of us resents it. A gift is an insult in disguise. 'Avenge the gift' is Nietzsche's advice. As quickly as possible, we should give a gift back, and preferably one of greater value. Thus we can switch the balance of power again. I would add that generosity can even be a form of evasion. How so? Giving provides a smokescreen for what is withheld.

Whilst Nietzsche may have a point about gift-giving on the human-to-human plane, when it comes to the exchange between human and divine his theory, like a Formula One car going off road, stalls. The human–divine exchange occurs on no 'plane'. The two parties operate on different levels, asymmetrically. Between god and mortal there cannot even be exchange. The gift goes one way. Avenging the gift is impossible because a human can never overtop a god. That's what makes us human. Instead, the challenge for us is to hold the gift, ablaze with light, in our hands. The fear in our hearts will tell us to drop it in case it burns a hole through us. The grace in our hearts tells us to let it. The result will be that transfiguring.

A sigil stamped on wax

Mother Meera's visit to London appeared to have been a one-off. Then two years later, in 2010, new London dates were announced. Word must have spread, for the Darshan was booked in at a larger venue. What's more, Mother would be running three sessions a day. In the perhaps too charitable assessment that it was my fault and not Mother Meera's that my first Darshan had been so underwhelming, I signed up.

The format was a carbon copy of what it had been in Chelsea. Rows of seats, people in silent contemplation, the unobtrusive entrance of Mother Meera. Knowing what to expect, I could be more patient. I set my inner alarm clock for much later and settled in. The silent sheep dip commenced.

Bearing in mind that lesson about grace, I had resolved to make myself as open as I could be. I would become the deserving vessel of spiritual beneficence. In practice what that meant was using the time before Mother Meera entered to 'empty the mind'. Then, as I neared the stage on my knees, I concentrated hard on her physical presence. Bowing before her, I tried to be as blank as possible. My conceit was:

Let me be the wax upon which she can impress her sigil.

I felt the touch of her hands on my head. Time slowed down. When one looked from the audience at the stage, each blessing had seemed to take about as long as it does for somebody to wash and dry their hands, and was no less perfunctory. Here, on the stage itself, with my head inclined towards the now golden fabric of Mother Meera's sari, there was as much time between each beat of my heart as there was ocean between islands in an archipelago. Sailing from one island to the next gave me time to feel the swell of the sea and watch the sun sparkle on its surface.

Then I looked up and felt the intensity of Mother Meera's gaze. Her head moved almost imperceptibly in slow nods, as if marking the tempo of her seeing. There was no smile, no social aspect to her countenance, none of the facial semaphores that human beings use as micro-signals when looking at each other. She was neither friendly nor hostile. There was simply a job to be done: the transmission, no less, of divine light.

As I rose to my feet, up rose within me a strange sensation originating in my viscera and issuing through my eyes as tears. Whether they were tears of joy or sorrow, I am not sure. Walking down the three steps that led off the stage, I felt unsteady. The feeling continued after I regained my seat. It wouldn't elapse before I left the hall that night.

Emmanuel Levinas, another French philosopher, explores the phenomenology of the face-to-face encounter between two people. His chief point is that to look at another person in the face is to look at *an other* person. The otherness, or ➡

◀ what Levinas calls 'alterity', is the dominant factor. As we
see them, and see them seeing us, and see them seeing us
seeing them, et cetera, we feel their difference. That difference
is important for Levinas because it echoes the asymmetrical
relationship between human and God. Drawing on
the Jewish mystical tradition, Levinas defines God as
'infinitely other'. So when we look at a human other, we are
experiencing an adumbration of that divine alterity.

Fibre-optic

I say that Mother Meera's Darshan produced in me a 'feeling'. But
that's not quite the word. Nor was it a thought. Only on the following morning, after sleep, could I get any measure of what had
happened. I would say that my inner geography had been rear-
ranged.

Later I would chance upon a slim volume of Mother Meera
interviews. In it she is asked about the two stages of the Darshan:
the touching of the head and the looking into the eyes. This is
what Mother Meera has to say about the latter:

> I am looking into every corner of your being. I am looking
> at everything within you to see where I can help, where I
> can give healing and power. At the same time, I am giving
> Light to every part of your being. I am opening every part of
> yourself to Light. When you are open you will feel and see
> this clearly.

I have to concede that I had neither felt nor seen the Light
during my Darshan. On Mother Meera's terms, therefore, I was

not 'open'. That made me feel like a failure. And since feeling like a failure felt bad, I deployed the standard defence mechanism of turning it back on her. The reason why I saw no Light was that there was no Light to be seen – neither by me nor by anybody else. Boasting about the Light (in capital letters, of course) and how she could open people to it was mere self-aggrandisement on Mother Meera's part. She was a fraud, after all.

Yet Mother Meera's account of the first part of the Darshan – the laying on of hands – fitted with my experience exactly. In the interview she describes her method as untying knots in the person's soul. That is not, to be frank, what I felt while kneeling at Mother Meera's feet. But it was what, the next day, I felt had taken place. The nearest physical equivalent that I can think of is acupuncture. The insertion of needles into nodes of the nervous system releases energy to flow throughout the body. Perhaps Mother Meera was cleansing my circuitry for the Light to pass as through a fibre-optic cable.

Yet I insist that my experience was neither a feeling nor a thought. It registered in neither the heart nor the head. So where did Mother Meera's intervention have its locus? My only resort was to take her at her word. Like a spiritual surgeon, Mother Meera had operated upon my soul. And although we can never say where the soul is, we always know whether we are aligned with it. Mother Meera had improved that alignment.

Spiritual but not religious

It would appear that an increasing number of people identify as 'spiritual but not religious'. They are turned off by the trappings of religion. Like archaeologists, they also wish to dig up a spiritual truth which they feel that religion has buried. The table overleaf breaks down their outlook.

SPIRITUAL...

Belief in a higher being or force, though not gendered and not anthropomorphic

Personalised practices such as meditation or mindfulness

Inclusive of all

Selecting what feels right from a variety of spiritual sources

Draws inspiration from meaningful music, poetry or art

Sexual honesty as a part of self-development

Ready acceptance of homosexuality as an expression of identity

In touch with nature

An appreciation for the just, benign and inscrutable workings of the universe

A recognition that people sometimes do bad things

Being true to oneself

Emotionally rich

It is on the last item in the list that I want to pause. One eschews religion because it fails to deliver the emotional satisfaction offered by the spiritual approach. In, for example, prescribing rules on where to pray, what to eat, when to wash and how to dress, religion feels less like a garden of emotional development and more like school. It is too dry.

Yet my experience of Mother Meera suggested that whatever

... BUT NOT RELIGIOUS
Belief in a father figure in the heavens
Institutionalised rituals such as Communion
A hierarchy run by old men
Obedience to a single religious dogma
Focuses on a primary religious scripture
Sexual hypocrisy and/or repression as evidenced by purportedly celibate priests abusing minors
Ambivalence or intolerance towards homosexuality
Disconnected from nature
A God who fails to intervene against war, pestilence and famine
A belief that there are forces of Evil at large
Being good
Emotionally avid

'spiritual' means, it has strikingly little to do with the emotions. As I say, I had had no feeling as such. It was more a retrospective recognition that my soul had been worked on, like leaving one's car at the mechanic's overnight. I make the point because those who call themselves 'spiritual but not religious' will often relay their spiritual experience in emotional terms. They will speak of feelings of profound peace when in touch with nature;

of deep empathy with other human beings; of awe at the vastness of space; of compassion for those in pain; or of being moved by the miracle of life. I have no beef with any of those emotions. My question is whether they count as spiritual.

An emotion such as profound peacefulness in the presence of nature might be special, but identifying it is not so hard. We feel it, we know that we are feeling it, and we are generally able to name it. Not so with the spiritual. If I am struggling to pinpoint the effect on me of Mother Meera's Darshan, it is not, I submit, because my powers of expression have inadvertently dried up. Nor am I trying to wrap what happened at Darshan in bands of mystique in order to enhance my personal kudos. My hypothesis, simply, is that the spiritual cannot be felt.

Nor can it be thought. Indeed thinking has even less to do with the spiritual than feeling. I say this because the focus of spiritual development is on the soul, and the soul has no concern with thinking or with thoughts. What use are thoughts to the soul? What use are ideas? Thoughts are not real. Ideas, insofar as they are speculative, are cousins of the lie.

The cloud of unknowing

I found two ways of making sense of it all – the Darshan, the Light, the absence of feeling and thought. The first was through a medieval mystical text that was on the syllabus at Oxford. Illuminatingly, the work is called *The Cloud of Unknowing*. In a key excerpt, the author says of God that 'He can be well loved, but he cannot be thought. By love he can be grasped and held, but by thought, neither grasped nor held.'

From those words I understood that unknowing is not a prick against which to kick. Unknowing might actually be that climacteric state at which we are most likely to discover the spiritual Thing. The cloud of unknowing is like the real cloud in which we lose our way on a mountainside moments before the summit reveals itself above. For somebody of my academic background, that was not easy to accept. Would I really have to put my brain to one side? At the very least, *The Cloud of Unknowing* helped me to realise that thought is only one medium for relating to the universe. If I could stop privileging thought above everything else, I might experience that universe in a richer way.

I also took the point about love: 'By love he can be grasped and held, but by thought, neither grasped nor held.' The enlightenment offered by the spiritual Thing is not to be confused with the Enlightenment by which name scientific progress made in the eighteenth century is identified. The latter is purely rational. Spiritual enlightenment, paradoxically enough, is closer to 'Endarkenment' – hence the cloud of unknowing. There is a sense of blindness in it, and that is its connection with love. Love is blind; it is no rational or cognitive state. What if not love would be the point of spiritual enlightenment anyway? It isn't to make us more brainy. It is to make us more loving.

Regarding Mother Meera's divinity, my position on the belief stick was one notch higher than agnosticism and one notch lower than outright faith. But even if outright faith were misguided, it does us no harm to be reminded that there might be things in the universe that we cannot know. It tempers our ego. The notion of ego was the second way I made sense of Mother Meera's disputable divinity. Remaining open to the possibility of the divine fosters humility. If nothing else, Mother Meera reminds us that we might not be lords of the world. Besides, you don't have to be a believer to acknowledge that the idea of God being dead is less powerful than the idea that God is alive.

That oceanic feeling

At the time I discovered Mother Meera, I had been seeing a psychoanalyst. Three evenings a week I would cycle to a townhouse in Soho, ring the buzzer, climb the steep stairs and stretch out on the couch. On a chair behind my head, out of view, sat my analyst, Flora. As I talked, Flora remained largely silent. Should I fall silent too, Flora would rarely break the ice. It was an odd way for two adults to spend an hour in each other's company. If you didn't know that it was psychoanalysis, you might take it for absurdist theatre.

But why consult an analyst at all? To put it a little sappily, I wanted to know myself better. When it comes to the unknowable, the greatest enigma is probably that presented to ourselves by ourselves. Hunkering deep inside is a heavily alarmed safe known as the Unconscious. Indeed its location within us is the chief reason why the Unconscious is so hard to see. We can't mark out sufficient distance from our Unconscious to get an objective view. It's like trying to step away from one's shadow. No less sticky is the fact that in analysing our Unconscious we become the subject of our own enquiry, police investigating the police. It's tempting to brush uncomfortable truths under the rug. With the help of an external observer, however, we have a fighting chance of achieving objectivity. Hence employing a psychoanalyst.

Other than absurdist theatre, the thing that psychoanalysis most resembles is confession. Although one does not lie down for confession, the priest's screen serves the same function as the couch-and-chair arrangement in psychoanalysis. It keeps the face of the analyst or confessor out of sight. With their reactions hidden, one's fear of being judged recedes. The environment becomes one of amnesty. The set-up is the opposite, say, of a newspaper, which frames all human behaviour in terms of good and bad. Talk to a journalist and not only will your story be splashed across the pages, it will be presented as either sympathetic or antipathetic to the paper's own stance. The paper's slavish readers will judge you in kind. With psychoanalysis and confession, by contrast, your unedited story is allowed to stand.

So there you are in analysis or confession. You are about to disclose in private what in public you would feel a thousand stabs of embarrassment to reveal. Disclosure is facilitated by the fact that in both psychoanalysis and confession the rules on censorship are relaxed. Yet the censor's withdrawal doesn't mean that you will automatically reveal all. Another censor remains.

Occasionally Flora would say to me, 'I can only analyse what you bring.' I took it as an admonition. *Don't waste your time and money by filtering your words,* she seemed to be warning. Once Flora told me that my behaviour was like that of a tennis player who, whenever the ball is hit over the net by his opponent, returns it with calm consistency. I took her to mean that my responses were too smooth, too controlled, too polite. And that I wouldn't allow myself to be beaten. The reason I kept playing the ball back was to stop it landing beyond the baseline, in my Unconscious – that area at the back of the tennis court where the nettles grow through the chainlink fence. Chatting to my shrink was fine, but was I ready for those nettles to be grasped?

There are differences between psychoanalysis and confession too, the most obvious being their take on religion. A confessor might allow your stream of filthy admissions to flow, but afterwards he will ask you to say a 'Hail Mary'. After all, confession takes place in a church. The effluent needs to be cleansed. So even if you are not judged in the moment, it is understood that you are confessing because you have done something bad. That is why confession opens with:

Forgive me, Father, for I have sinned.

Forgiveness would not be called for had no sin been committed. Confessing in church and talking to a journalist are in the end quite similar. In both cases, there is a set of norms from which any deviation on your part will be mathematically measured.

Psychoanalysis is a stridently secular practice. Psychoanalytic theory construes God as a mere psychic projection, a laser show beamed from earth onto the cosmos for the wonderment of humans. What gets projected is that father figure listed in the table on page 313 concerning those who are spiritual but not religious. God, for psychoanalysts, is the ideal father whom we never had, as opposed to the real father who disappointed us. We would rather believe in an ideal than accept the inadequacies of the real.

For all the father's fatherly dominance, there is a psycho-analytic interpretation of the divine mother too. She is connected with spiritual feelings. Should we ever experience spiritual infinity, we will be unconsciously reanimating the succour given us as infants by the mother's body. Freud describes such feelings as 'oceanic'. There is a benevolent entity larger than us. She offers an enveloping warmth. Her mysterious power lies not least in having existed in the legendary time that preceded our own appearance on earth. She gave birth to us. I couldn't help but wonder if that was the need satisfied in me by Mother Meera. 'Mother' was the idealised maternal figure by whom I was lovingly held.

The secularism of psychoanalysis also helps in the session. Where in exchange for disclosure confession offers forgiveness, psychoanalysis has no such bargaining chip. In order to encourage disclosure and discourage self-censorship, psychoanalysis is obliged to offer alternative inducements. Chief among those inducements is deodorising the room of the slightest whiff of moral judgement. The environment should smell as little of church as possible. That way, the patient knows that no matter how transgressive their revelations, they are safe from judgement and the presumption of sin. In other words, the ideological secularism of psychoanalysis delivers the tangible benefit of helping the patient to open up.

But even with the room swept of social and religious listening devices, opening up isn't easy. We continue to judge ourselves. We have made those external judgements internal. Regardless of the shrink's neutrality, we deem ourselves to be bad or wrong or shameful – or inadequate or failing or imperfect. We ourselves are the ones who fear what lurks in the undergrowth at the back of the tennis court, and so we fear reaching in our hand. Better to keep returning the ball.

In short, the problem is less that the Unconscious is hard to know and more that we are afraid to look. Within us all, like a stagnant pond, there exists material that at first sight may not be so edifying. Freud's great contemporary, Carl Jung, called it our 'shadow'. The shadow brings together aspects of our personality and behaviour that in moral or social terms would be deplored. A list might include:

- vengeful thoughts about somebody who has wronged you
- sexual desire for somebody who is not your partner
- times when you have affected liking somebody in order to win their approval
- feelings of hatred towards somebody in your family
- bearing a grudge against somebody at work
- envying the success of somebody who is supposedly a friend
- lies you have told about somebody in order to advance your own cause
- fantasies about hurting somebody who has not returned your love.

It isn't wholesome reading, that list. At least, not from a moral perspective. From a non-moral viewpoint, however, it merely seems human. Take the bearing of grudges. We don't hold grudges against people who are weaker than us. What the grudge secretly expresses is a weakness of our own. That makes us feel vulnerable. It is a bit scary.

Fear probably lies at the root of all those items in the list. Envying the success of a friend is based on the fear that you are not as good as them. Wanting to hurt somebody who has not returned your love stems from the fear that you will be lonely. And so on. About such fears there is nothing morally bad. Again, they are human. The moral of the story being that if we wish to increase our self-knowledge, the language of 'good' and 'bad' is of little use. Judging ourselves prevents us from seeing ourselves.

> And I have felt
> A presence that disturbs me with the joy
> Of elevated thoughts; a sense sublime
> Of something far more deeply interfused,
> Whose dwelling is the light of setting suns,
> And the round ocean, and the living air,
> And the blue sky, and in the mind of man,
> A motion and a spirit, that impels
> All thinking things, all objects of all thought,
> And rolls through all things.
>
> William Wordsworth

9

Portraits of Love

What his time spent with women offered was the opportunity to be embraced by reality, on the one hand, while negating it entirely on the other.

Haruki Murakami

Helen and I split up in the spring of 2015. I moved out of our London home. While sorting out the sale of the house and the legalities of the divorce, I took up a short-term rental on a flat in Brighton.

Perfect symmetry

My flat was located on the occidental side of Oriental Place. The street had no obvious right to call itself a 'Place' as it is a straight length of two hundred metres with an exit at each end. But the original sketches had figured Oriental Place as an approach to a pleasure garden. A shortfall in financing meant that the designs were never realised. As for the word 'Oriental', that came from the exotic vision for the garden's layout and planting. The oriental style was all the rage in the Regency period when architect A. H. Wilds designed the street.

The buildings, dating from 1825, were subsequently Grade II listed on account of their splendour and coherence. They are still adorned with their ironwork balconies, double-height pilasters, ammonite capitals and carved scallop shells. Uniformly their façades wear the Regency coat of butter-yellow paint. And whilst along each side of the street the buildings vary, every individual structure mirrors the one that it faces. Referencing the principles of 'oriental' design, Oriental Place is a showcase of perfect symmetry.

Oriental Place, Brighton 2015

'Regency' refers to the Prince Regent, later King George IV. It was he who commissioned Brighton's famous Royal Pavilion, the construction of which began in 1787. A gateau of dainty minarets and onion domes, the Pavilion was where the oriental style – technically 'Indo-Saracenic' – achieved its most ornate expression. That suited His Royal Highness' taste for extravagance. It was to the Pavilion, its rooms bedecked with scarlet hangings, that he would take his entourage for pleasure by the sea.

That association with royalty, added to the fancy architecture and the seaside amusements, ensured that Brighton became a nineteenth-century destination. But there was a more industrial catalyst of Brighton's boom. In 1841, a railway line began operating from London Bridge. That made the coastal city a destination in the prosaic sense too. A journey beginning after breakfast in London could now end at Brighton's airy station in time for lunch. The railway broadened the city's visitor base to include ordinary folk alongside the elite. And although the social classes remained predictably stratified, in their pursuit of the hedonic they were one.

By the mid twentieth century, the press of visitors had made Brighton a beacon of the leisure industry. The city enjoyed a reputation as a resort where families went on their summer holidays; children went for rides on the pier; day trippers went for fish and chips; seagulls went to pinch those fish and chips; and couples went for dirty weekends.

Those couples weren't always legitimate, and Brighton became a byword for adultery. The townhouse hotels that sprang up in the city's multiple squares would soon be turning seedy. The unsavoury atmosphere wasn't improved by the infamous running battles between Mods and Rockers in the 1960s, parkas skirmishing with leather jackets, Vespa versus Villiers.

That violence was largely offset by the hippies who flocked to Brighton preaching peace. With their homegrown cannabis and a disdain for the Establishment, the hippies served as path breakers for a generation advocating alternative lifestyles. Homeopaths, yogis, Tarot readers, clairvoyants and a gaggle of gurus made Brighton their home. Sandals and vegetarian shoes became the approved footwear, second only to going barefoot. The hash of streets comprising North Laine filled with the commingled scent of incense, patchouli oil and dope.

When in the 1970s package holidays began luring tourists away to the Med, Brighton suffered along with other British resorts. Unwanted Brighton rock piled up in the souvenir shops. Unsold seaside postcards yellowed and curled on their rotating stands in the sun. The Regency residences, now derided as old-fashioned, were broken up into bedsits. Many became squats. No less dispiriting was the erection of tower blocks and concrete edifices that stood among Brighton's elegant terraces and squares like bullies in the playground.

One of those supervening structures was the Brighton Centre, bang on the seafront. Built in 1977, it symbolised the city's attempt to reinvent itself. The fact that it was opened by the then Prime Minister, James Callaghan, signalled the nature of that reinvention. Brighton was to become a conference hub for politicos. It was at the Brighton Centre that the Conservative Party met for its ill-fated conference of 1984. Staying up late in her room at the nearby Grand Hotel to work on the keynote speech, Margaret Thatcher narrowly escaped an assassination attempt. At 2.54 a.m. a bomb planted in the hotel by the IRA went boom.

That rebranding of Brighton as the venue of choice for your conference was not unsuccessful as such. But it was a boring way to market a city with a record for fun. The city's liberal culture meant that what eventually won out in terms of an identity for Brighton was the gay scene. That scene took root in the 1980s and has flourished ever since. In one of the few British towns where the neighbourhood pub does not seem to be in decline, every third hostelry displays a gay-friendly rainbow. On the streets, men hold hands with men, and women with women, in a way that is freer than anywhere else in the country. Brighton has also taken over from London as the birthright host of Gay Pride.

Seashells near the seashore

Brighton's associations with gayness meant that when in May 2015 I moved there after breaking up with Helen, I received some inquisitive looks from family and friends. Was the reason I couldn't sustain relationships with women that I was a closet homosexual? Had my decamping to the south coast been motivated by a need to express my sexuality beyond the prying eyes of my London network? Might I be on the verge of coming out as gay?

Finding myself single for the first time in my adult life, I did take the opportunity to interrogate myself about my sexual preferences. The interrogation lasted all of twenty minutes. Search as I might through the contents of my erotic drive for material featuring males, I could find nada. If I wasn't repulsed by the idea of gay sex, nor could I be bothered to use my newfound freedom to make sure. I was sure already. So no: my removal to Brighton was not about giving rein to the sexuality I had unconsciously repressed.

That said, parts of my unconscious must have been involved in choosing Brighton for a bolthole, because they surfaced only after I had arrived.

Those carved seashells that decorate the buildings of Oriental Place allude to the beach at the south end of the road. From that spot you can see the West Pier, the rusting pleasure dome now marooned just out to sea. It was to the shore there, exactly a decade before, that I, despondent because of my job at Burton Harcourt, had repaired in order to assess my future.

I was dimly aware of a further link with the city. The link became clear when I telephoned my Uncle Rowley. He reminded me of the family's associations with Hove – to which Brighton is seamlessly joined. It turned out that the house where he grew up with his father (also his half-brother, my father's father) was a bare ten minutes' walk from my new abode. Anticipating a mansion, I went to check it out. The reality was a nondescript 1950s semi. When I spoke to my mother in turn, she recalled visiting the house when she was pregnant with me.

The first time I took the car rather than the train to Brighton, I also saw road signs for Hurstpierpoint, on the north fringe of the South Downs. That was where my father had been sent to boarding school after the war. The route led down the A23 from south Croydon, so I would drive past my prep school on the way. I wondered if crossing and recrossing the Brighton Road in Croydon as a child had wired a connection with Brighton into my brain. The city was turning out to be like the bulletin board in *The Usual Suspects*, where all the clues are gathered in one place. Brighton was a collage of my history; the centre of a maze; my psychic city.

On an expedition through Brighton's Kemp Town district – the gay scene's epicentre – I even happened upon the road where Helen had been lodging when we first met in the year 2000. I would swing down to visit her there in the blue Saab 9-5 that I was driving at the time. But that wasn't the last of Brighton's spooky connections. Uncanniest of all was the fact that the woman with whom I would next become involved lived, of all the places in all the world, on the parallel street. This was Colette.

A broken plate

Along with, say, the *Song of Songs*, Plato's *Symposium* stands as one of the founding discourses on love in the Western tradition. The two texts concur on the simple truth that love involves the longing to be with the beloved. In the *Song of Songs*, that longing is voiced by a bride and groom anticipating their wedding night. The young woman's words are soaked in vulnerability and desire:

All night long on my bed
I looked for the one my heart loves;
I looked for him but did not find him.
I will get up now and go about the city,
through its streets and squares;
I will search for the one my heart loves.
So I looked for him but did not find him.
The watchmen found me
as they made their rounds in the city.
'Have you seen the one my heart loves?'
Scarcely had I passed them
when I found the one my heart loves.
I held him and would not let him go
till I had brought him to my mother's house,
to the room of the one who conceived me.
Daughters of Jerusalem, I charge you
by the gazelles and by the does of the field:
Do not arouse or awaken love
until it so desires.

Plato's version also stresses that compulsion in love to join with the other. It does so through the retelling of a Greek myth. Originally, human beings were like a man and a woman of today stuck together, with both male and female genitals. Nervous of our conjoint power, the gods decided to sunder us in two. We were cut down the middle, and the skin of each person tied up to form their belly button. Men and women have been trying to reattach to one another ever since. Like pieces of a broken plate, they are searching for their other half.

It is the looking for love which provides the subject of this, the final chapter. I say 'final' fully aware that a book exploring what it means to be human can never be finished. One might question whether love merits a chapter at all. Does 'looking for love' deserve a place in the definition of what it means to be human? Where would love fit into Maslow's famous hierarchy of needs? Is love a necessity or a luxury? We don't need love in the way that we need food and shelter. On the other hand, not to experience love leaves a sense of potential untapped. And potential, whether it be maximised or misspent, must surely count as a core human attribute. We can always grow a little bit more. Of course, the cost of fulfilling potential is to lose it. But potential is never absolutely fulfilled. So even if love doesn't belong in the definition of what a human being *is*, it is part of what a human being, at their most realised, *can be*.

Abandon all hope

I had met Colette in the summer of 2014. Though an artist by trade, she attended a workshop that I had run for aspiring authors on how to write autobiography. Her stated reason for enrolling was to work on a memoir about an ex-boyfriend. He had killed himself.

I confess that I felt attraction towards Colette. I say *confess* because Colette was my student, albeit a 'mature' student in her thirties. Plus I was still married to Helen. Those two facts came together like the doors of an automatic gate as it is closing. I was shut out. Besides, Colette had been testy with me at the workshop. When it finished, I simply went home.

Then, out of the blue in early 2015, Colette made contact. She had just moved from London to Brighton. There in the city of faded grandeur she could more easily afford a studio in which to paint. Also, for an artist, the bohemian milieu of Brighton was congenial.

Colette hadn't given up on the writing project, however. That was still on her mind and was why she was reaching out to her former tutor. Like all autobiographers, Colette was obliged to juggle two stories. There was her story as in her lived experience (Story 1). Then there was her story as in what she might or might not transpose into the written version (Story 2). Colette was seeking further advice on how to manage the interplay between the two.

Over tea at the Rosewood Hotel in Holborn, Colette regaled me with her story in the first sense (Story 1). In her twenties she had briefly gone out with an older man named Josh. Although the relationship centred around sex, it wasn't devoid of sentiment. So when Josh later gassed himself to death in a south London flat, it had its impact on her. The given reason for the suicide was that Josh couldn't pay his bills. But Colette fearfully wondered if she had been a factor. Regardless of what would go into her memoir, she sensed that in her soul were stones that needed turning over.

As for the written narrative (Story 2), the question was one of focus: narrow versus wide. Colette could certainly restrict the scope to Josh's demise. The material was fecund enough. On the other hand, that event was an episode in a longer tale that was asking to be told about Colette's loves. For there was a second man in the mix. This was Sam.

Also much older than Colette, Sam had been her on-off lover for years. The reason why Colette hadn't committed to Sam in any sustained way was that she wasn't as into him as he was into her. Both in parallel to, and in the gaps between, periods with Sam, Colette would explore other amatory interests at her discretion.

In effect, Sam was only one-third boyfriend to Colette. The second third was older brother. The third third was provider. But if on one level that division of Sam's status bought Colette some freedom, on another level it felt like a burden. Ambiguous relationships absorb more energy than the unambiguous type.

And Sam's hopes for a long-term future with Colette remained inextinguishable. It had all begun to get on Colette's nerves. In the run-up to Christmas 2014 she drew a line in the sand. Colette informed Sam that he never would be her boyfriend proper, let alone her husband. *Abandon all hope* was the essential message. She urged him to move on.

It was in the following February that Colette and I had our tea in Holborn. Colette had been seeing a third man. His name was Jamie. But Jamie too was not allowed to be a full-blown boyfriend. Where to Jamie he and Colette were an item, to Colette they were merely lovers. Like Sam, Jamie was more into Colette than she was into him. By the time Colette and I sat down for tea that afternoon, she had determined to distance herself from Jamie and his hopes.

But for one tiny detail, Colette's attempt at putting clear blue water between Jamie and herself would have been unproblematic. Tiny as in the size of an embryo. Colette was pregnant with Jamie's child. She had the option to abort. But because she had had two terminations in her twenties, her conscience felt under scrutiny. Or perhaps it was her conscience that was scrutinising Colette. Either way, a third procedure would have been a procedure too far. Jamie's baby was the one that she would keep. Not that Colette was at all clear about how to work it vis-à-vis Jamie. She was serious about not wanting him romantically. Perhaps they would live together as parents if not as partners. Perhaps there was some other twenty-first-century model to be looked into.

When Colette got in touch, a part of me hoped that she wanted to see me for reasons beyond soliciting my advice. And as the two of us talked, the professional question about what should go into Story 2 (the memoir) got lost in the personal recounting of Story 1 (the life). I was craftily recusing myself from my advisory role and ushering forwards my fantasy of the two of us as lovers. Then, on hearing Colette's revelation about the pregnancy, I was put in my place. I was a sounding board, no more. My hopes, having only just bobbed away from the jetty, sank like a punctured dinghy. When the tea was over, I bade goodbye to Colette with a chaste kiss on the cheek.

The artist's way

Walking away from that tea I had an intuition about Colette that I was able to articulate only much later. That was thanks to a psychotherapist friend, Daniella. Naming no names, Daniella was musing on the several artists whom she had treated in her consulting rooms. Most had had tempestuous, short-lived, adulterous or in other ways suboptimal love lives. Daniella's conclusion was that you can never marry an artist, you can only accompany them. It's not that they are incapable of making a commitment. If anything they over-commit. But what they commit to is the artist's way. That takes priority. Any marrying that they undertake with a human being comes second.

Daniella and I went on to talk about Picasso and his string of relationships. The majority of women with whom the Catalan artist became involved also appeared on his canvases. That made them a resource for his art in the practical sense that they gave their bodies to be portrayed. They sat, stood or reclined while Picasso rendered their fleshly reality into images in oil that would survive them. To accuse Picasso of seducing them so as to have subjects to paint would be captious, however. For his women were more than the human equivalent of a jug in a still life or a haystack in a landscape. It seemed that Picasso's relationships with them were part of his creative process, the fertile ground from which his ideas would spring.

Yet Picasso hopped from one woman to the next without looking back, as if over stepping stones. That in itself says something about the creative process. For every new relationship that Picasso started, an existing relationship was brought to an unceremonious finish. As in his artistic transition from, say, the Blue to the Rose Period, there had to be an ending before there could be a beginning. So yes, Picasso's women were integral to the creative process, but each had an expiry date invisibly branded on her, courtesy of the artist. The departure of one heralded the arrival of the next. My point being that the creation in the creative process was facilitated by a preceding destruction.

All this I was thinking in its inchoate form after I said goodbye to Colette. Even if the way wasn't clear to Colette herself, she was on an artistic journey of her own. The first gift she would ever give me was a copy of *The Artist's Way*. The message seemed to be 'I'm on a creative path. Maybe you could start on a creative path too.' In other words, various men might accompany Colette for a few miles en route. Some she might even stop to paint. Then she would let them go. None would become her destination.

I didn't know if I would hear from Colette again. Then two weeks later she emailed to say that Sam had been found dead. In the intervening fortnight she had also changed her mind about keeping Jamie's baby.

High windows

Colette gave two reasons for the volte-face on the pregnancy. The first concerned Jamie himself. Whatever domestic arrangement they might contrive, he and Colette would be co-parents. They would be tied to each other in that responsibility at least until the child became an adult. That was not a scenario to be entered into lightly. It was best not entered into at all. The prospective mother really did wish to put some distance between herself and the prospective father, not become more embroiled with him.

The second reason for changing her mind about keeping the baby concerned Colette's conscience. A friend had counselled her to look at the pregnancy on its own merits, not in the context of the previous two terminations. Was it in itself a good decision to have Jamie's offspring? Colette's misgivings about Jamie implied that it was not. Imagine the child discovering that it had been given life not out of the mother's love but out of the mother's fear of feeling guilty. By trying to be good this time and keep the baby, Colette was doing good by no one. She was acting out of a fearful wish to be innocent. She hoped that going through with the birth of the third child would repay a debt to the two half-siblings who hadn't made it to that point. But where exactly were the recipients of that repaid debt to be found? They were gone. It was time for such moral fantasies to stop.

Then came the news of Sam's death. He had fallen from the kitchen window of his flat in south London. The window was brand new. The previous window had been cracked and Colette had hired a glazier to replace it. That was Colette's way of thanking Sam for letting her stay in the flat rent-free before her move to Brighton. It was her reciprocal gift to him. Did Sam avenge the gift by smashing it?

Sam's body had been discovered in the back garden. There was an obvious explanation. Sam was hypoglycaemic and given to seizures. In her time with him, Colette had witnessed all too many of Sam's 'hypos'. He would thrash about uncontrollably and sometimes black out. The risk of such spasms was increased by Sam's tendency to binge drink. He had probably got drunk, had a hypo, and fallen flailing through the window to the ground. The impact had killed him.

Obvious, maybe. Satisfactory, no. That explanation didn't account for how somebody could die falling from a first-floor window into a garden. Maybe the impact hadn't been the cause of death. Maybe Sam had died after lying for a while unconscious. Maybe he had already been dead or dying in the kitchen when his body slumped and folded through the window like a sack of coal.

Though taboo, there was also the possibility of suicide. Sam had set his heart on golden years with Colette. A few weeks earlier she had ruled that out. Sam can't not have felt bereft. Colette having withheld the romantic future at which he clasped, had Sam decided to take his own life? Perhaps Sam was getting hammered to numb the pain of Colette's rejection. He was aiming for the temporary oblivion of a drunken blackout, not the permanent oblivion in which forgetting itself is no longer possible. But did the former accidentally lead to the latter?

There was a further taboo, still more delicate to mention. If Sam had killed himself, he would be the second of Colette's former partners to have done so. That might have been coincidence. It might have been bad luck. But in both having been lovers to Colette, Josh and Sam had a common denominator.

Josh and Sam's terrible lot became a terrible lot for Colette. She had already suffered the grief of losing not one but two ex-lovers. Now she had that last taboo to worry about. Was there something in her to which both men had reacted? What was that something? Was it really in her? Self-doubt self-seeded. It was like having to keep watch on a snake moving through the nearby rushes. Most likely the snake would pass on by without incident. Alternatively it might swivel its head, stare for half a minute with its forked tongue tasting the air – then pounce.

In a short story entitled 'Men Without Women' by Haruki Murakami, there is the following passage:

This woman was the third woman I'd gone out with who'd killed herself. If you think about it – and you don't really need to, since it's obvious – that is an extremely high fatality rate. I couldn't believe it. I hadn't gone out with that many women in my life. Why these women, all still young, felt *compelled* to take their lives, was beyond my comprehension. I hoped it wasn't because of me, or in some way connected to me.

Overdetermined

The year 1900 saw the publication of the world's first full-blown psychoanalytic text. This was *The Interpretation of Dreams* by Sigmund Freud. The title advises that dreams are not fripperies to be shooed away like Victorian children. They warrant interpretation. So they must have meaning.

Unfortunately, teasing out the meaning of a dream is no walk in the park. Dreams are, to use the Freudian term, 'overdetermined'. They don't just have meanings, they have *too many*. A dream serves up a cornucopia of edible interpretations. We unlock one door only to see another door ahead. We unlock the second door only to see a third. Or, to use a third metaphor, one of Freud's own, we will never find the 'navel' of the dream. Trying to settle on the definitive interpretation is a fool's errand.

I light on the word *overdetermined* because I think it relevant to the multiple repetitions, coincidences and ironies surrounding Colette's story and its links to my own. To list them:

(a) Colette was living in Brighton. Brighton was my psychic city. It was the delta where a myriad undercurrents converged.
(b) Colette's Brighton home was round the corner from where Helen had lived when we were courting. Also, Colette's studio happened to be a stone's throw from Oriental Place.

(c) Brighton beach was where I had been involved in filming the trailer for 'Sex Lives of the Philosophers'. The sex life of this philosopher was about to start a new chapter in Brighton with an artist in residence there.

(d) Colette had grown up on the farm next door to where my godfather Uncle Rowley had moved, in middle-of-nowhere Suffolk.

(e) As a teenager, Colette had later moved to go to school in south London, where we had beaten the very same streets.

(f) Colette was planning an autobiography. Autobiography was my specialism. This very book is an autobiography. Colette is in this very book, in this very sentence. Her autobiography was going to be about her lovers. I was on the point of becoming the next. I might therefore be included in her autobiography.

(g) Colette had previously been a lover to two different men who had died unnaturally early. At least one of those deaths was suicide. I had had suicidal leanings of my own.

(h) Colette's lovers had been significantly older than she was. I too was older than Colette.

(i) Colette had not managed to sustain any of her relationships. I had not managed to sustain any of my relationships, even if mine had lasted considerably longer.

(j) Both Colette and I had had to wrestle with our conscience regarding babies who would or wouldn't be brought to term. As the result of decisions taken, I had ended up with three children to Colette's none. Yet she had had three in the womb.

Like a dream, that list is alive with symbolic collisions. They create an intoxicating sense of portent, of meanings inexhaustible. In other words, they are overdetermined. For example, one might speculate as to whether in Colette's psyche there was a standing slot for an older man. When Josh died, that slot was filled by Sam.

When Sam died, it was filled by me. Just as destruction precedes creation, so the deaths made space for new love. And if I was to fill that slot next, would I thereby make the bringing-forward of my own death more likely? Did I strap myself so readily into that seat because it was such a snug fit for my psyche?

Or take the notion, common to Colette and me, of being unable to sustain a relationship. In entering through the front door with each other, were we both reassured to know that the back door had been left unlocked? Was a transient connection what we both secretly sought? Were we compatible precisely because our compatibility would be time-limited?

Such speculations could go on for ever: that is the nature of the overdetermined. But rather than risk getting mired in them all, I draw a single superordinate conclusion regarding what causes us to fall in love. It is a matter of weirdness.

Weird artefacts of attraction

The adjective 'weird' has become so common that we forget its pedigree. This can be traced back to the Anglo-Saxon *wyrd*. The word makes an appearance in a poem called *The Wanderer* whose text is over a thousand years old. The original reads:

Wyrd bið ful aræd

The academic translation has:

Fate remains wholly inexorable.

More conversationally one might say:

There's no avoiding fate.

What is fate if *not* unavoidable? That line of Anglo-Saxon verse is a tautology. The more important point being that 'fate' was the original meaning of 'weird'. Even today when we say 'It's weird', the phrase is sometimes short for 'It's weird how things turn out'. The idea of fate has left its vestiges in the modern word. What we find weird is how fate deals out its deck. What makes events weird is that we hadn't foreseen them.

The semantic depth of the word *weird* doesn't end there. If in the Anglo-Saxon period 'weird' came to mean 'fate', it is because the 'weir' in weird indicates 'turning'. For fate is the turn taken by events, a turn for which we hadn't planned. Finally, at the very source of the word weird is *wer*, which is Proto-Indo-European. It was first enunciated by what would today be Iranians, and their Neolithic neighbours. *Wer* means 'to watch out for'. Fate's ability to turn events in unpredictable directions is based on its watching out for what lies ahead. To be weird is to be both prophetic and powerful.

That lesson in etymology is offered as a way of comprehending the overdetermined connections between Colette and me. Those connections are weird in the sense that they turned our fates towards each other. Indeed 'connections' doesn't do them justice. The weirdness had not just a connecting but an attracting force. That force moved near-identical elements in Colette's life and mine to lock together. Neither of us could have predicted it. It was a case of weird attraction.

The elements of that weird attraction are those that appear on the overdetermined list – Brighton, older lovers, autobiography and so forth. Though I'd argue that better than the word 'elements' to describe them is 'artefacts'. For, like anthropological artefacts, the phenomena subliminally coupling Colette with me were highly specific to times, people and places. Hence 'weird artefacts of attraction'.

But just because those weird artefacts were particular to us, it doesn't mean that other relationships won't gather artefacts exclusive to them. The proviso being that their subconscious quality can delay the weird artefacts' identification. As in the diagram below, weird artefacts of attraction hang beneath our optic range.

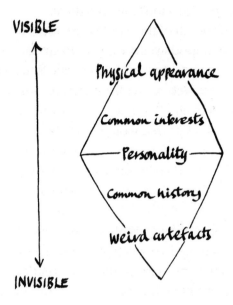

The diagram maps out what attracts people to each other romantically:

- At the top, and most clearly visible, is physical appearance. Being at the top does not imply that physical appearance trumps everything else. Physical appearance is merely the easiest to see.
- Next down come common interests. Again these are not hard to spot. We go to galleries together, we play backgammon, we like the same cuisine, and so on. It's all there on show.
- Personality too is largely evident. It will be the personality of our partner with which we mostly engage. That is why in the diagram it occupies the widest point. The width is a measure

of how much time we spend on it. We tend not to dwell on the other's physical appearance once it is familiar. That is why physical appearance sits in a narrow part of the rhombus. But our partner's personality, yes. It's what takes up the bulk of our attention. How they behave, what they say and do, whom they talk about. And yet we never quite know what they are thinking. We cannot read our partner's mind. One hears anecdotes about people whose partners up and leave without forewarning. All along they were in love with somebody else or were secretly gay or wanted to find themselves spiritually. So the personality of our partner has something of the invisible to it. That is why in the diagram it sits on the cusp.

- Common history gets added over time. It's not something of which we are actively conscious. But common history counts as an attractor because it creates a bond. The history shared by two lovers forms the foundation upon which the relationship is built. I am thinking of holidays taken together, in-jokes, the times when one of us fell ill, the song that captured a moment.

- Weird artefacts of attraction are the most invisible because they are the least conscious. They might include back-of-the-mind coincidences in our family history; fantasies from when we were children that are oddly alike; joint attachments to a certain word or phrase; or a shared fascination with a person from the past. Those are just examples of weird artefacts of attraction. Every couple will have a singular set of its own. They are like objects dropped separately by each partner over the side of a boat at different times. Those objects have drifted to the bottom of the deep ocean yet settled side by side on the sandy floor. They make a heap of psychic treasure that the couple will either delight in rediscovering or, more likely, continue to forget. The forgetting is of no consequence. What matters is that those objects have silently collected in the same place.

The attraction between Colette and me would work on all of those levels. So how to account for her spiky behaviour towards me during the autobiography workshop the previous summer when we first met? I was later to quiz Colette on the matter. We were out for a stroll along the beach huts by Hove Lawns, joggers and dog walkers before and behind us. The reason for being off with me at the workshop, conceded Colette, was that she too had felt attraction. But having learned that I was married, she sent barbs in my direction both to attack me and to defend herself. Better to reject the unobtainable loudly than to suffer a humiliation quietly. Her spikiness was still flirting, just in its negative form.

Monochrome paint-balling

By the time Colette and I had that conversation, in the late summer of 2015, I was settled in my Oriental Place apartment. From the ceiling-to-floor windows in my living room, I had an ample view of the goings-on on the street.

The balcony diagonal to mine would sometimes be draped with a large Union flag. Out would step a man with a moustache and mutton chops, like a Victorian constable from a cuckoo clock. Blaring from behind him came Elgar's *Pomp and Circumstance*. He would survey the scene as if he were Lord Kitchener addressing the troops. Except that Kitchener would not have stood in his underpants, as was this good gentleman's preference.

Next door to that colonial outpost was a three-star hotel arranged over the full five storeys. Every Friday night a hen party would check in. The young women with their wheelie bags would arrive at about six o'clock. Two hours later they would emerge in their team kit. This usually comprised a T-shirt with wording such as 'Jade's Hen, Brighton 2015'; a sash, typically pink;

kitten heels; tiaras; and joke erotica such as an inflatable penis. In the small hours of the morning, I'd hear them return, drunk and ragged, belting out a karaoke classic. The next time they appeared on the steps of the hotel, in daylight, they would naturally be hungover. What was the plan again? Oh yeah, full English breakfast on the seafront.

Oriental Place also featured a hostel for those trying to re-assimilate into normal life. One man had in his possession a single NHS crutch. Since I would hear that crutch clacking up and down the road at speed, it didn't seem strictly necessary. That provoked in me the supercilious thought that the crutch served a need in the man to identify as a victim. The hostel's denizens would get into altercations on the street and, with the wide sea serving as a screen behind him, he would shake his crutch like a crazed lobster waving a claw. Often I would be disturbed by the caterwauling of his friend, a woman who had been turfed out of the hostel for the umpteenth time. With limp brown hair and a missing tooth, she would plant herself on the road outside the hostel with one fist clenched and the other gripping a lager. Over and over she would moan, 'I fucking hate you lot! I fucking hate you lot!'

Brighton had more than its fair share of beggars and street sleepers too. I couldn't help wondering why itinerants are so drawn to the seaside. There was, I reasoned, the relatively clement weather. Also, the footfall from visitors increased the likelihood of a handout. I was forever being asked to 'spare some change' by homeless people camped at the cashpoint on Western Road. But those two reasons seemed overly pragmatic. What about the way the sea has of making us contemplative? Those whose fate has steered them onto the touchline of society have plenty to contemplate. Is living by the beach the geographical embodiment of having been shunted to the social margin? Mercifully the ocean, the wind, the birds – they make no judgement. To look out to sea is to have your back to the land and thus to the landlubbers with their values and biases and disapproving looks. The shoreline offers respite.

Colette semi-adopted one of those rough sleepers. His name was Herbert. In his sixties, Herbert was tall, broad and handsome. He had long silver hair and crystalline blue eyes. Together with his flea-bitten garb, those features meant that he could have been mistaken for an actor from the Royal Shakespeare Company doing the heath scene as King Lear. Herbert's life had taken a not dissimilar twist from riches to rags. He moved from South Africa's wine lands to England to take up a job. He got married and had kids. But over time it fell apart. His home was now the bus shelter facing the lower end of Oriental Place. It was near the bandstand where, if you squinted hard, you could see the ghosts of an Edwardian brass ensemble tooting a bright march for the passers-by. If ever she cooked a stew at mine, Colette would make extra for Herbert. She would ladle it into a takeaway tub and shuttle it down the road for him. By the end of that summer, the local council had made Herbert's wish come true by finding him accommodation. His eyes glistened at the thought of a hot shower. But even after moving in, Herbert could still be seen the odd night back on his bench. That was his terroir.

If Brighton had a large transient population, there was one demographic that was not part of it: the seagulls, permanent residents. The avian equivalent of Hell's Angels, the city was theirs in which to run amok. Their shrieks pitched between affront and lamentation, they would cruise the skies unchallenged, dive-bomb kids with ice creams, gather on pavements to tear at bin bags, and shit over anything and everything. Parked outside my flat, my silver sedan would get so liberally spattered that it looked as if it had been driven in slow motion through a monochrome paint-balling battle.

At night, all that kinetic activity would die down. The birds assembled like elders at council, discussing their young. They would glide in white flurries over what Homer called the 'wine-dark sea'. I pictured them pulling back the skin of the water with their beaks for their offspring, then pulling it back over them again like a blanket.

The pink whiteboard

Colette's studio teetered like the crow's nest of a ship at the top of a ramshackle courtyard. You accessed it from a flight of vertiginous wooden stairs with a rickety handrail. I was forced to go up and down with my feet turned sideways, so narrow were the steps. One time, carrying a box of art supplies for Colette, I nearly slipped. Inside the studio, there was no central heating. Electricity cabling looped downwards from coarse holes in the fibreboard wall. The roof was a corrugated iron sheet that let the rain in. The toilet was unspeakable. I exaggerate only slightly. Still, it was cheap.

Colette showed me her works. Painted as if seen from the doorway was a half-naked woman on a bed, the atmosphere disjointed between the erotic and the foreboding. Then there was a self-portrait of Colette swimming in Brighton's salty sea, and delving with the fleetness of a scallop harvester beneath the cold cerulean waters. A third painting showed a round iron table with a box of Nike trainers on top, forlorn emblem of consumer desire.

What struck me throughout were the colours. The cadmium red of that shoebox. Tropical greens springing forward like foliage. The ultramarine blues depicting pine forests, cooler but no less insistent. And rose pink, the artist's signature colour.

I especially admired a canvas called *Theory*. The subject matter was as pedestrian as could be: a whiteboard. Here was a pink painting of a whiteboard. A whiteboard being a teaching tool, it provides the surface upon which a theory might be transcribed. Hence the title, I presumed. A whiteboard is also the epitome of a blank canvas, yet Colette's painting was saturated with energy and invention. Mathematical symbols in the shape of etched pyramidal objects like moon-landing craft hovered over the central pink field. A pistachio slab, both advancing and receding, formed the unstable ground between the whiteboard's legs. A green circle balanced on the whiteboard's left shoulder as though it might boing out of the frame.

I persuaded Colette to let me hang *Theory* on the wall behind my bed at Oriental Place. The pink seemed to answer the blue of the sky through the bedroom window. Eighteen months later, in December 2016, I purchased the painting from its creator. Colette and I had long parted company; I had moved back to London; and the painting was to go in my new flat by the river. I had hoped that Colette would give me *Theory* as a gift. But by then the gift-giving that comes so naturally to lovers had been overtaken by the contractual exchange that resumes once those lovers have separately returned to the market. It was like the Monday after a weekend. The romantic snaps back to the economic.

The question of ownership was to nag at another painting by Colette. During that summer of 2015, she painted a watercolour of a kiss. The painting featured the head of a man and the head of a woman facing each other. Both were in profile as on a coin. The two heads were joined at the picture's centre – its navel perhaps – by their lips. Colette's painting exhibited that longing-to-be-with-the-other by which love is defined.

I didn't recall posing for any portrait. Yet the painting seemed to represent Colette and me. Of course, with a modern artwork the notion of representation is far from simple. In what sense were Picasso's portraits 'of' his subjects? It was because those portraits were anything but faithful reflections that they caused controversy. Was Picasso painting (a) the women as they were in real life; (b) the women in his mind's eye; (c) a combination of the two; or (d) a fourth possibility? In relation to Colette's painting, one could phrase that fourth possibility as the following double negative:

> *Even if the painting wasn't of her and me, it wasn't not of us either.*

And if it wasn't not of us, it wasn't not of me. So did I have any rights over Colette's watercolour of a kiss? Could the work be said in any sense to be mine? Not the painting as a whole, but the representation of me within it? And what if that representation wasn't accurate or flattering: did I have any recourse? Perhaps I could have bought that painting too, like I would buy *Theory*, thus taking it off the market and pre-empting any wider consumption of my image.

It was not the first time that I had been represented in a creative work. I had been the subject of an abstract sculpture by Adeline de Monseignat, simply titled *Robert*. I feature briefly in Monique Roffey's memoir, *With the Kisses of his Mouth* – which, with further irony, was the way in which Colette, as a reader of that book, would first hear about me.⬇ I am one of Rose Rouse's walking companions in her *A London Safari*. And I make a cameo appearance in *An English Guide to Birdwatching* by Nicholas Royle, which despite the factual title is a fiction. The difference with Colette's watercolour was that it seemed to be a depiction of our relationship *per se*. Although it wasn't exactly biographical, the picture had a documentary quality that made me feel that

⬆ The phrase 'With the kisses of his mouth' comes from the *Song of Songs*.

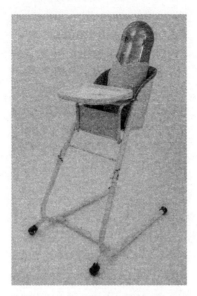

Adeline de Monseignat, 'Robert', 2013

I was part owner. No gift could have been made to me of this particular work since it was to some degree already mine.

Hence the questions. Did I have any rights over *The Kiss*? Did I deserve a say? Whatever the validity of those questions, they would rebound. They are rebounding right here, right now. Does Colette have any comeback over the representation of her in this chapter? How reliable a portrayal is it? If she were concerned, perhaps Colette could herself buy a copy of this book, just as I could buy *The Kiss*. But no. Unlike a painting, a modern book has no original. Colette's purchasing a copy would not take this book out of circulation. But why should Colette need to make a purchase? She might rightfully expect a copy from the author as a gift.

There was a final reason why I found *The Kiss* disconcerting. It was akin to the feeling of having been objectified. I wondered whether the fact that Colette had painted me meant that my usefulness to her as a man was exhausted. Now that she had decanted my image, would she feel freer to toss out the dregs of my reality?

Three love-frames

The image that Colette created of me was real. It was made of watercolour and paper, and could be physically seen. But you don't need to be an artist and make tangible paintings in order to create images of your lover. One often creates an idealised picture of the other that remains inside one's head. Even in the presence of the beloved, one will see them through this inward frame. That is Frame 1.

The course of love usually involves a fading of that ideal image. The watercolour becomes faint on the mental page. Oxytocin subsides and reality resumes. One sees one's lover more or less as they are. That is Frame 2. The test will be whether there is enough genuine love in the relationship to ride that disappointment out.

During a relationship that continues for any length of time, one is likely to generate a third frame. It is filled with theories that we hold about our lover. In unhappy relationships, such theories typically manifest in sentences beginning with, 'You always' or 'You never'. For example: 'You always put yourself first' or 'You never think of me'. The natural disappointment of Frame 2 is no longer tolerated. Frame 3 is constructed. But it is worse for the partner being framed than the one doing the framing. When one partner decides to leave the other, it is often because they cannot stand to be seen through the other's Frame 3. The image that the other holds of me is now too far from reality, and I cannot bear it.

The 'solus'

The chromaticism, verve and immediacy of Colette's painting combined on the palette to produce a distinctive style. Just as a writer will have a 'voice', so Colette had developed a painterly idiom that was unmistakably hers. One could still detect influences on her work. Colourists such as David Hockney and Henri Rousseau stood about in its corners. But they were only whispering. The voice that you heard was Colette's.

Colette had succeeded through her art in expressing herself. For that is what creativity is supposed to be: expression. Particularly self-expression. Material that would otherwise be suppressed or repressed is let out. Hence the creative 'outlet'. As with a boiler, the pressure of repression rises to a level where not expressing it could be dangerous. Pressure, repression, suppression, expression: the family of metaphors points to a swelling force that needs its valve releasing or else.

Yet arguably it is in *non*-expression that we find the secret to creativity. After all, the language of art is more compressed, allusive and deictic than the language that we use in everyday life. There are few straightforward expressions in modern art. Picasso's works might be indisputably expressive, but try putting down on paper what it is exactly that they express and you will likely hesitate. Ordinary, non-artistic language is different. We express ourselves perfectly well in everyday communication when we say 'I'd like a coffee', or 'I'm going to the supermarket'. Such sentences are easily expressed, and once we've expressed them, we're done.

Artists achieve a style of their own by doing the reverse. Rather than say something once and be finished, they keep repeating certain tropes. Indeed it is the repeating of those tropes that makes the artist's style identifiable to us punters. A style without consistency is no style at all. We recognise a Picasso as a Picasso thanks to the recurrence of distorted faces, say, or the familiar appearance of a bull, or of a tongue shaped like a cone, or of hands with preternaturally fat fingers.

Tropes like those go to make up Picasso's language. The language once developed, Picasso can't stop speaking it. The compulsion to repeat suggests that he hasn't quite expressed himself. He has to keep going back. And if they demand constant repeating, those tropes can't be fully expressible. Counterintuitive though it may be to say it, creativity lies in the failure of expression. That is what makes creativity so restless. The artist keeps scratching the itch. As Samuel Beckett notoriously put it: 'Try again. Fail again. Fail better.'

The name that I give to this principle of inexpressible creativity is the 'solus'. The solus evokes 'solitary' and 'solitude' because the creativity is unique in each case. Picasso has his bulls, Hepworth her smooth monoliths, Monet his hazy flora, and so on. The tropes differ because they come from a wellspring in the unconscious, and no two unconsciouses are alike. 'Solus' also alludes to 'solar' as in the sun. Both the sun's creative energy and its capacity to keep returning are features shared with the artistic sensibility. In all cases, the solus is that dense artistic material whose ineffability provokes the artist to continuously restate it in near-identical terms. The solus is the source of the artist's style.

Creatures of love

What has creativity got to do with the theme of this chapter, which is love? There is an empirical link to be found in my falling for an artist in the shape of Colette. I would also argue that love is itself a form of creativity, on the grounds that love both can and can't be expressed. That contradiction is set out in the two columns on the right.

A. Love can be expressed

Part of the joy of falling in love lies in the generating of new in-jokes, new terms of endearment, new forms of affection. There is also the coming up with new plans: let's travel the world; let's build a house; let's just run away. The fledgling couple will talk for hours on the phone or in bed, hearing in each other's words ever more to add to. That generative urge in love begins in those minor ways and in many cases carries through to the major generative urge to start a family. In the making of love, one is creating a new world. To fall in love is to clamber aboard the supercharged vehicle of generation. It is like a ride on Brighton Pier: the adrenalin makes you shout your heart out. Nothing is left unexpressed.

B. Love cannot be expressed

The phrase 'I love you' has a quality similar to that of an artistic trope. The expressing of it doesn't use it up. It needs repeating. The repeating, though joyous, is almost painful. We tell the person with whom we are in love that we are in love with them. It is at once totally true and utterly inadequate. If only there were an intenser phrase to match the intensity of the love that I feel for you. I would say it a million times over. All the dictionaries in the world fall short. My love for you is so great that I need an entirely new language. Bring me that new language now and I will wear it out.

Creativity, in other words, need not be confined to the making of art. To be creative is to stand at the generative fount of our being. How and where that fount ultimately issues will vary according to the person. Should it issue as falling in love, that person will likely experience it as a co-creative joy. Among other things, love is the delight in making a shared world: two creativities come together. Unlike the production of much art, love is no lonely enterprise. One's own creative self and that of one's lover come into alignment. Together they bloom as a form that neither had foreseen.

Moreover, the words 'creativity' and 'creature' hail from the same linguistic tribe. We are human *creatures* insofar as we were *created*. We didn't fall to earth like an asteroid. As creatures, as created beings, we remain ontologically in touch with the act of creation. We know what it is not to have been in the world, then to have been there. When we engage our creativity, particularly the creativity of love, we are tacitly reprising and honouring that coming-to-be.

In sum, there is a creativity of art and there is a creativity of love. Both are concerned with generating the new. Both are open to what may come. One could say that, in deferring to the unknown ahead of them, both art and love allow themselves to be guided by the soul. The creative person, whether it be art or love that they create, is somebody who has given the soul the keys to the car. As the soul takes charge of the controls, the self moves over into the passenger seat.

Yet as we know from the example of Picasso, the self doesn't shyly retire. The self as the ego, as the personality and as the will of the artist remain firmly in the vehicle. As in the diagram below, creativity is where self and soul converge.

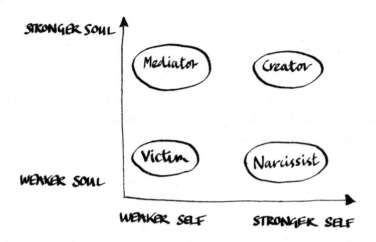

When a person's soul and self are both strong, that person is likely to become a creator. But that doesn't happen often. Most of the time our self dominates our soul. We are led by the demands of our ego to feel better about ourselves. It is an essentially narcissistic position. We might not be vain as such but we are seeking affirmation or reward. We lack the courage to give our soul its space. We are afraid that in ceding to the soul, all those things that the self has identified as desires will not be satisfied. Put another way, our self looks out for our wants where our soul looks out for our needs. Both are met in acts of creativity.

Rarer than the narcissist but less rare than the creator is the mediator. This is the person who seeks consensus, sees all sides of an argument, suffers discomfort in conflict situations, and prefers to broker the peace. Their soul overrides their self. The mediator plays a vital role in society – especially in a society overrun by narcissists – but pays a personal price. They put their wants behind the wants of other selves, with the result that they are less sure of who they are. The mediator risks simply mirroring those around them.

Then there are the victims. What defines victimhood is passivity. The victim shares with the mediator the conviction that agency lies more with others than with themselves. But their souls are too weak to do much about it.

Creativity, in short, is that state in which we as humans are most activated. Self and soul are equally alive. Love is one of creativity's preferred channels.

Suppose the man should fall asleep

The last time I heard from Colette was after she too had transferred back from Brighton to London. It was 5 June 2017, the Monday following the terrorist attack on London Bridge and Borough Market. Three men had hired a white van and driven it as a weapon into pedestrians enjoying a Saturday night on the town. The attackers then jumped out of the vehicle and knifed as many people as they could before being shot dead by the police.

Although not directly affected, Colette like many Londoners felt shaken up by the news. As the events took place in the vicinity of London Bridge, they seemed uncomfortably close to me too. It wasn't that I was nearby on the night. It was rather that London Bridge represented 'my' London. As a boy, I had on my bedroom wall a picture three feet wide of London Bridge in medieval times. The bridge was then a thoroughfare bustling with horses, carts and merchants. As I gazed at it falling asleep, the picture came alive like a widescreen musical that entered my dreams. My mother would sing 'London Bridge is Falling Down' as a lullaby. Tooley Street, which runs perpendicular to London Bridge, is where Rowland Smith & Son Ltd. had had its offices. When still employed, my father would drive his Jaguar there every day after dropping me at Dulwich. That daily journey pinned London Bridge in my mind as an adult destination beyond the range of a schoolboy, as if that was where I would one day reappear as a man. And by now, in my early fifties, I was a regular at the food stalls and eateries of Borough Market. The hospital next to the bridge is where I had been anaesthetised for my heart investigations. The railway station was one that I as a south Londoner had relied on for years. Headquartered between the station and the bridge, cheek-by-jowl with The Shard, is the publisher of this very book.

All that Colette wanted to know was whether I was still alive. What would have been an innocent question from anybody else, coming from Colette was unusually freighted. Had I perished that night, Colette would have been obliged to chalk up the third death of an ex. That snake of self-doubt would have throbbed with redoubled intent. Colette was getting in touch partly to make sure that the snake had no such need.

'No, this is a prerecorded message,' I texted back to Colette in answer to her question.

'Silly bugger,' came her reply. While ticking me off for being facetious, Colette was expressing a complex relief.

At the time of asking, I was indeed still alive. But the life that I was now living, back in London and alone, was new. It was the latest in a series of lives that I had lived:

1. Croydon as an infant;
2. Dulwich as a schoolboy;
3. Oxford as a student;
4. Perpignan as an illegal immigrant and dropout;
5. Oxford as a Fellow and a father;
6. Los Angeles as an illegal immigrant with an American wife;
7. London as a consultant and an Englishwoman's husband;
8. Brighton as a divorcé and follower of an artist;
9. London as a bachelor writer.

Like a cat I had had my nine lives. Each life had been built up only to fall down and be replaced by another. Which is exactly what that nursery rhyme about London Bridge is about. It ends with a man smoking a pipe. The man is charged with keeping watch in case the bridge collapses one last time.

> London Bridge is falling down,
> Falling down, falling down.
> London Bridge is falling down,
>   My fair lady.
>
> Build it up with wood and clay,
> Wood and clay, wood and clay,
> Build it up with wood and clay,
>   My fair lady.
>
> Wood and clay will wash away,
> Wash away, wash away,
> Wood and clay will wash away,
>   My fair lady.
>
> Build it up with bricks and mortar,
> Bricks and mortar, bricks and mortar,
> Build it up with bricks and mortar,
>   My fair lady.
>
> Bricks and mortar will not stay,
> Will not stay, will not stay,
> Bricks and mortar will not stay,
>   My fair lady.
>
> Build it up with iron and steel,
> Iron and steel, iron and steel,
> Build it up with iron and steel,
>   My fair lady.

Iron and steel will bend and bow,
Bend and bow, bend and bow,
Iron and steel will bend and bow,
    My fair lady.

Build it up with silver and gold,
Silver and gold, silver and gold,
Build it up with silver and gold,
    My fair lady.

Silver and gold will be stolen away,
Stolen away, stolen away,
Silver and gold will be stolen away,
    My fair lady.

Set a man to watch all night,
Watch all night, watch all night,
Set a man to watch all night,
    My fair lady.

Suppose the man should fall asleep,
Fall asleep, fall asleep,
Suppose the man should fall asleep?
    My fair lady.

Give him a pipe to smoke all night,
Smoke all night, smoke all night,
Give him a pipe to smoke all night,
    My fair lady.

Afterword

In the last chapter, I referred to a distinction between 'Story 1' and 'Story 2'. The former denoted Colette's life as lived; the latter, the editing of that life into written form. The distinction applies no less to me. To recycle a metaphor from the chapter titled 'A Love Quadrangle', the writing is to my life as a Tube map is to the terrain. Editorial choices have been made for the sake of a tidy read.

In fact, that distinction between the life lived and the life recorded is common to us all. We may never write an autobiography as such, but from time to time we will reflect on our lives; and in reflecting, we will be no less selective than the autobiographer. We leave periods out, we emphasise events, we zero in on individuals. One side of the family receives more attention than the other. The lover who left us, compared to the one whom we left, gets an unfair share of our thoughts. Certain years in our past stick out whilst others leave barely a trace. A thousand schooldays, a thousand meals, a thousand dreams are left off the record.

As well as *what* to select, there is *when* to make the selection. For our lives do not sit on a single plane before us, like a canvas on an easel. They concertina back into the past. My sojourn in

Brighton, for example, is far more recent than my escapade in Perpignan. Inevitably I have had less time to process the former than the latter. Which raises again the issue that I address in the passage about splitting up with Simone. When is hindsight at its clearest? Were I to rewrite the story of Brighton in ten years' time, how different would it be? This text has been published at a given point in time. Whether it is the right point remains open to question; as does the very notion of a 'right time'.

So selecting material implies deselecting. That might sound like a problem, yet if we didn't make cuts, we would be swamped. Conducting a truly comprehensive review of one's life could take as long as it did to live it. Above all, it would leave no room for sense-making. It is precisely by sifting material that we make sense of our lives, sorting the meaningful from the mundane. And insofar as autobiography is a meaning-making exercise, we are not just autobiographers, we are all philosophers too. #AutoBioPhilosophy

Where this autobiography goes a step further, perhaps, is in taking autobiography itself as a theme. That makes the book doubly reflective. If it is a self-portrait, it is also a self-portrait of a self-portrait. In the opening pages, for example, I refer to Zadie Smith and the similarities between one's life and a book. In a later chapter, a discussion unfolds around Derrida and autobiography. Those sessions on the psychoanalytic couch were nothing if not moments of self-exploration. And there is the question of Colette's story and its links to mine. Autobiography is not only the genre but the meta-theme of this book.

There are several themes of the ordinary type too. Indeed, themes are vital to sense-making. By connecting one part of the book to another, they create narrative coherence. And although the repeating of a theme is artificial, it contributes to a feeling of a natural whole. In this book repetition itself is a major theme, as in my repeating the fate of my father; the repeating of the purchase of the engagement ring; or the repeating in reality of the dream of three daughters. Ranging from the most to the least prominent, other themes include:

- fate
- cars
- Freud
- the number three
- the soul
- death/suicide/terminations
- Shakespeare
- Brighton
- gold
- labyrinths, mazes, the Minotaur and bulls
- staircases/falling/vertigo
- immigration/borders/transit/train stations
- pine trees
- architecture
- the planets and stars

As well as their connective function in the book, such themes are supposed to hint at the uncanny way in which motifs recur in reality. One's life is like a dream in this respect. Reality is so unreal. Although in the daytime we are supposedly conscious, our experience often operates on a level below the cognitive. The classic distinction between conscious and unconscious, day and night, might be too black-and-white. I have tried to bring out what I would call the 'mid-conscious' level on which we often live. I have done so not just with themes but by identifying semi-strangers, Real Imaginaries, everyday angels, world-forms, soul knowledge and adaptive fantasies. All belong in the mid-conscious. We spend more time there than we think.

That, if I had to say, would be my short answer to the exam question set in the Foreword: 'What is it to be human?' Being human is a dwelling in the mid-conscious. As a rule, we are neither comatose nor 100 per cent alert. Surprise, by definition, is rare. We go about our lives getting lightly tangled in patterns like ribbons draped from the clouds. The light in this mid-conscious space is neither bright nor dark, but diffuse and refractive. Our minds fill with a liquid that enables us to identify things, while keeping us underwater where the sounds wobble. People, shapes and movements are recognisable enough for us to function, but not always sharp. We don't know very much, but we know a few things, and fill in the blanks where necessary. We take action and make decisions as if steering a boat on top of that water, as on a lake. Every now and then we look further out to realise that we are not on a lake but on the sea, and that the sea has a current that has pulled us elsewhere.

Part of the point of self-reflection is that it makes the mid-conscious conscious. The more aware we become of our repetitions and tendencies, the less likely we are to be blindly controlled by them. Autobiophilosophy is the practice of waking up. I would encourage my readers to become autobiophilosophers in turn. Again, that doesn't have to involve writing a book. It is more a question of listening to the stories we tell ourselves about ourselves; of spotting the patterns and exclusions in such stories and how they have shaped our sense of self. The implication being that if we can change the story that we tell ourselves, we can also change who we are.

Having finished the book, I realise that it was about closure. The self that I was for the first fifty years of my life is not the self that I will be going forward. A skin has been shed, a mask has slipped, a door has shut. Dante talks about the first half of his life as taking place in a *'selva oscura'*, a dark forest. I feel like I am leaving the forest behind. That is both scary and exhilarating. I am stepping into open country.

Acknowledgements

For helping me in various ways with the making of this book, I would like to thank the following people who appear in the text undisguised: Patricia Smith, Rowley Smith, the Fellows of All Souls College, Jacques Derrida and Mother Meera.

As regards the vast majority of the other individuals discussed, I have changed their names to preserve anonymity. Thanking any of them by name would blow their cover. Nevertheless my gratitude is sincere.

Those not in the text whom I also thank wholeheartedly for their help are: Susanna Abse, Fahd Al-Rasheed, Paul Alexander, John Ash, Björn Atterstam, Jake Attwell, Mihaela Berciu, Daniel Crewe, Gervase de Wilde, Stephanie Ebdon, James Fulton, Louise Haines, Terry Ingham, Tom Jarvis, Matt Kingdon, Anna Murray, Carrie Plitt, Andrew Scott, Dan Simmons, Leonie Tayler, Sarah Thickett, Sarah Tyler-Walters, Mark Vernon, Patrick Walsh and Andrea Wulf. I offer special thanks to Mia Levitin for her unflagging interest, practical help and moral support.

Finally, a word of love to Anna, Ruby and Greta. This book would not have been possible without the gifts that you have brought into my life.

Epitaph

Colin Rowland Smith passed away
on 2 September 2017.

Illustration Credits

All illustrations drawn by Joe Bright.

p. 2 The British Home and Hospital for Incurables © Robert Rowland Smith

p. 5 Hurstpierpoint College, reproduced with kind permission from Hurstpierpoint College Archives

p. 41 Chrysler car © Robert Rowland Smith

p. 101 All Souls College © Robert Rowland Smith

p. 109 Derrida inscriptions © Robert Rowland Smith

p. 110 Red Renault 5 © Rudolf Stricker

p. 141 Park Town © Robert Rowland Smith

p. 176 C-class Mercedes © Rudolf Stricker

p. 237 West Pier © Robert Rowland Smith

p. 302 Mother Meera, reproduced with permission by Mother Meera

p. 322 Oriental Place, Brighton © Robert Rowland Smith

p. 347 'Robert' by Adeline de Monseignat (hand-blown glass, mirroring chemicals, fabric, name-tag and found chair). 2013, 2843gms, 48.5cm